making a movie in iMovie HD and iDVD 5

Visual QuickProject Guide

by Jeff Carlson

Peachpit Press

Visual QuickProject Guide

Making a Movie in iMovie HD and iDVD 5

Jeff Carlson

Peachpit Press

1249 Eighth Street
Berkeley, CA 94710
510/524-2178
800/283-9444
510/524-2221 (fax)

Find us on the World Wide Web at: www.peachpit.com
To report errors, please send a note to errata@peachpit.com
Peachpit Press is a division of Pearson Education

Editor: Nancy Davis
Production editor: Lisa Brazieal
Copy editor: Liane Thomas
Compositor: Jeff Carlson
Cover design: The Visual Group with Aren Howell
Cover photo credit: Dynamic Graphics
Interior design: Elizabeth Castro
Indexer: Caroline Parks

Notice of Rights

Notice of Liability

Trademarks

ISBN 0-321-33018-8

9 8 7 6 5 4 3 2 1

Printed and bound in the United States of America

For Janet and Linda

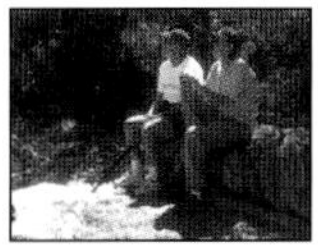

Special Thanks to...

Kimberly for her ceaseless love and support, and for taking me to Arizona in the first place;

Janet and Linda for being excellent tour guides;

Lisa Brazieal for assistance in producing the book and listening to my layout ideas;

Liane Thomas for being the sharp eyes of this book, even while chatting via iChat at 2 a.m.;

Caroline Parks for indexing the book in record time;

Everyone at Peachpit Press for helping me enjoy what I do for a living;

My officemates Glenn, Jeff, Agen, Larry, and Kim for encouragement and conversation;

Diva Espresso for delicious consciousness in a cup (or two, or dozens);

and to Nancy Davis: I don't know how you do it all, but I'm glad that you do.

contents

introduction ix

what you'll create	x	the web site	xiv
how this book works	xii	the next step	xv

1. project overview 1

project overview	2	movie editing overview	4
project materials	3	dvd creation overview	5

2. create an iMovie project 7

the iMovie interface	8	extra bits	10
the Timeline	9		

3. import video into iMovie 11

connect the camcorder	12	timecode	15
review your footage	13	extra bits	16
import your footage	14		

4. assemble your movie 17

add clips to timeline	18	extra bits	23
arrange the clips	20		

contents

5. add photos and music 25

import photos 26
add motion to photos 28
add music from iTunes 30
extra bits 31

6. edit clips 33

direct-trim clips 34
split clips 35
crop and trim clips 36
copy and paste 37
paste clips over clips 38
create blank clips 39
revert clip to original 40
change clip volume 41
extract audio 42
lock and unlock audio 43
extra bits 44

7. add transitions 47

edit settings 48
add the transition 50
extra bits 51

8. add titles 53

create a title 54
style the text 56
add the title 57
extra bits 58

9. add effects 59

edit effect settings 60
apply the effect 61
extra bits 62

10. share your movie 63

share via email	64	create an iDVD project	68
share via a web page	65	extra bits	69
share via QuickTime	66		

11. explore iDVD 71

the iDVD interface	72	extra bits	74

12. choose and customize a theme 75

apply a theme	76	add drop zone media	82
edit the title	77	use animated drop zones	84
edit the buttons	78	change background	85
edit motion buttons	80	apply submenu theme	86
set background audio	81	extra bits	87

13. add more content to the DVD 89

create a submenu	90	add DVD-ROM content	94
add movies	91	extra bits	95
create a slideshow	92		

14. burn the DVD 97

preview the DVD	98	save project to disk	101
set encoding options	99	extra bits	102
burn the DVD	100		

contents

appendix a: troubleshooting 103

improve performance 104
troubleshoot burning 105
troubleshoot system 106

appendix b: resources 107

reference and tutorials 108
iMovie software 109
iDVD software 110

glossary 111

index 115

introduction

The Visual QuickProject Guide that you hold in your hands offers a unique way to learn about new technologies. Instead of drowning you in theoretical possibilities and lengthy explanations, this Visual QuickProject Guide uses big, color illustrations coupled with clear, concise step-by-step instructions to show you how to complete one specific project in a matter of hours.

Our project in this book is to edit a home movie and put it on a DVD that can be viewed using most consumer DVD players. Why go to the trouble of editing? After all, the footage shot on the camcorder's tape is a movie—all the pieces are there, and can be played back from start to end. However, the video you shoot invariably includes rough patches that always crop up: blurry shots when you were trying to locate something in the viewfinder; sections of time when the camera was inadvertently recording the ground as you were walking; and, for lack of a polite way of saying it, those parts that seemed interesting at the time but on reflection are now just boring.

With iMovie HD, you will take that footage and easily shape it into a movie that your friends and family want to watch. In addition to assembling and trimming scenes, you'll add music, sound effects, and still photos. Once the movie is edited, you'll be able to post it on the Web, send it to someone via email, and burn it to a DVD using iDVD 5. What's great is that you don't have to be a professional video editor or even a computer expert to accomplish this task. Better still, it's fun: you get to shape your own movie, with tools that are easy to understand and use.

what you'll create

Import your video footage from a digital camcorder into iMovie HD.

Add photos from iPhoto with the Ken Burns Effect applied to create a sense of motion in the still images.

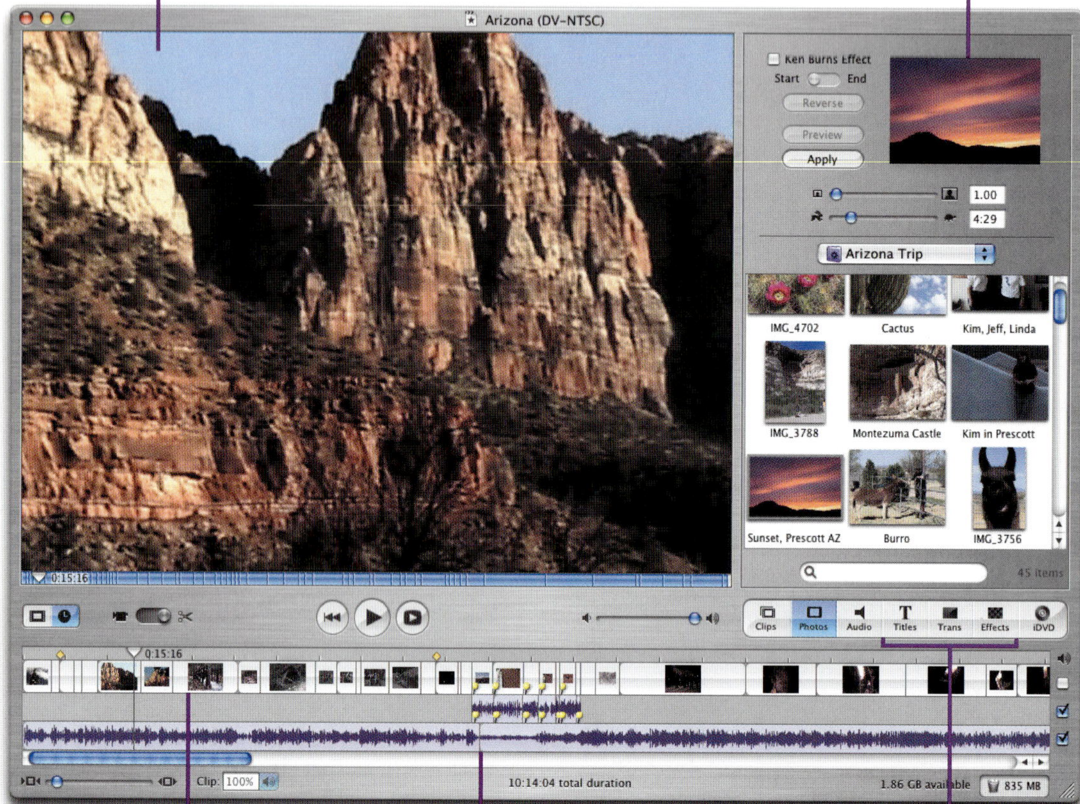

Edit video clips to tighten the action, eliminate boring parts, and tell a story.

Add music from iTunes to play in the background.

Create titles, transitions, and effects to produce a more professional-looking movie.

Create a project in iDVD that includes the movie you edited in iMovie.

Increase visual interest by adding a movie or photos to a drop zone.

Choose one of 73 attractive, motion-enabled themes for your DVD's menu.

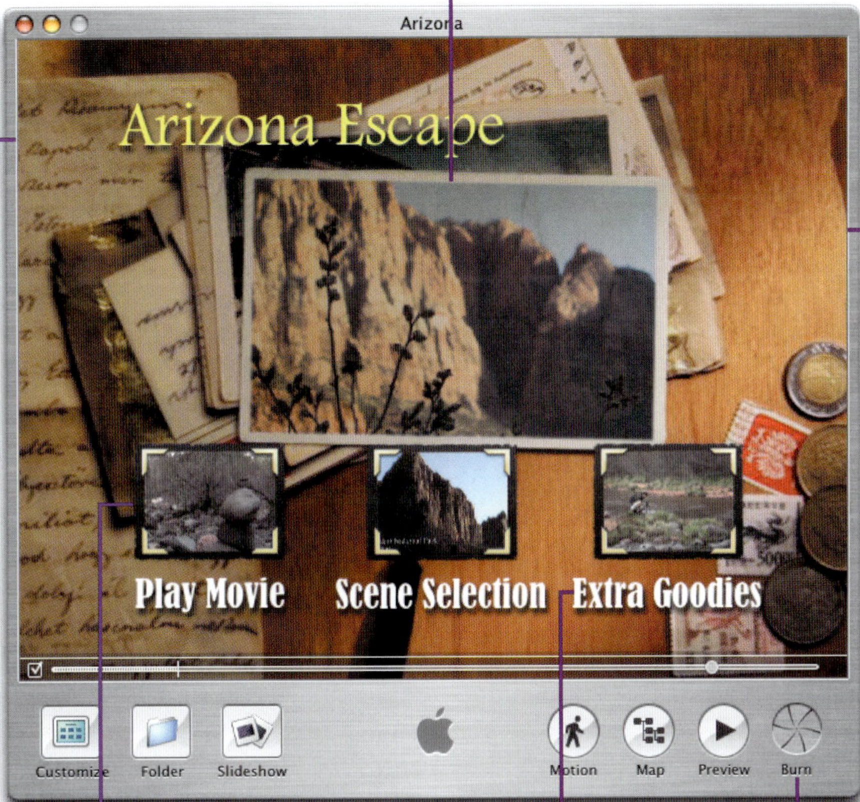

Customize the appearance of navigation buttons based on your movies and photos.

Create submenus that contain more content, such as video or slideshows built from iPhoto.

Burn a DVD disc of your project that can be played in consumer DVD players.

how this book works

The title of each section explains what is covered on that page.

Numbered steps explain actions to perform in a specific order.

Important terms and Web site addresses are shown in orange.

Captions explain what you're doing and why. They also point to relevant sections of the interface.

A dotted arrow indicates movement you need to make, such as dragging an object to an area of the interface.

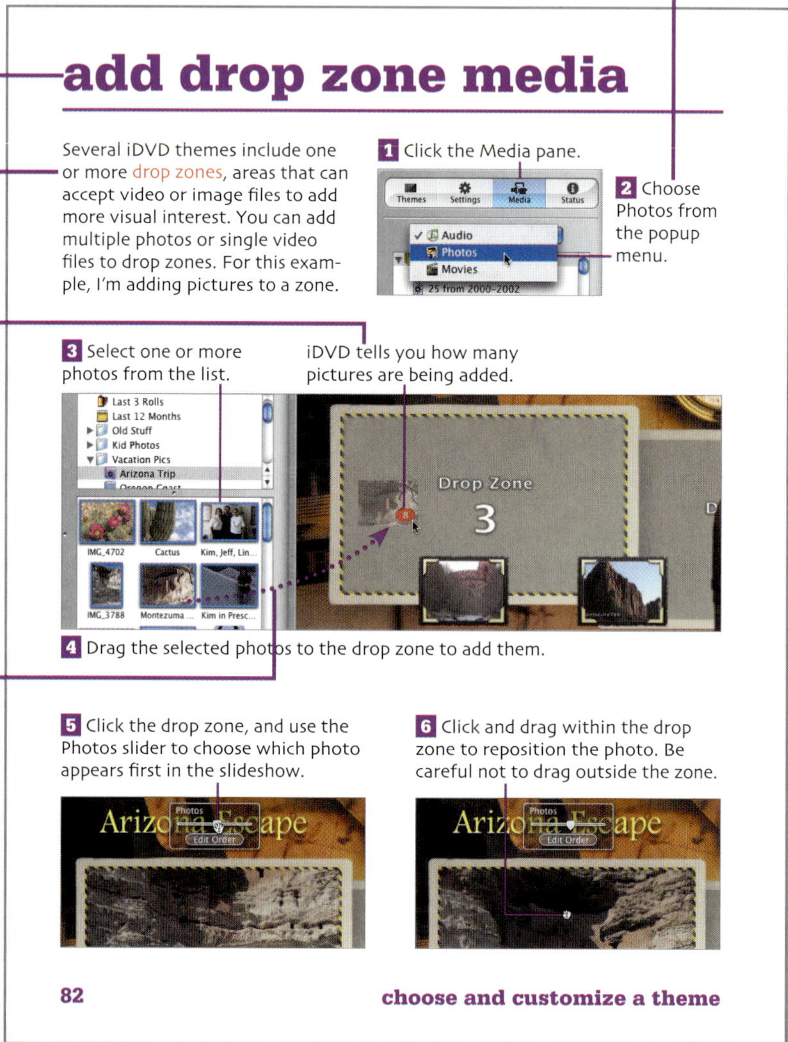

add drop zone media

Several iDVD themes include one or more drop zones, areas that can accept video or image files to add more visual interest. You can add multiple photos or single video files to drop zones. For this example, I'm adding pictures to a zone.

1 Click the Media pane.

2 Choose Photos from the popup menu.

3 Select one or more photos from the list.

iDVD tells you how many pictures are being added.

4 Drag the selected photos to the drop zone to add them.

5 Click the drop zone, and use the Photos slider to choose which photo appears first in the slideshow.

6 Click and drag within the drop zone to reposition the photo. Be careful not to drag outside the zone.

82 choose and customize a theme

The extra bits section at the end of each chapter contains additional tips and tricks that you might like to know—but that aren't absolutely necessary.

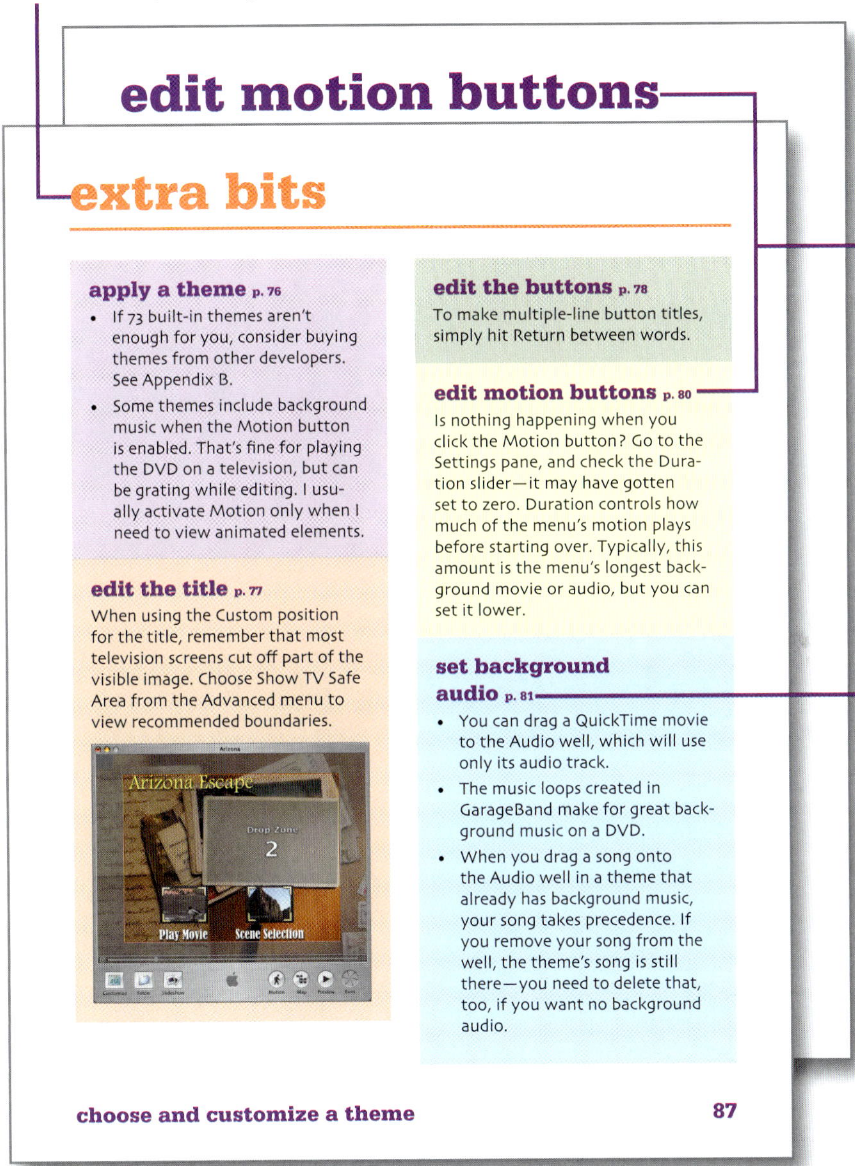

edit motion buttons

extra bits

apply a theme p. 76

- If 73 built-in themes aren't enough for you, consider buying themes from other developers. See Appendix B.
- Some themes include background music when the Motion button is enabled. That's fine for playing the DVD on a television, but can be grating while editing. I usually activate Motion only when I need to view animated elements.

edit the title p. 77

When using the Custom position for the title, remember that most television screens cut off part of the visible image. Choose Show TV Safe Area from the Advanced menu to view recommended boundaries.

edit the buttons p. 78

To make multiple-line button titles, simply hit Return between words.

edit motion buttons p. 80

Is nothing happening when you click the Motion button? Go to the Settings pane, and check the Duration slider—it may have gotten set to zero. Duration controls how much of the menu's motion plays before starting over. Typically, this amount is the menu's longest background movie or audio, but you can set it lower.

set background audio p. 81

- You can drag a QuickTime movie to the Audio well, which will use only its audio track.
- The music loops created in GarageBand make for great background music on a DVD.
- When you drag a song onto the Audio well in a theme that already has background music, your song takes precedence. If you remove your song from the well, the theme's song is still there—you need to delete that, too, if you want no background audio.

choose and customize a theme 87

The heading for each group of tips matches the section title.

The page number next to the heading makes it easy to refer back to the main content.

the web site

Find this book's companion Web site at http://www.necoffee.com/imovievqs/

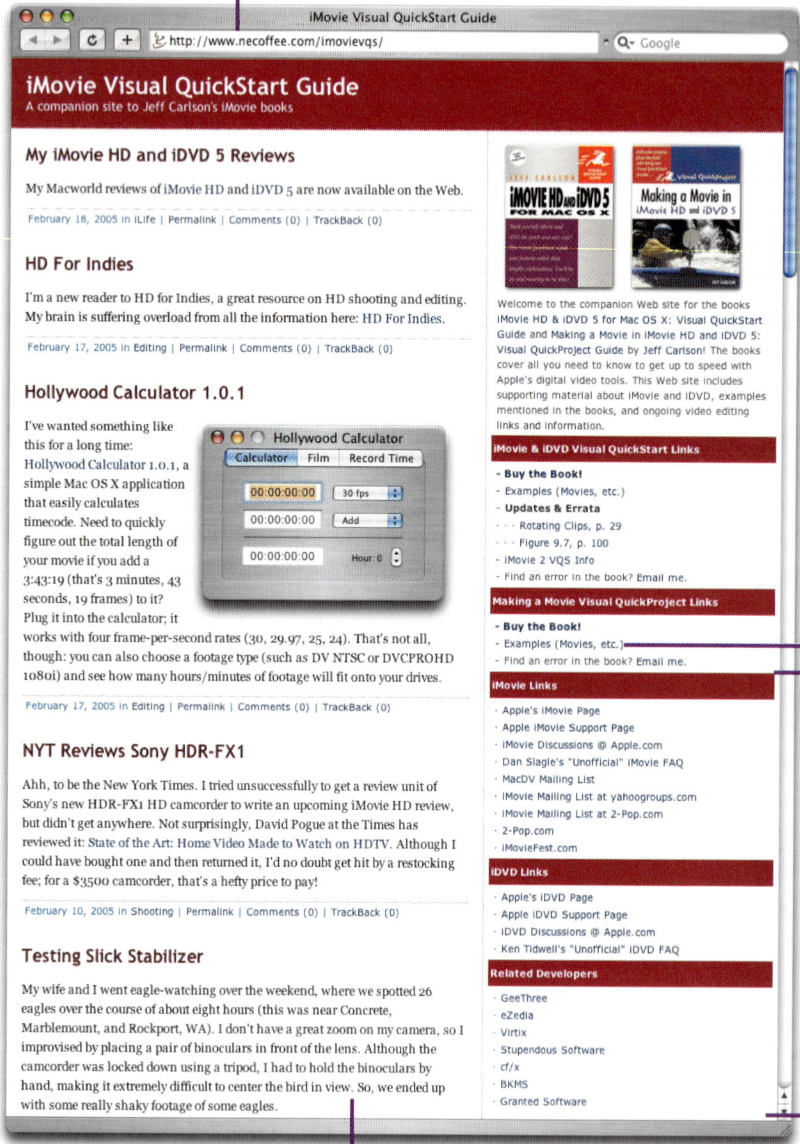

View examples mentioned in the book.

Get fast access to iMovie and iDVD resources.

Stay current with iMovie, iDVD, and iLife-related news, tips, and opinions, updated regularly.

the next step

While this Visual QuickProject Guide will walk you through all of the steps required to edit a movie and burn it to a DVD, there's more to learn about iMovie and iDVD. After you complete your QuickProject, consider picking up my book iMovie HD & iDVD 5 for Mac OS X: Visual QuickStart Guide as an in-depth, handy reference.

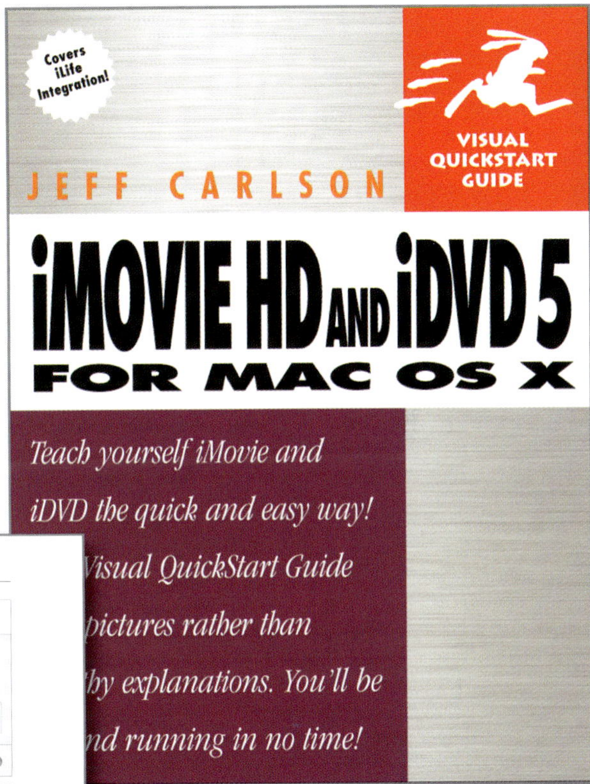

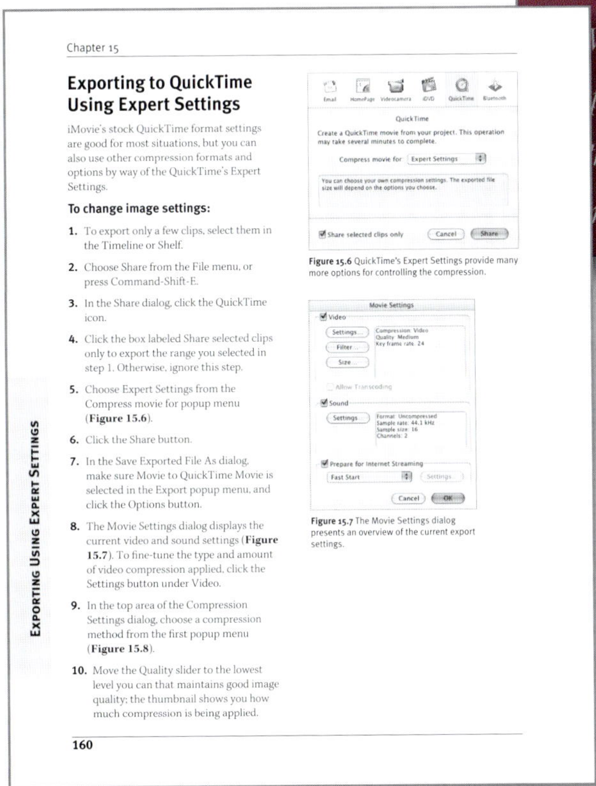

Chapter 15

EXPORTING USING EXPERT SETTINGS

Exporting to QuickTime Using Expert Settings

iMovie's stock QuickTime format settings are good for most situations, but you can also use other compression formats and options by way of the QuickTime's Expert Settings.

To change image settings:

1. To export only a few clips, select them in the Timeline or Shelf.
2. Choose Share from the File menu, or press Command-Shift-E.
3. In the Share dialog, click the QuickTime icon.
4. Click the box labeled Share selected clips only to export the range you selected in step 1. Otherwise, ignore this step.
5. Choose Expert Settings from the Compress movie for popup menu (**Figure 15.6**).
6. Click the Share button.
7. In the Save Exported File As dialog, make sure Movie to QuickTime Movie is selected in the Export popup menu, and click the Options button.
8. The Movie Settings dialog displays the current video and sound settings (**Figure 15.7**). To fine-tune the type and amount of video compression applied, click the Settings button under Video.
9. In the top area of the Compression Settings dialog, choose a compression method from the first popup menu (**Figure 15.8**).
10. Move the Quality slider to the lowest level you can that maintains good image quality; the thumbnail shows you how much compression is being applied.

Figure 15.6 QuickTime's Expert Settings provide many more options for controlling the compression.

Figure 15.7 The Movie Settings dialog presents an overview of the current export settings.

160

The book includes information on using expert settings when exporting QuickTime movies, using GarageBand to score background music, shortcuts for working in the Timeline, and more. It also features a whole section on the basics of video editing, including using camcorders, composing shots, moving the camera, lighting scenes, and capturing audio.

1. project overview

You can shoot and edit all kinds of movies: wedding videos, fictional stories, scripted documentaries, sporting events, or just in-the-moment scenes of babies, pets, landscapes, clouds...your only true limits are the amount of tape and the camcorder's battery life. For this Visual QuickProject Guide, I'm creating a vacation video from a recent trip to Arizona. Nearly every task I show in this book applies to other types of movies, so don't worry if the movie you're editing isn't a vacation video. Then again, if you've been itching to go on a vacation anyway, maybe this is a good excuse to get out there and capture your own footage!

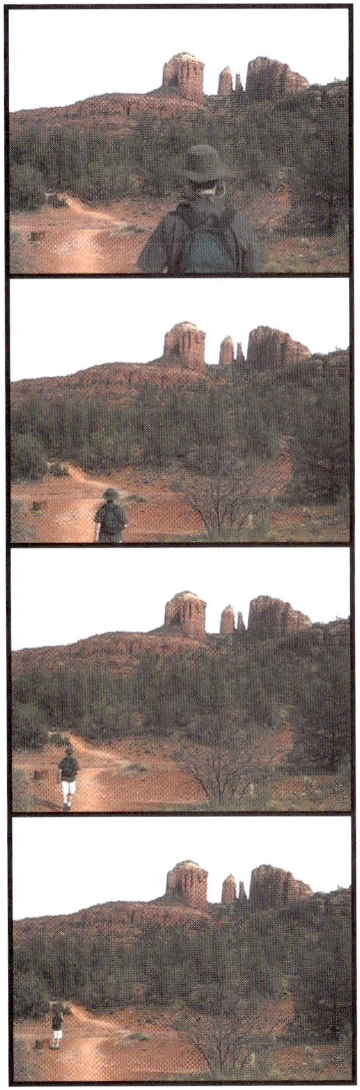

project overview

Here's what you'll be able to do by the end of the book:

1 Import the video footage from a digital camcorder into iMovie (see Chapter 3).

2 Assemble the movie by choosing the order of the video clips, adding audio, and importing some digital still photos (see Chapters 4–5).

3 Edit the clips to remove footage you don't need and improve the movie's timing and flow (see Chapter 6).

4 Add titles, transitions, and effects to the movie (see Chapters 7–9).

5 Share the movie with others by creating a QuickTime version that can be burned to a CD-ROM or uploaded to a Web site, such as an Apple .Mac HomePage (see Chapter 10).

6 Create an iDVD project that contains your movie (also in Chapter 10).

7 Edit the project in iDVD by choosing a new menu theme and personalizing its appearance (see Chapters 11–12).

8 Add more media to the DVD, such as other QuickTime movies and a slideshow of some of your digital still photos, which can be viewed separately from your main movie (see Chapter 13).

9 Burn the project to a DVD disc that can be played back in most consumer DVD players and DVD-equipped computers (see Chapter 14).

Editing video in iMovie, and creating DVDs in iDVD, is fun, easy, and even slightly addictive. With this initial project under your belt, you'll be ready to tackle others on your own.

project materials

A Macintosh computer (desktop or laptop) with a PowerPC G3, G4, or G5 processor running at 400 MHz or faster. iDVD 5 requires a G4 processor at 733 MHz or faster.

A 1 GHz or faster G4 processor is needed to take advantage of HD editing in iMovie HD. Both applications require Mac OS X Panther version 10.3.4 or later.

At least 10 GB of free space on your hard drive.

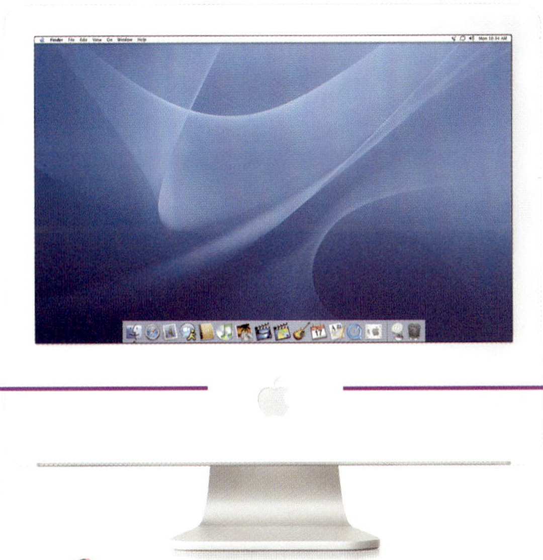

A built-in SuperDrive if you plan on burning DVDs.

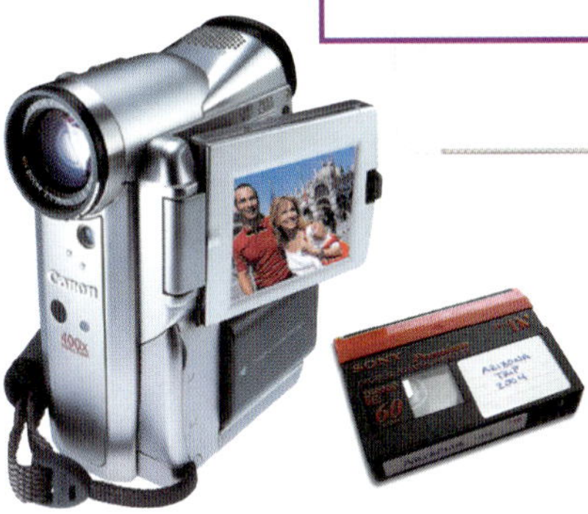

A digital camcorder and MiniDV tapes for shooting video footage.

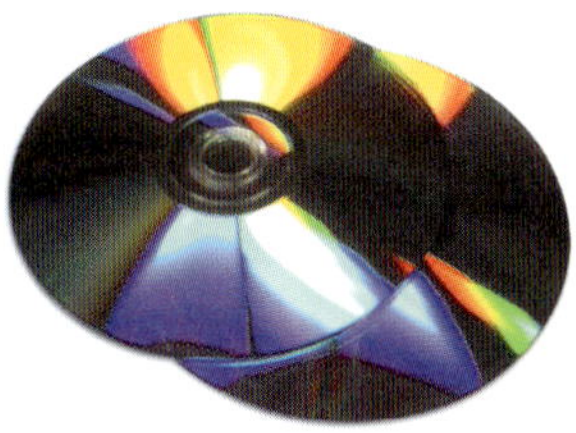

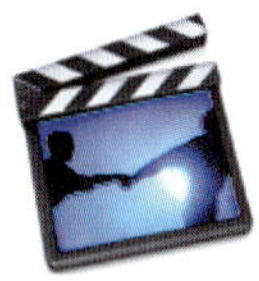

iMovie HD

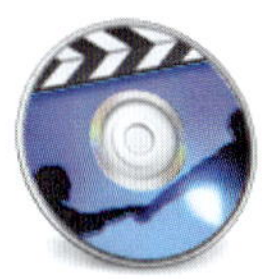

iDVD

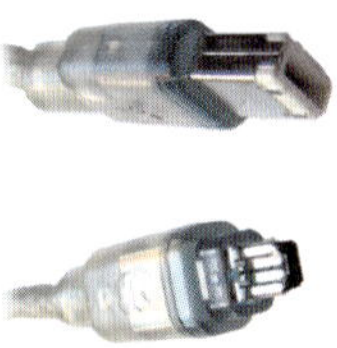

4-pin to 6-pin FireWire cable to connect the camcorder to the Mac.

Blank DVD discs (DVD-R, DVD-RW, DVD+R, or DVD+RW), if your Mac contains a SuperDrive and you want to burn DVD projects.

iMovie HD 5.0.1 or later, and iDVD 5 or later (part of the iLife '05 package).

movie editing overview

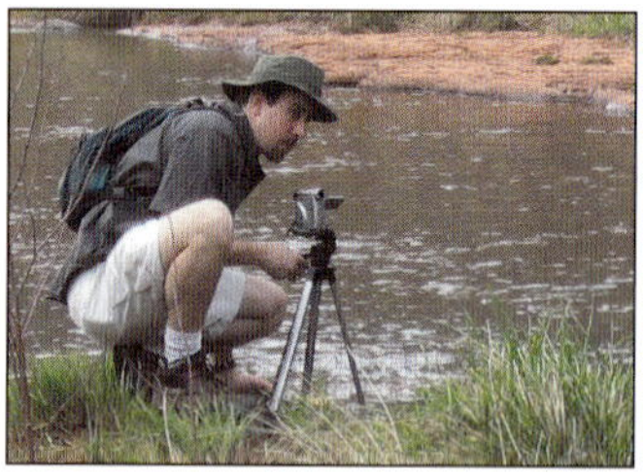

1 Shoot Video. Go into the wild (or just into the living room) to capture video footage that you will edit later in iMovie.

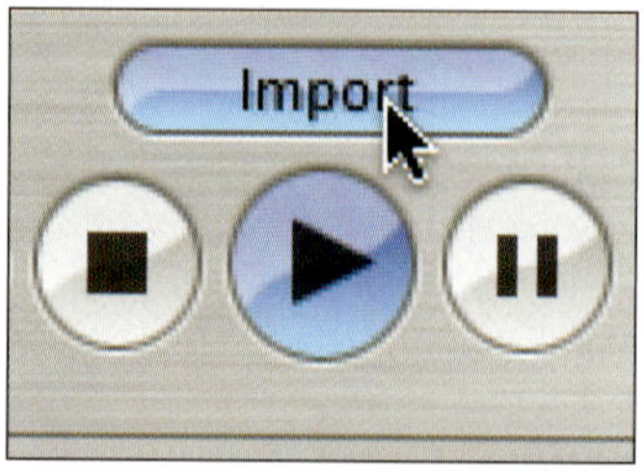

2 Import Footage into iMovie. Use iMovie's Import feature to save the footage to your hard disk as clips.

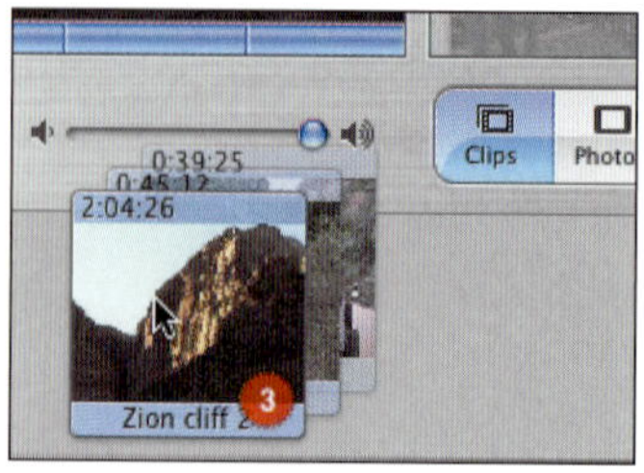

3 Assemble Your Movie. Drag movie clips to the Timeline to determine their order of appearance. Also, add audio (such as music or sound effects), digital still photos, or other content that appears in the movie.

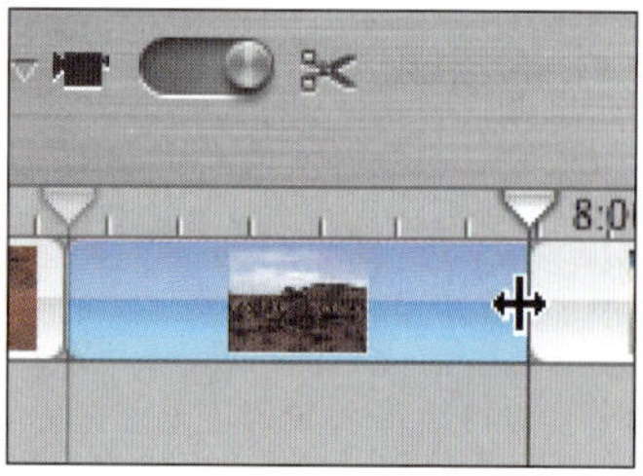

4 Edit Clips. With a rough version of your movie in place, edit the individual clips to remove unwanted frames, trim clips for timing, and add transitions, titles, and effects. This is the polishing stage, where the movie really comes together.

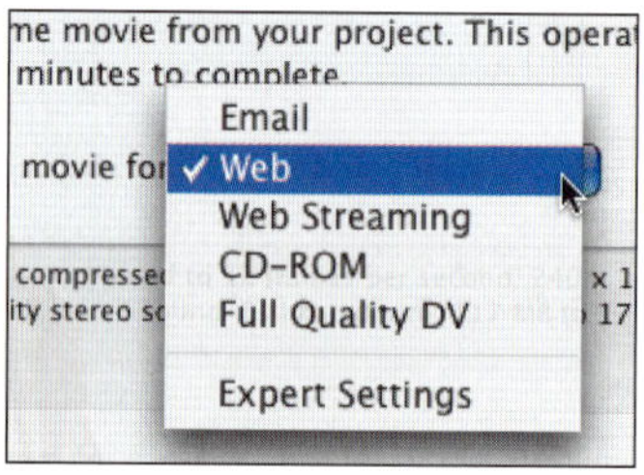

5 Share Your Movie. It's done! Now, save the movie out of iMovie into a format that other people can view, such as a QuickTime file, .Mac HomePage, or iDVD project.

dvd creation overview

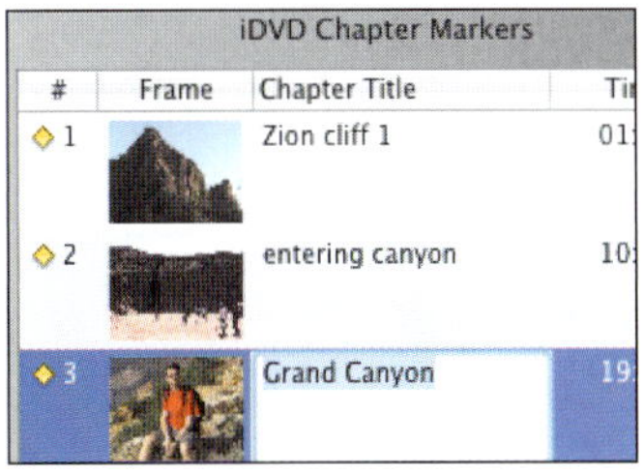

1 Prepare in iMovie.
Create iDVD Chapter Markers in iMovie to access individual chapters within the movie when you play the DVD.

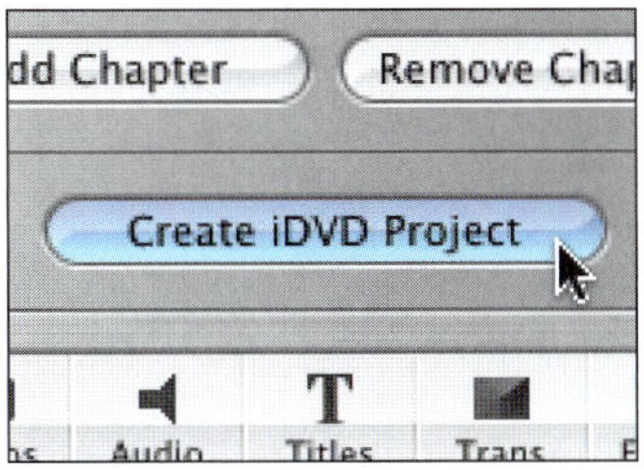

2 Create iDVD Project.
The easiest way to move from iMovie to iDVD is to use the Create iDVD Project command. iMovie prepares the data, launches iDVD, and saves a new iDVD project containing your movie.

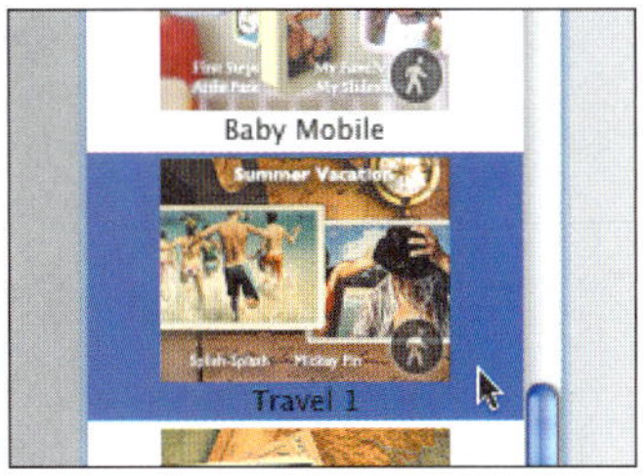

3 Edit the DVD Theme.
Each DVD menu has a visual theme that not only makes it attractive, but provides links and folders to your movie and other content. Choose one of iDVD's existing themes and then customize its appearance.

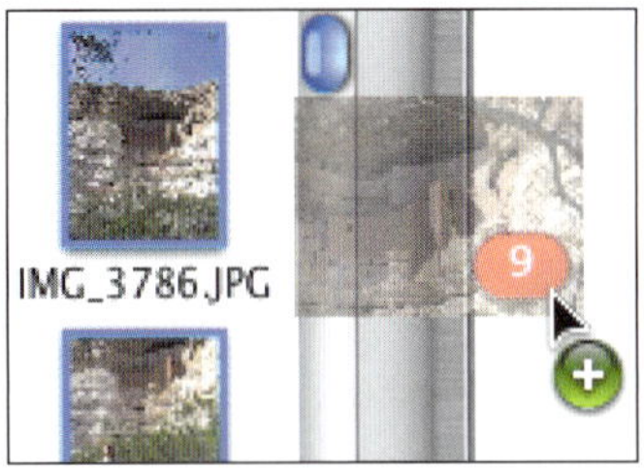

4 Add Other Content.
Your DVD can include just your movie, but if there's enough room on the disc, you can add QuickTime movies, photo slideshows, and other data.

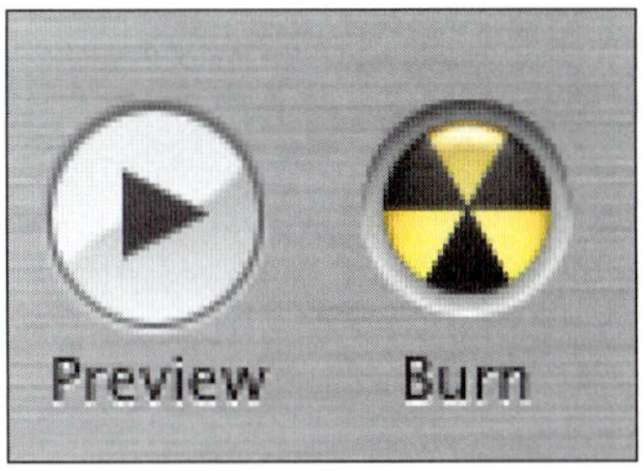

5 Burn the DVD Disc.
Time to etch your project into a disc's surface. Choose the type of encoding, double-check that everything is set, and then burn the disc in a SuperDrive.

2. create an iMovie project

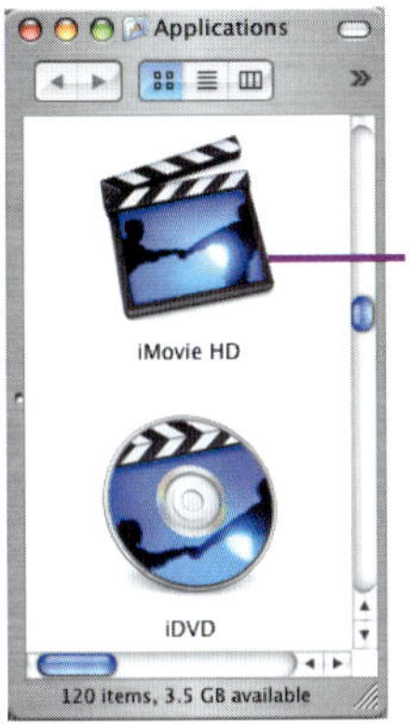

1 Double-click the iMovie HD icon in your Applications folder. If the iLife '05 installer placed iMovie HD onto the Dock, you can also single-click it there.

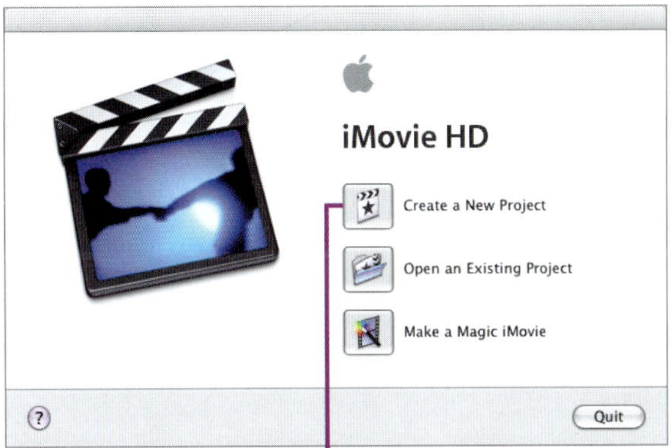

2 This dialog appears the first time you launch iMovie HD. Click the Create a New Project button. (If you previously opened iMovie, the last active project opens automatically.)

3 In the Create Project dialog that appears, type a name for your project and choose a location to store it on your hard disk.

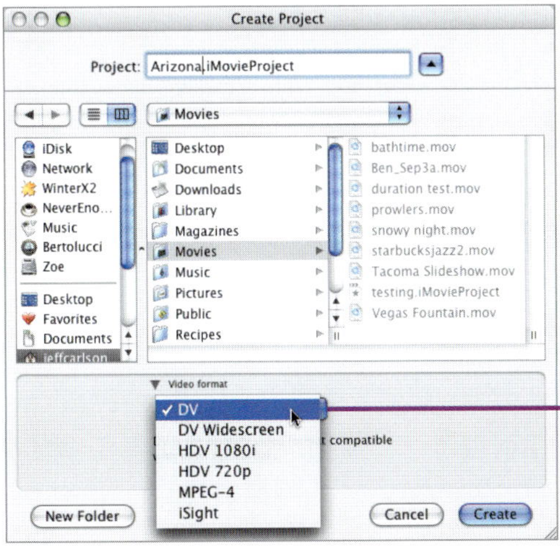

4 From the Video Format popup menu, choose the type of project that corresponds to the type of video footage you shot: Most camcorders record in DV (digital video); DV Widescreen accommodates film shot using a DV camcorder's 16:9 feature; HDV 1080i and HDV 720p are for video shot with a high-definition camera; MPEG-4 is used by camcorders that record to internal memory instead of a MiniDV tape; and iSight is Apple's compact camera used mainly with iChat AV.

the iMovie interface

The Monitor is where you preview and edit clips and play back the entire movie.

The Shelf (also known as the Clips pane) is a virtual storage area where all your video clips are held before being added to the movie. This is also where other panes, such as Titles and Transitions, appear.

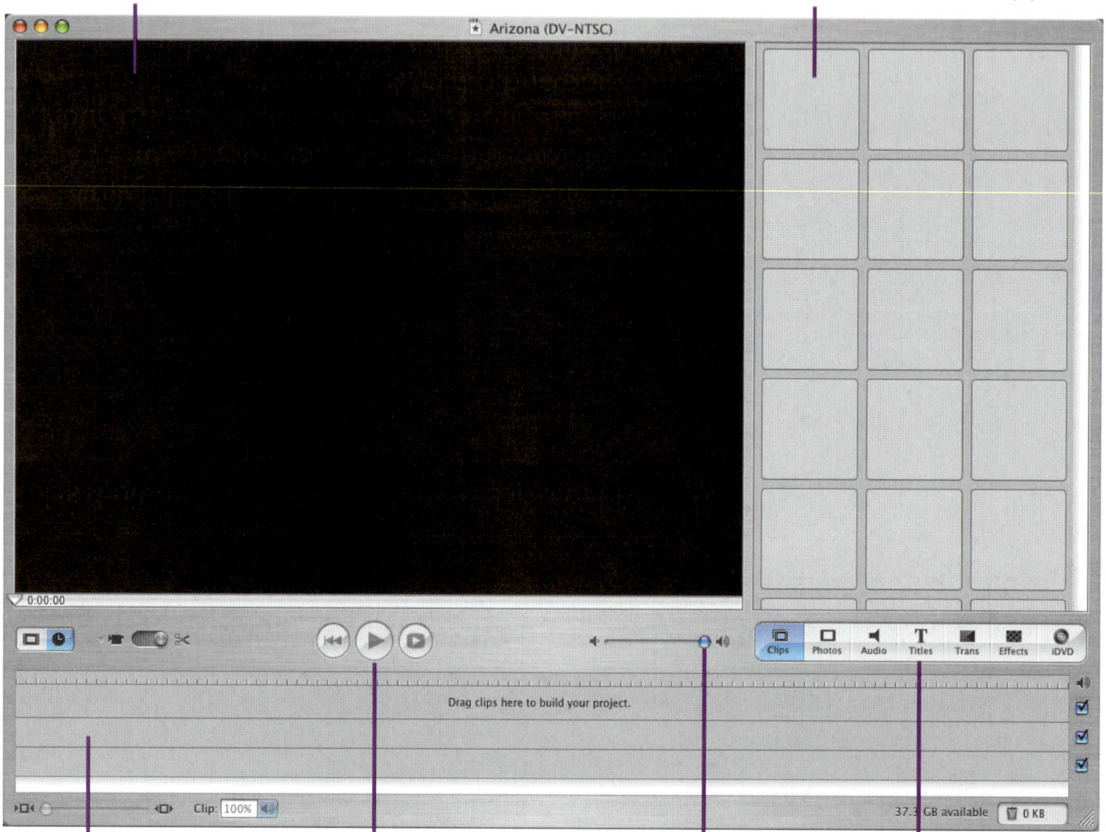

Assemble your clips in the Liquid Timeline, placing them left to right in the order you want them to play.

The playback controls jump to the beginning of the movie, play the movie in real time, or play the movie in full-screen mode.

The Volume slider controls the volume of movie playback. It doesn't affect the volume level of individual clips, however.

The buttons below the shelf access panes that control features such as creating titles and accessing photos.

the Timeline

The Timeline uses two views of working with your clips, each with its own advantages: the Clip Viewer and the Timeline Viewer.

Clip Viewer button

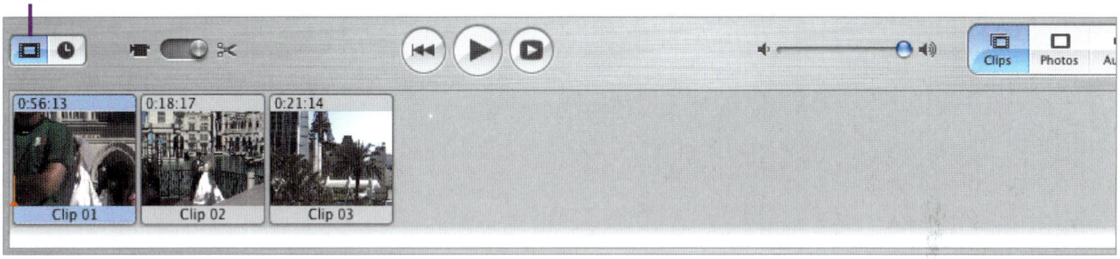

Click the Clip Viewer button (or press ⌘-E) to display the Clip Viewer component of the Liquid Timeline. In this mode, clips appear as thumbnails of the same size, which can be rearranged by dragging them (see Chapter 4).

Timeline Viewer button   Video track   Audio track 1   Audio track 2

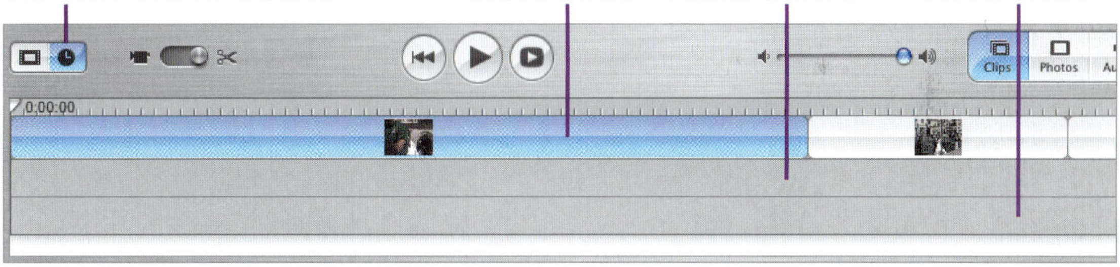

Click the Timeline Viewer button (or press ⌘-E) to display the Timeline Viewer. This mode displays clips sized according to their duration (which can also be rearranged by dragging). The Timeline Viewer also includes two audio tracks below the video track for adding audio files (see Chapter 5). This is the component you will use most when trimming clips and editing audio.

As you'll see in Chapters 6–9, you can use both Viewers to add and delete clips, titles, transitions, and effects.

extra bits

create an iMovie project p. 7

- Remember to save your project often. Choose Save from the File menu, or press ⌘-S. In the unfortunate (but possible) event that iMovie crashes, you'd lose any changes made since the last time you saved the project. Trust me, I've been burned by this too many times in the past; now I think of myself as a serial saver.
- You don't have to save your project into your Home folder. When you create a new project, feel free to save it anywhere on your hard disk.
- When working on a project, I usually save it to an external FireWire hard drive (you can get 80 GB models now for around $100) or to a partition on my computer's hard disk where I keep some works in progress. A partition is basically a section of your hard disk that appears on the desktop as if it were a completely different volume. (If you want to partition a drive, use Apple's Disk Utility application. Be sure to back up all of your data, because partitioning a drive erases it first!)

  Why use a partition or external hard disk? In addition to providing more storage, it is disk space that won't get as fragmented (i.e., pieces of data are written to lots of different areas on the disk). When data is fragmented, it takes longer for the drive to locate the data—granted, it's usually a matter of milliseconds, but if a drive is severely fragmented, iMovie can drop frames and otherwise not behave nicely.
- Mac OS X 10.3 Panther includes a feature called FileVault, which promises to increase the security of your data by encrypting the contents of your Home folder. Unfortunately, that's where Apple's programs store video files, iTunes music, and other large files. If you're running an iMovie project stored in the Home folder and have FileVault enabled, every byte that iMovie uses must be decrypted on the fly. The result is poor performance and potentially bad data loss. I really like the idea of FileVault, but its current incarnation is just too poorly implemented for real-world use.
- Depending on the size of your screen, you can play back your movie in its native resolution by choosing Show Full Video Resolution from the Window menu. It's great on a 30-inch Apple Cinema Display (I wish I had one)!

3. import video into iMovie

Although the video footage captured by your digital camcorder is recorded as long series of ones and zeros, it's written on magnetic tape (which is still the best way to store the vast amount of information that digital video occupies). To turn that footage into a malleable form you can edit, you need to bring it from the camera's tape to your hard disk. iMovie calls this process importing.

Before you start, make sure you have plenty of free space on your hard disk: importing a typical 60-minute MiniDV tape takes up roughly 13 gigabytes (GB) of hard disk space (1 second of DV video equals 3.6 MB). If you're importing HD footage, plan on using about four times that amount of disk space.

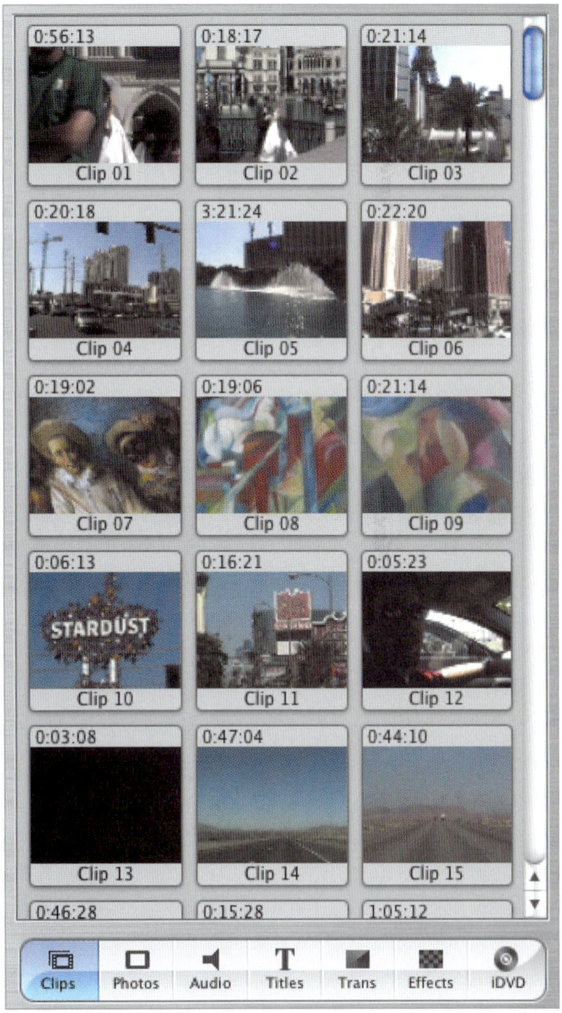

connect the camcorder

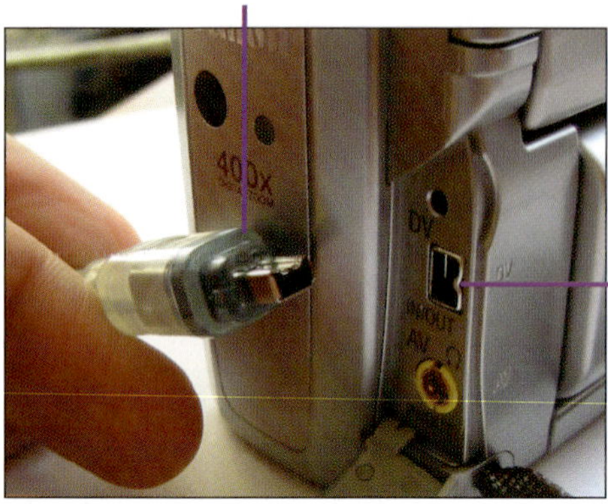

1 Connect the FireWire cable to the camcorder and your Mac.

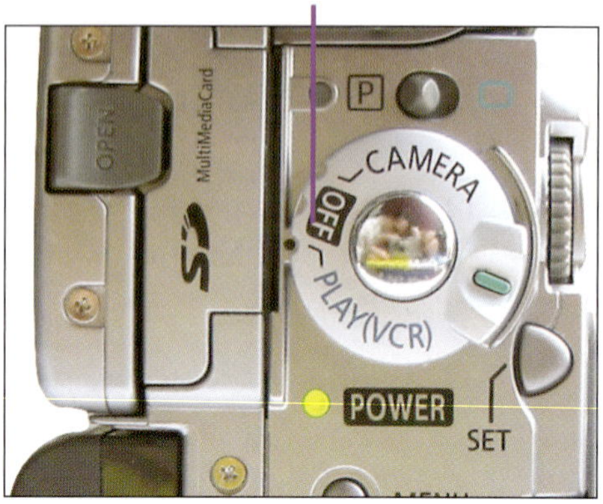

2 Switch the camcorder to Play/ VCR mode (the name can vary among camera manufacturers).

3 Launch iMovie. It should go into Camera mode automatically; if not, click the mode switch to change from Edit mode to Camera mode.

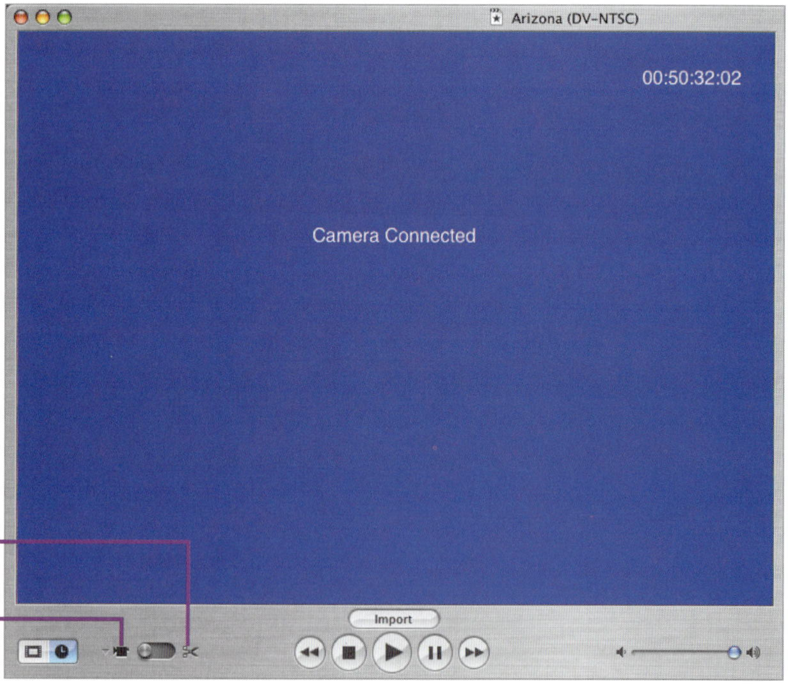

review your footage

When the camera is connected, you can use iMovie's controls to rewind, fast-forward, and play through the footage on tape. This lets you locate footage without fiddling with the camera's miniscule buttons. If nothing else, I find it easier to rewind the tape using iMovie.

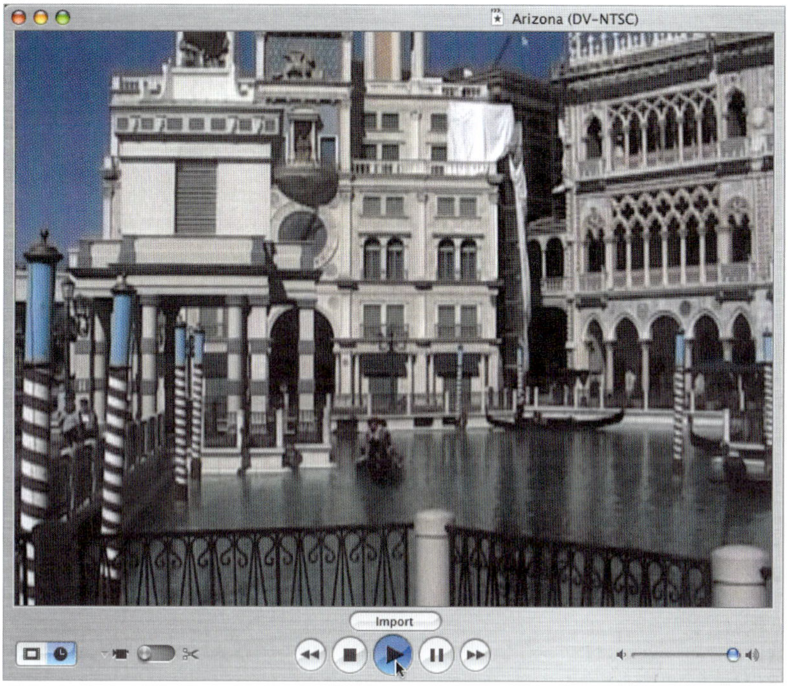

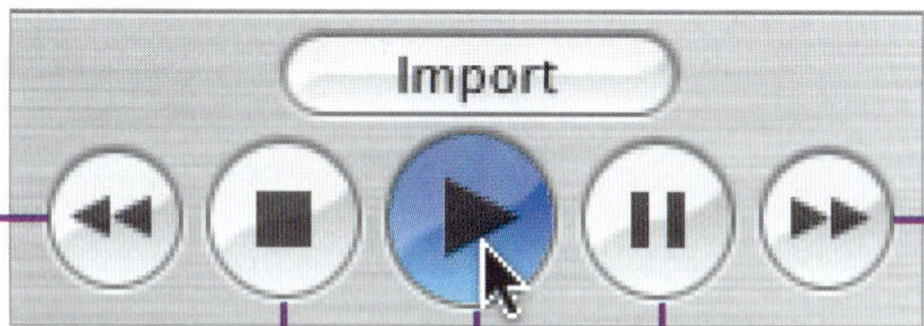

Press Rewind or Fast-forward while the video is playing to review the footage sped up.

import your footage

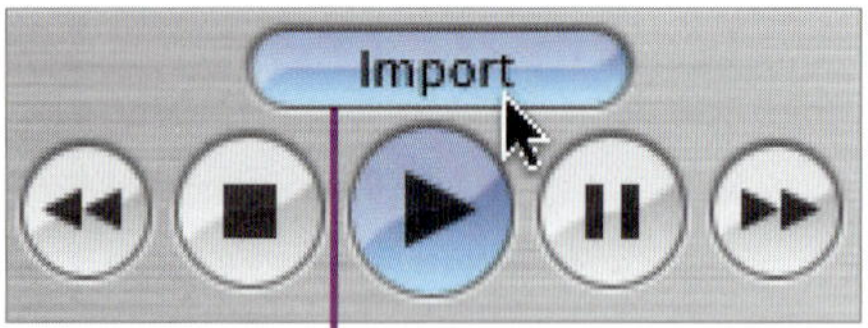

Here's the (not so) hard part: click the Import button to start importing your footage. iMovie automatically starts playback on the camcorder.

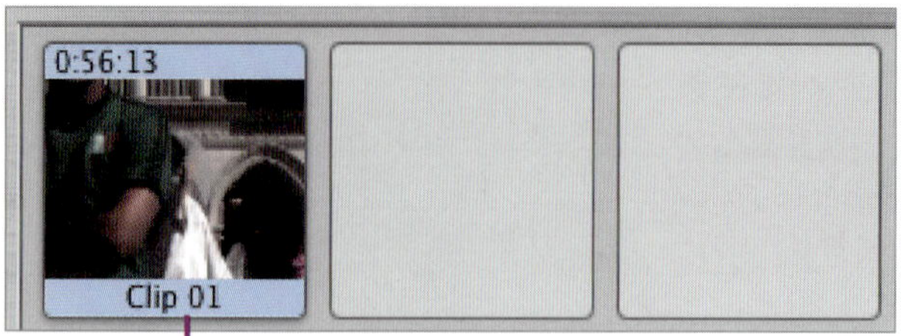

Footage appears on the Shelf as a clip.

As you import, iMovie identifies the moments in your footage when you stopped recording one scene and started recording the next. When such a break is encountered, iMovie creates a new clip for each scene.

New clip created for next scene.

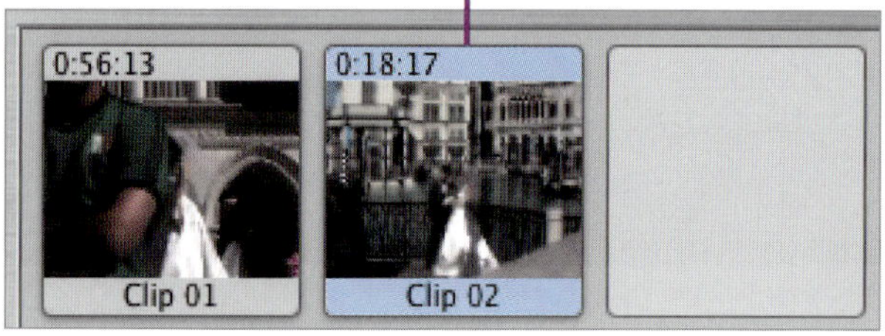

After importing the clips you want (the entire tape, in this case), click the Import button again to stop.

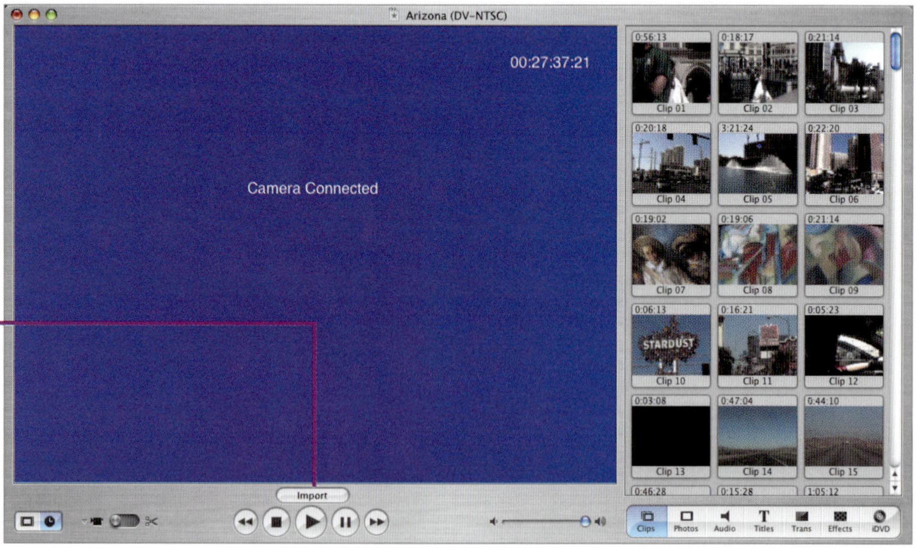

timecode

Now that your footage is in iMovie, you need to become familiar with the way video is measured: timecode. A movie is made up of thousands of frames, so clips are measured in terms of minutes, seconds, and frames.

In NTSC video (the standard for television in North America), 30 frames equals 1 second; so, for example, a timecode value of 1:23:15 is equal to one minute, twenty-three and a half seconds.

Many European countries use the PAL standard, which is 25 frames per second. In PAL format, our example of ten and a half seconds would be a timecode of 1:23:12.

iMovie automatically determines which type of camcorder you're using (NTSC or PAL) and creates a project matching that rate.

As you start working with clips, timecode will soon become second nature.

Length of clip in timecode: 1 minute, 23 seconds and 15 frames

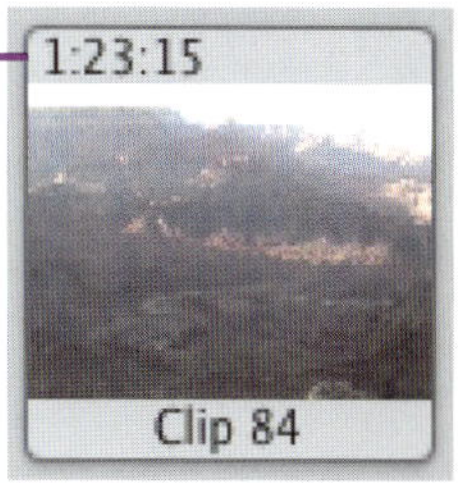

Timecode notation

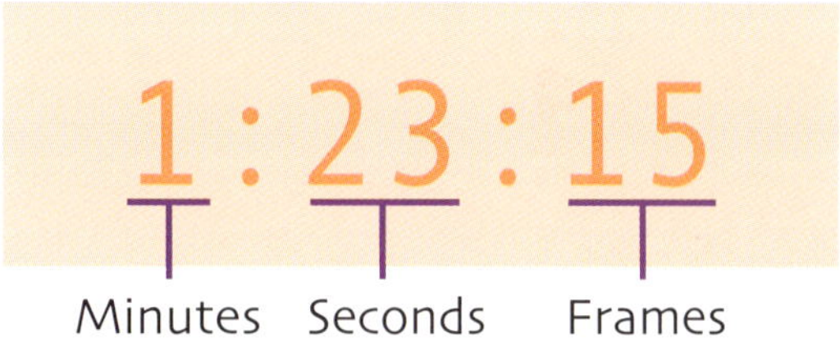

extra bits

connect the camcorder p. 12

- Quit other applications before importing to make sure that their actions in the background (such as checking email, playing music, etc.) don't interfere with the import process. Otherwise, you could encounter dropped frames or stuttery playback.
- If you have an iSight camera that's connected at the same time as your camcorder, and you want to capture live video with it, click the camera icon next to the mode switch and choose iSight from the popup menu that appears.

review your footage p. 13

- If you're importing sections of your tape (instead of the entire tape), rewind to a few seconds before the start of what you want to capture. This gives you some buffer while editing.

import your footage p. 14

- Press the spacebar in Camera mode to start importing footage. Press it again to stop.
- The free space indicator in the lower-right corner of iMovie's window keeps tabs on how much room is left on your hard disk. As the disk fills up, the indicator text changes from black to yellow to red. When no more space is free, iMovie stops the import process.
- You can also import QuickTime movies (or other formats that are compatible with QuickTime, such as AVI movies) from your hard disk. Simply drag the QuickTime file from the Finder onto the Shelf or the Timeline. However, since most QuickTime movies are smaller in size, the resolution may not be as good as your camcorder's footage.
- You can buy analog-to-digital converter boxes, which enable you to connect an analog camcorder or VCR to your Mac and import that footage into iMovie. I used one recently to digitize and edit the video from my wedding, since VHS tapes noticeably deteriorate.
- If, as you import, you hear an echo, check your camera's volume level. If it's audible, you'll hear the footage's audio first from the camcorder's speakers, and then from your Mac's speakers a fraction of a second after.
- iMovie HD's Magic iMovie feature imports video and adds transitions automatically. However, since we're editing manually, we don't need to use Magic iMovie.

4. assemble your movie

Your footage is now in iMovie, but you don't have a movie quite yet. To borrow from another art form, your project is now a block of marble just waiting for the chisel that will reveal the statue within. And like a sculptor, you need to reveal your movie gradually, creating a rough shape before refining the details. In this chapter, you'll move your clips from the Shelf to the Timeline and put them in order.

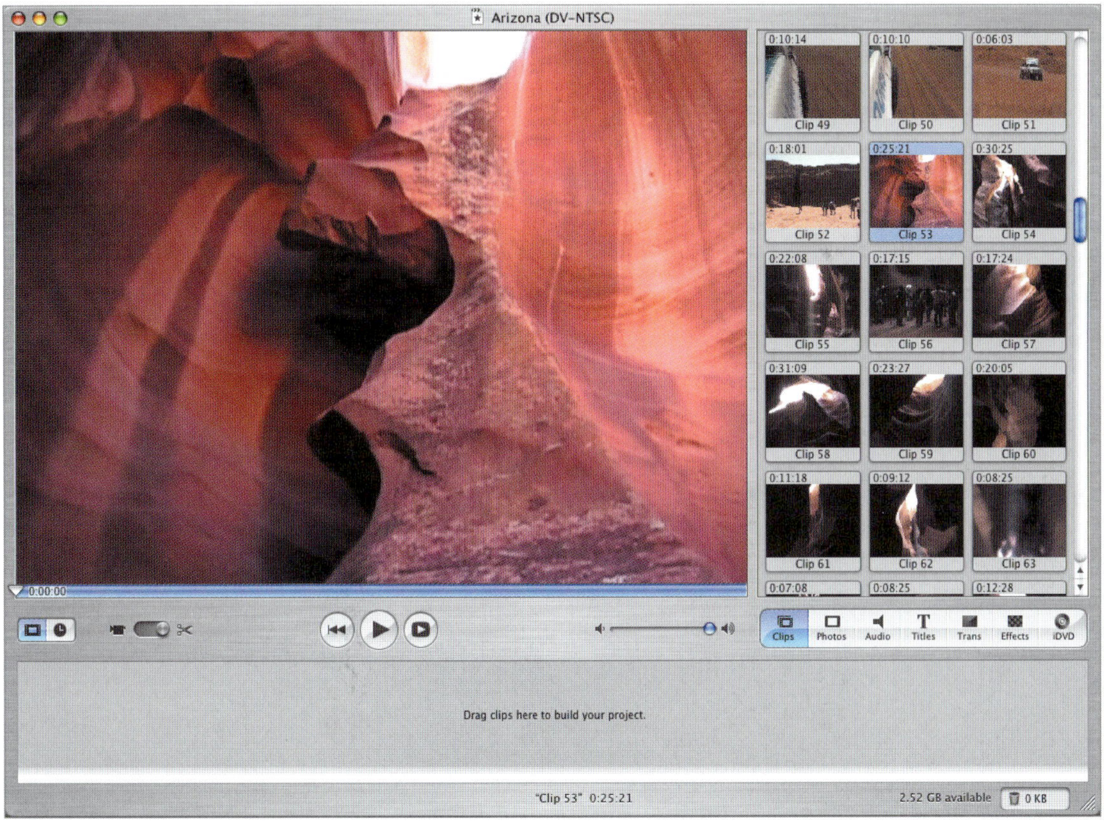

add clips to timeline

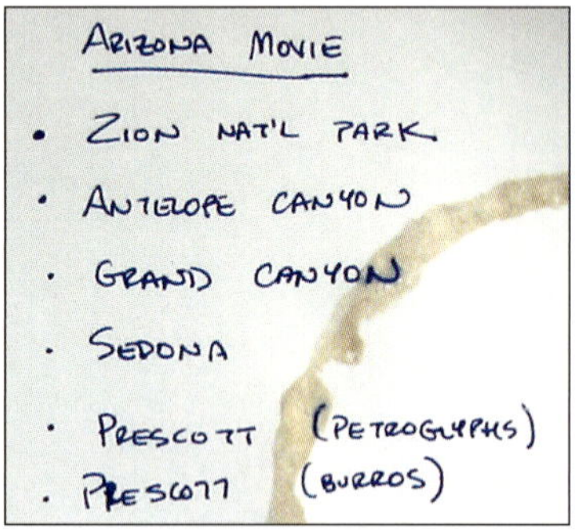

It may not be high-tech, but I find it essential to make a quick outline of the movie's high points to use as a road map.

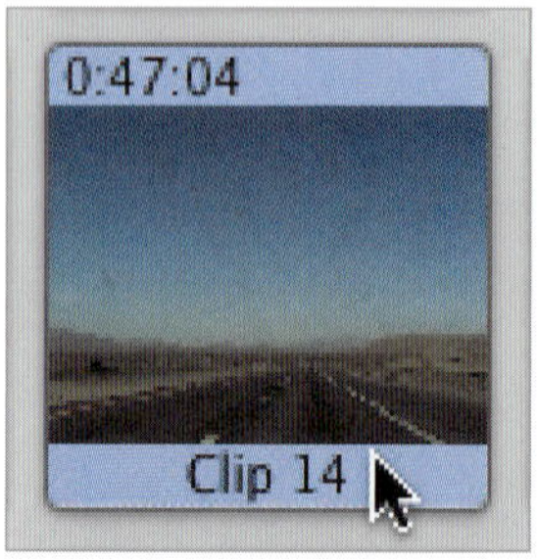

I also spend some time renaming significant clips to help identify them while editing.

Click once on the clip's name to edit.

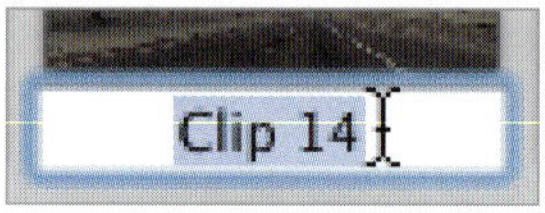

Highlight the current name.

Type a new name, and press Return.

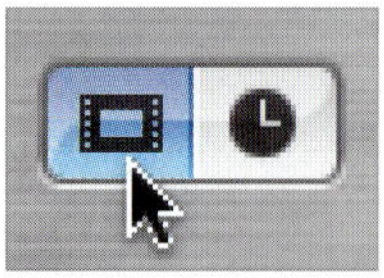

1 Click the Clip Viewer button to display that mode of the timeline.

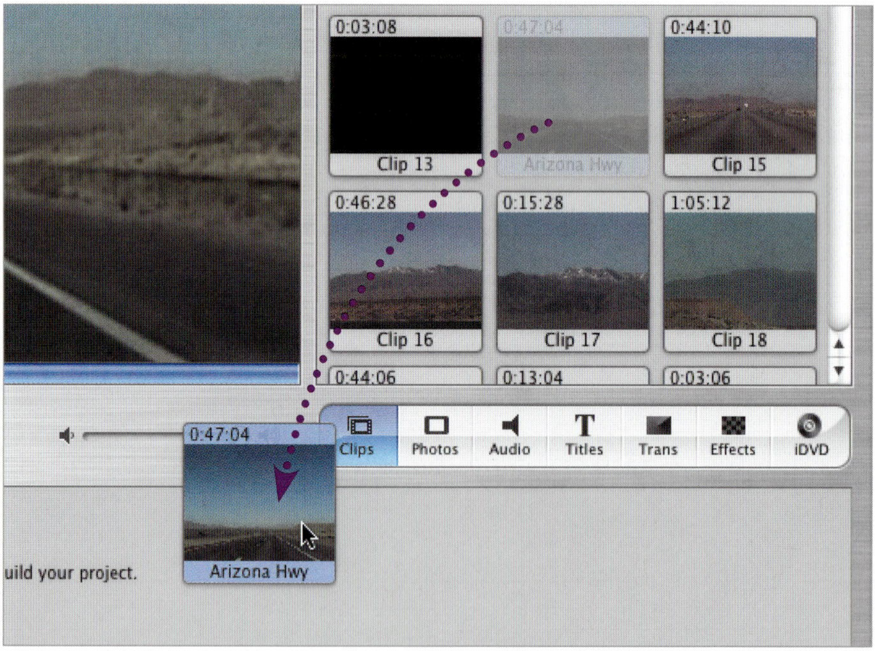

2 Drag one or more clips from the Shelf to the Clip Viewer. Congratulations, you've just made a (rough) movie!

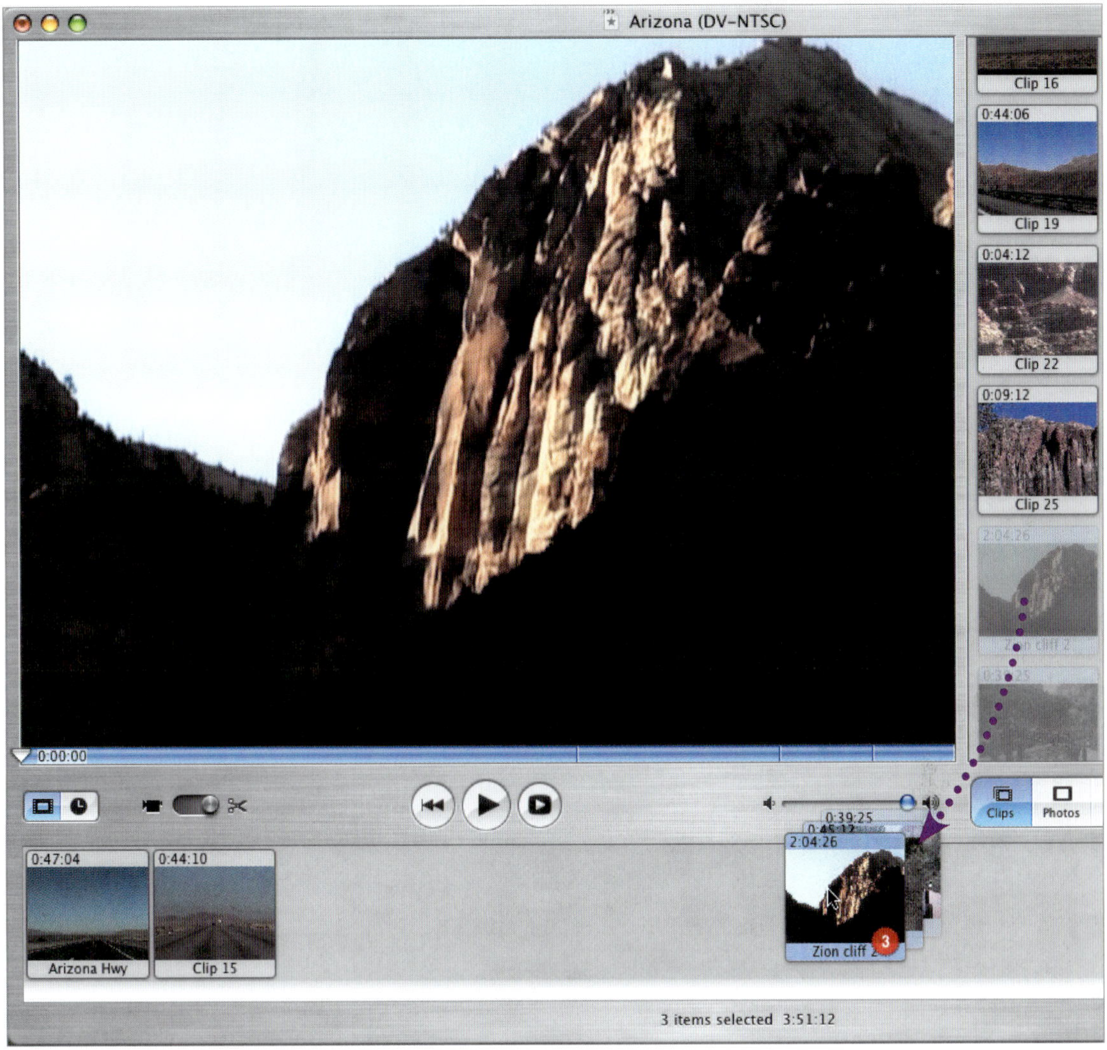

3 Continue to drag the clips you want to use into the timeline. Don't worry about the order that they're in—your goal at this point is to put together a rough assembly of the raw materials you'll be working with. Any clip added to the timeline becomes part of your movie.

arrange the clips

iMovie is nonlinear: you can arrange clips in any order you wish. Reposition clips in the Clip Viewer (shown here) or Timeline Viewer to determine the order they will play.

1 Click and hold on a clip to select it.

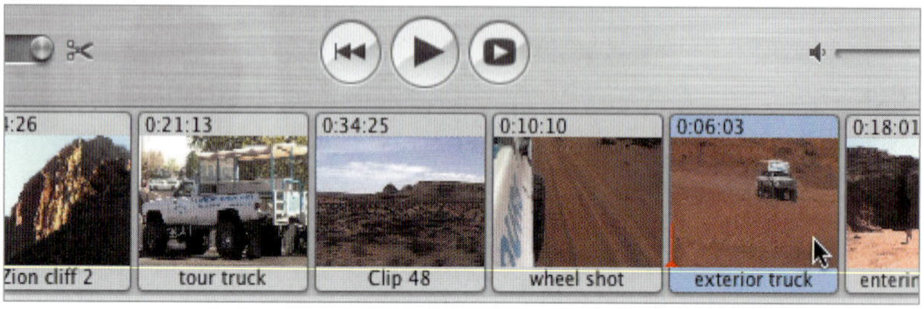

2 Drag the clip to a new location in the Clip Viewer.

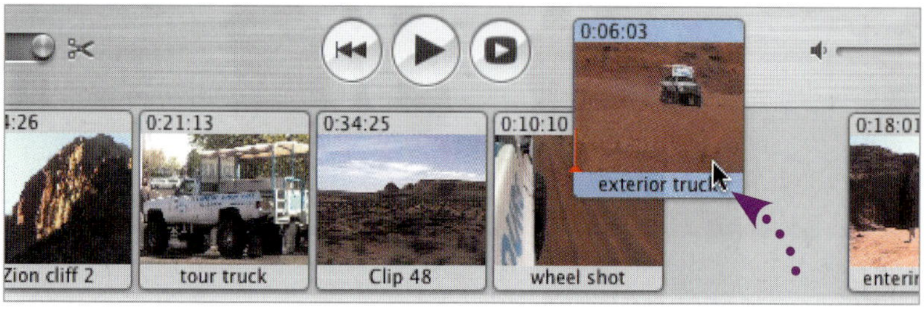

As you drag, other clips automatically slide out of the way of the selected clip.

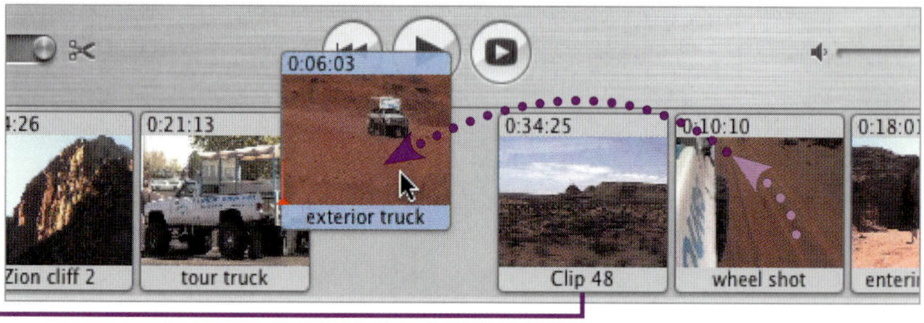

3 Release the mouse button where you want the clip to appear. It falls into place.

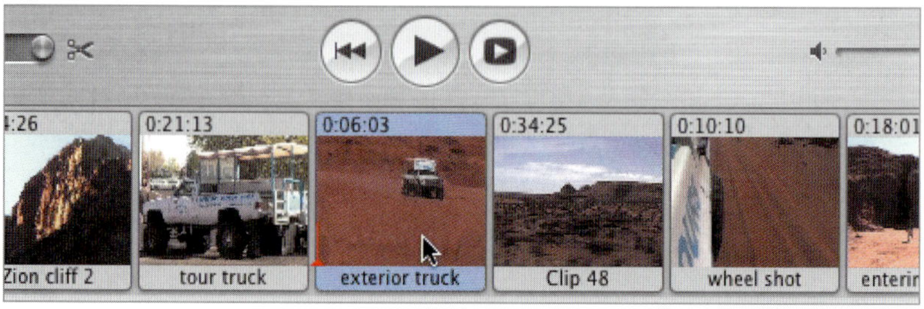

As you're arranging your clips, use the Shelf as a convenient holding area. For example, I've found two clips that I know would be great as the beginning (where I will want to add my titles later) and closing scenes in the movie.

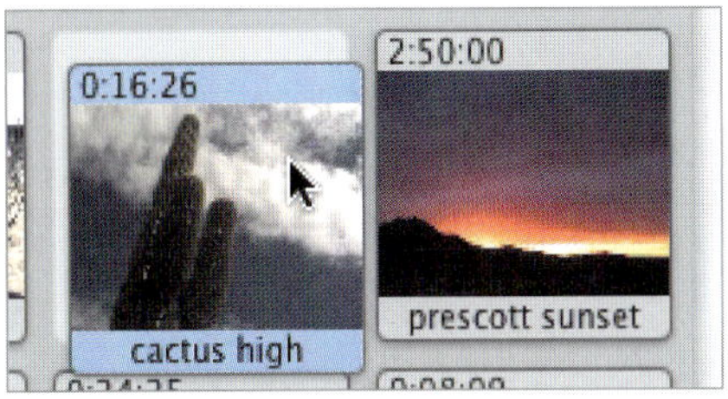

This cactus clip actually appeared at the end of the tape, so first I reposition it on the shelf for easy access...

...and then later drag it to the beginning of the timeline to appear as the first clip.

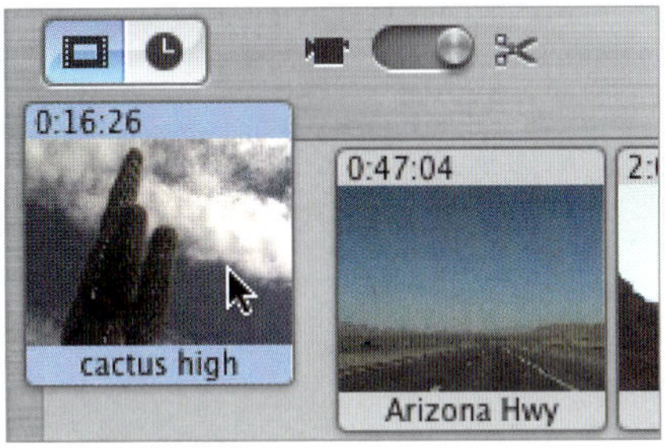

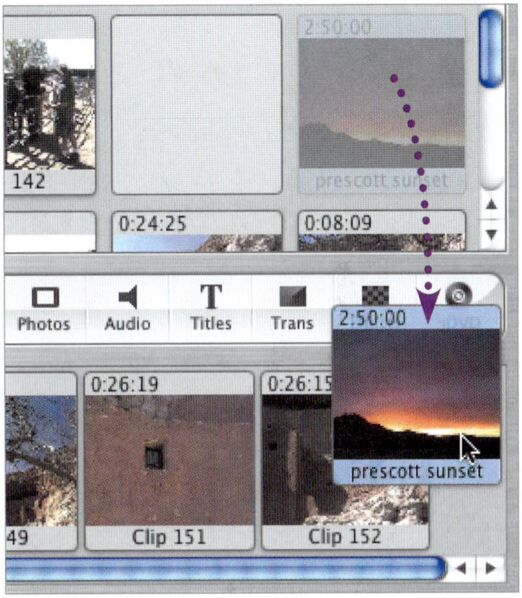

The sunset clip, meanwhile, goes to the end of the timeline.

If you don't need a clip, drag it to iMovie's Trash (or press the Delete key). However, I recommend that you not empty the Trash while you're in the middle of an editing project (see the extra bits section at the end of this chapter).

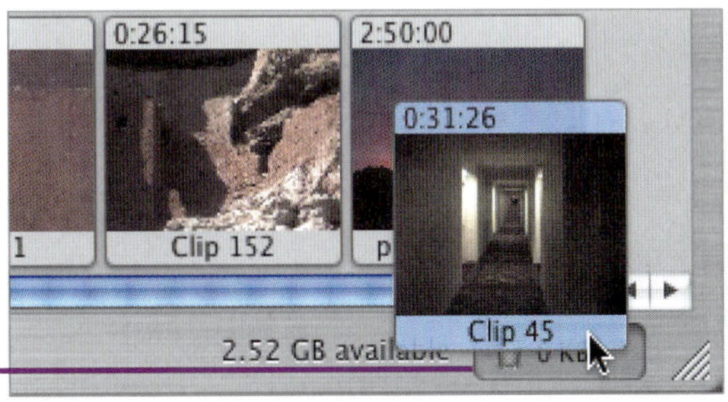

arrange the clips (cont.)

With all of our clips added to the timeline, you can see that the total duration of our movie is just over 45 minutes! But that's okay, because as we start editing the individual clips, we'll soon trim the movie down closer to a goal of 10-15 minutes.

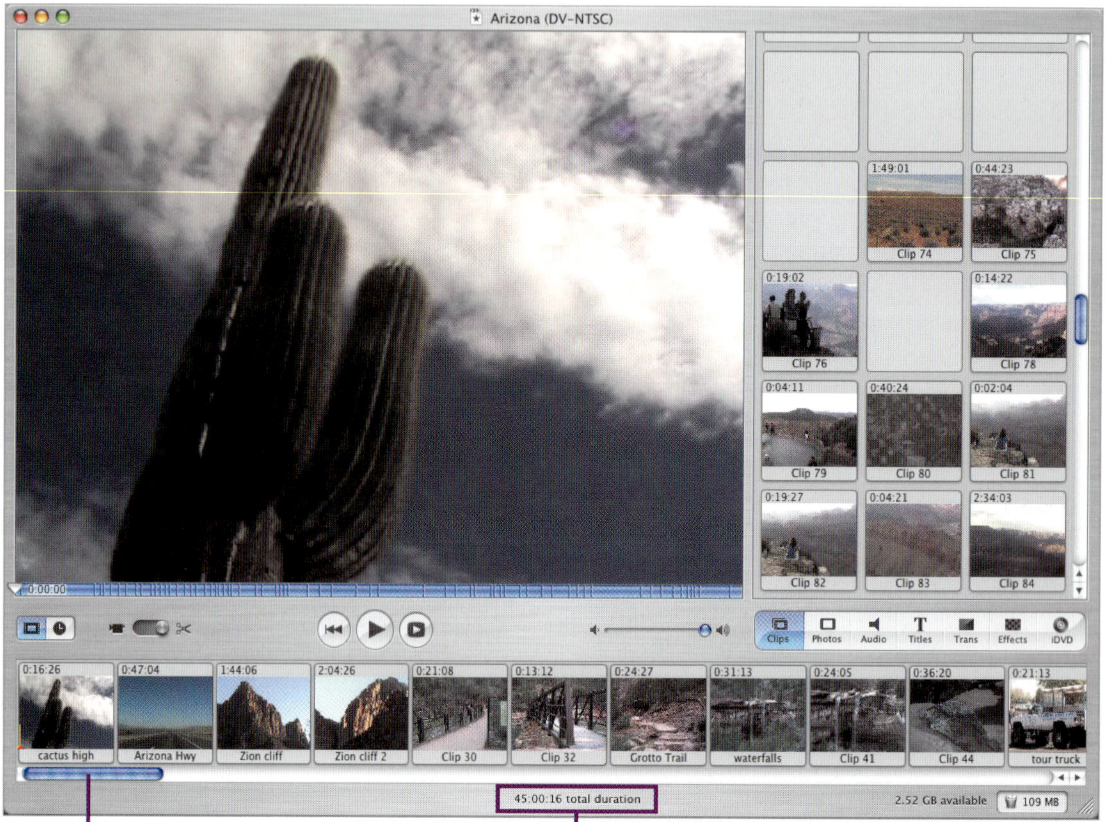

Drag the horizontal scroll bar to view all of your clips.

45:00:16 total duration

Keep track of the movie's duration here.

extra bits

add clips to timeline p. 18

- Don't forget about Copy and Paste. In iMovie HD, you can copy clips in one project, and then paste them into another project to add them.
- In general, I don't recommend that you empty the Trash while working on a project. Although iMovie HD improves on previous versions by enabling you to pull clips out of the Trash, you may throw something away that you need later. At that point, the only way to get it is to re-import the original footage from tape.
- If you do need to grab clips out of the Trash, simply click the Trash icon or choose Show Trash from the File menu. Select the clip you need and drag it to the Shelf or the timeline; the window at right lets you preview the clip.

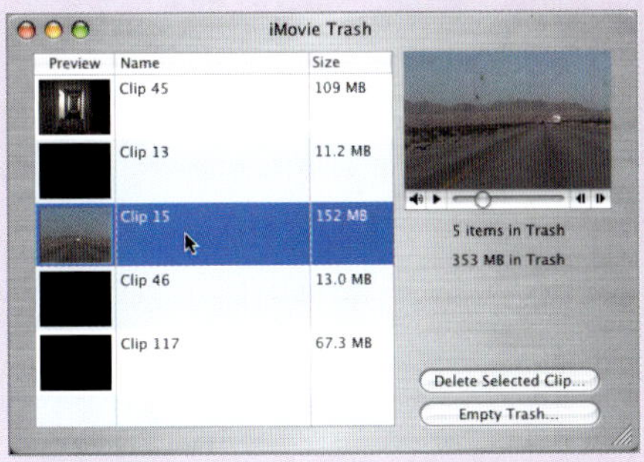

arrange the clips p. 20

- In earlier versions of iMovie, the Clip Viewer was the only mode of the timeline that allowed you to rearrange clips. However, now you can move them in the Timeline Viewer, too. You may not think that's a big deal, but it saves you some work and frustration by not having to switch between viewers just to slide a clip into a new location.
- If you do move clips in the Timeline Viewer, it helps to drag them slightly up above the timeline before moving, to make sure you rearrange the clips, and not just create a blank space (see Chapter 6 for more on blank clips).
- Although I've structured this book so that all the clips are added in this one stage of editing, you can drag clips in and out of the timeline at any time.

5. add photos and music

Even when I'm not on vacation, I like to keep a digital still camera close at hand. A typical still camera captures more image resolution than a camcorder; plus, I like to send snapshots to friends and family.

Most camcorders sold today can also shoot still images, so you've no doubt accumulated a bunch of photos. If you use iPhoto to organize your pictures, you can easily grab them from within iMovie and add them to your movie. And with the Ken Burns Effect, you can add some pan and zoom effects to make the photos more interesting.

At this stage, it also helps to add background music to your movie (if you choose). Later, you can edit your clips so they're timed to your tunes.

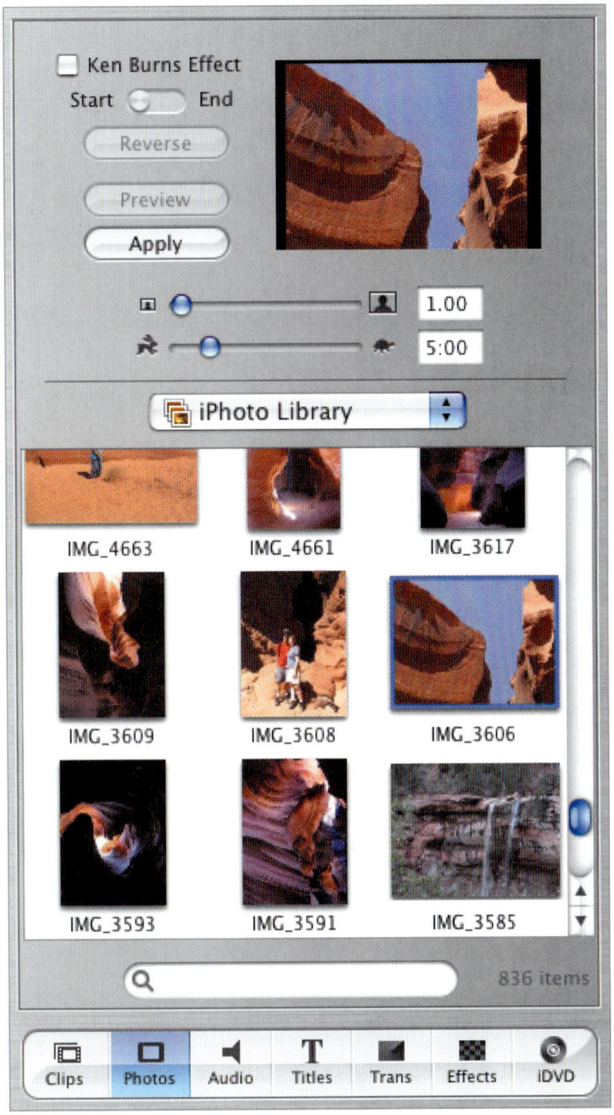

import photos

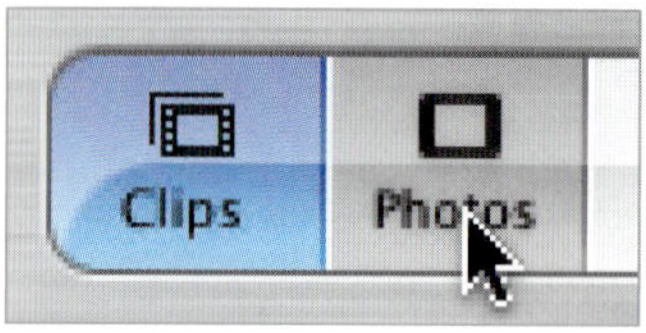

1 View the Photos pane by clicking the Photos button.

2 Make sure the Ken Burns Effect is disabled (we'll cover this feature on page 28).

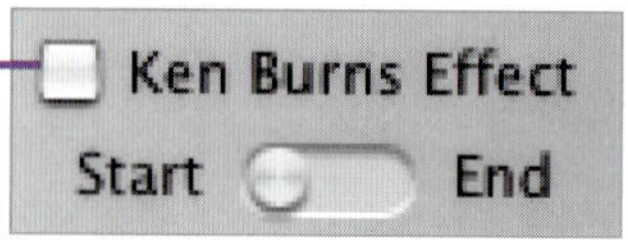

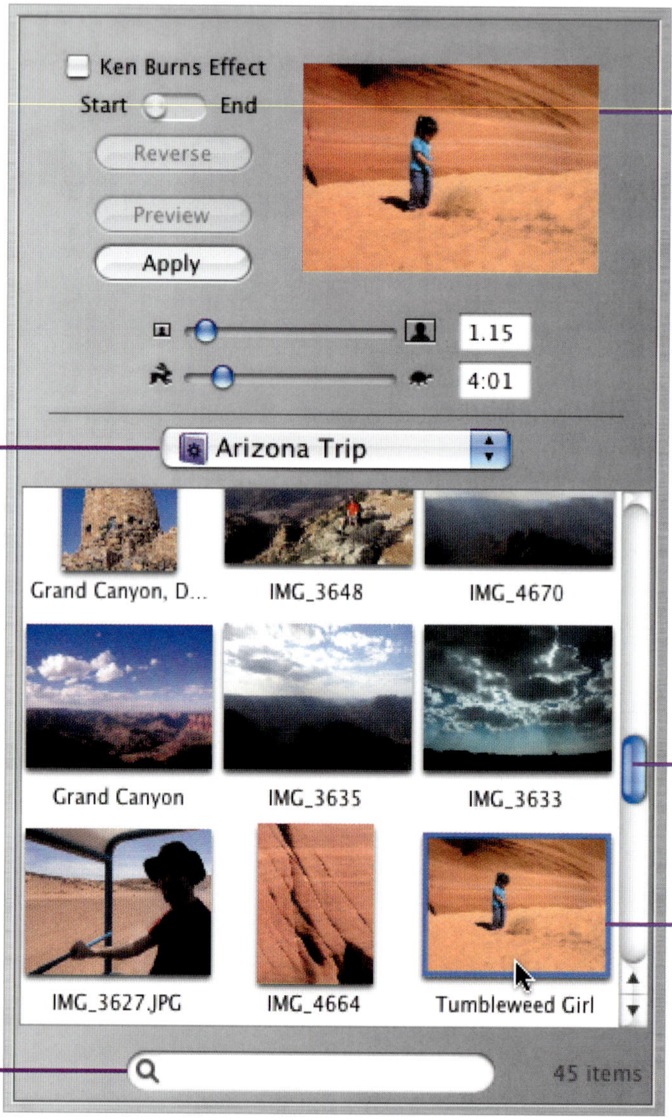

The photo you select appears in the preview area.

I created a new album in iPhoto for my vacation pictures. Choosing the album name from the popup menu displays only those photos.

3 Scroll through your iPhoto pictures to find one to add to your movie.

4 Click a photo to select it.

Type within the Search field to find photos that match titles and keywords (which you can set up in iPhoto).

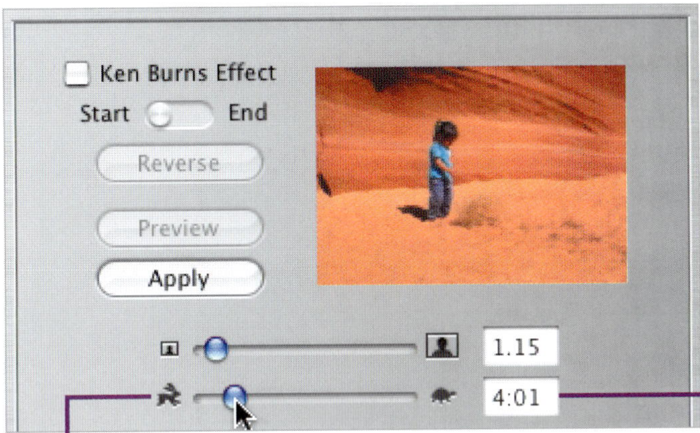

You can also type a new time value into the Duration field.

5 Move the Duration slider to specify how long the still photo will appear in the movie.

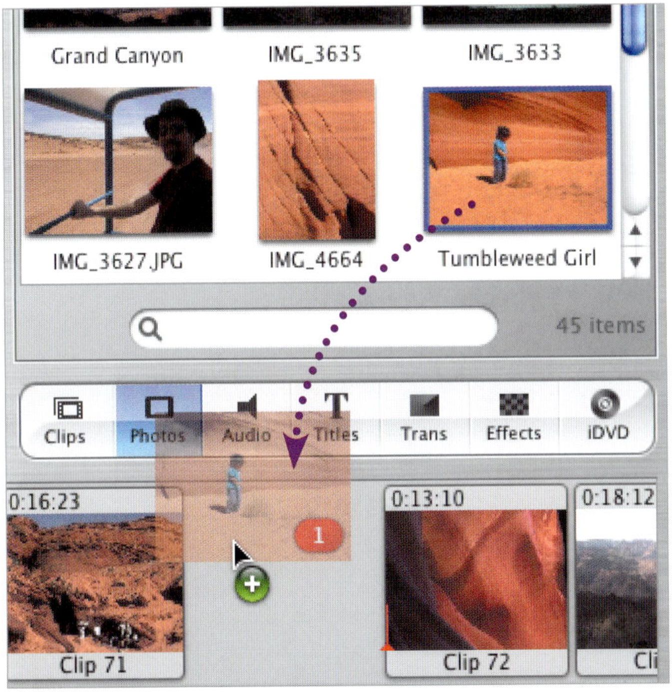

6 Drag the photo to the Clip Viewer (shown here) or Timeline Viewer to add it to your movie.

This icon, shown in the Clip Viewer, indicates that the clip is a still photo.

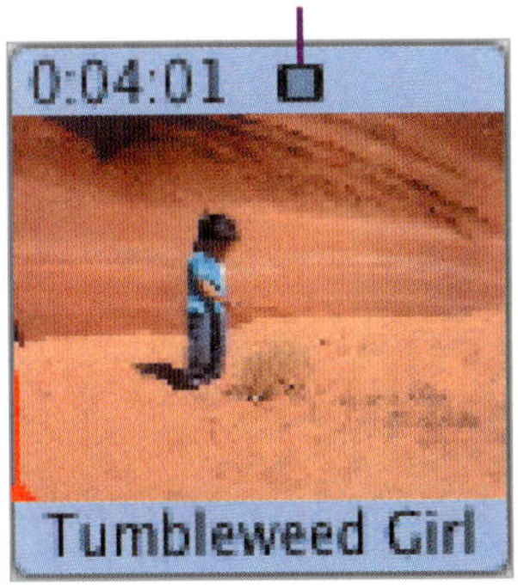

add motion to photos

The Ken Burns Effect (named after the documentary filmmaker who popularized the technique) adds motion to still pictures by panning and zooming: focusing on a portion of the image and moving the camera over it. To do so, set the appearance of the first frame of the effect (the Start), and then set the last frame (the End). iMovie then calculates the frames in-between to produce the effect. For this example, I want to start zoomed in on a photo of a handsome tourist, then zoom out to reveal the Grand Canyon.

1 Click here to enable the effect.

2 Move the switch to Start to set up the first frame of the effect.

3 Change the zoom amount by dragging the Zoom slider, or typing a value into the Zoom field.

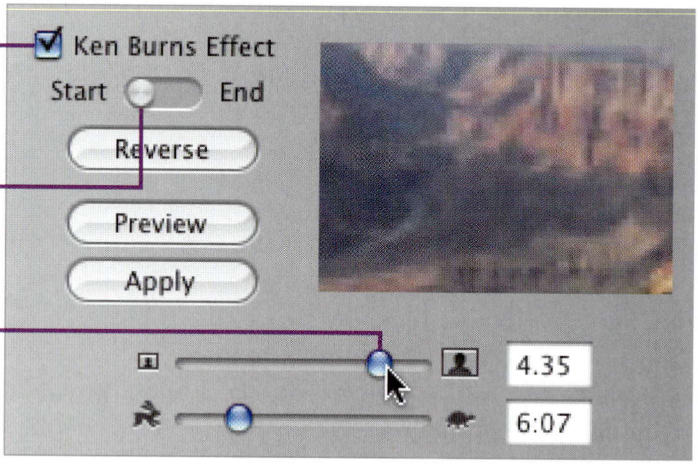

4 Click and drag in the preview area to locate the section of the image you want visible.

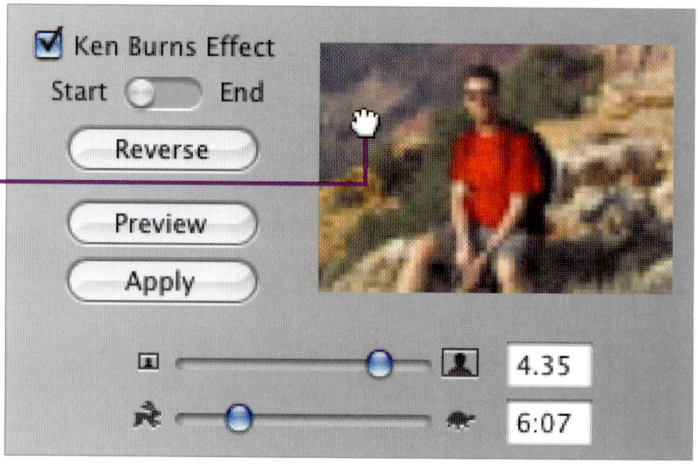

5 Move the switch to the End position to set up the last frame of the effect.

As you work, click here to preview the effect.

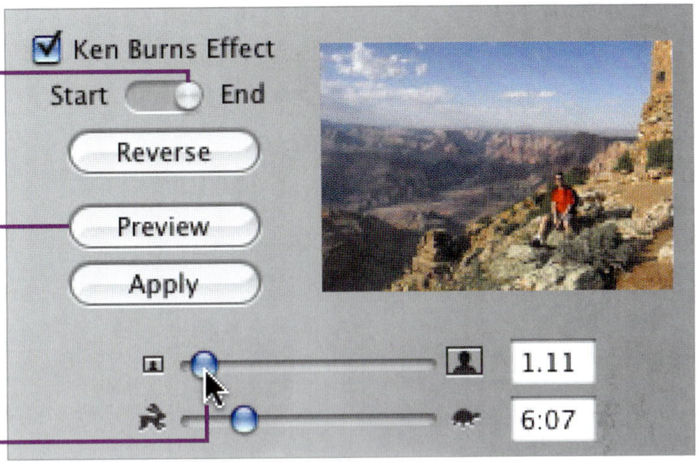

6 Change the zoom amount. In this case, I'm zooming almost entirely out.

7 Drag the image to the Timeline to add it to your movie.

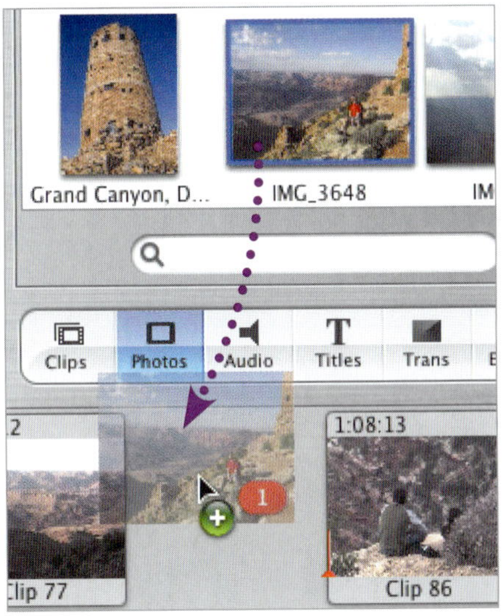

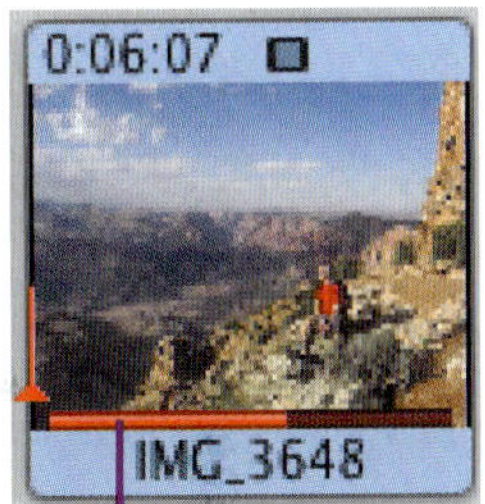

iMovie renders the photo as a video clip; the red line indicates rendering progress.

The completed effect:

Start

End

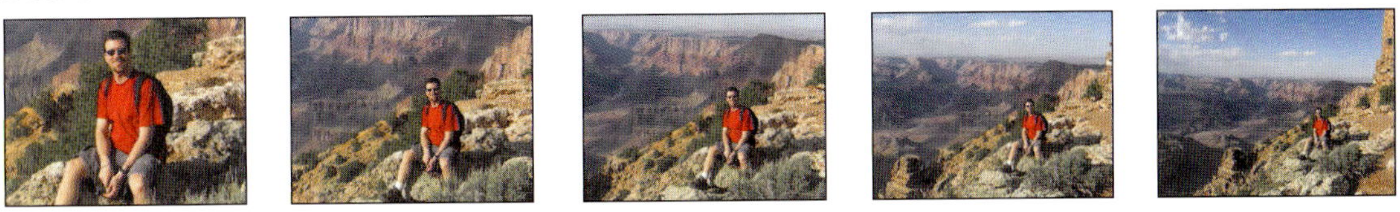

add music from iTunes

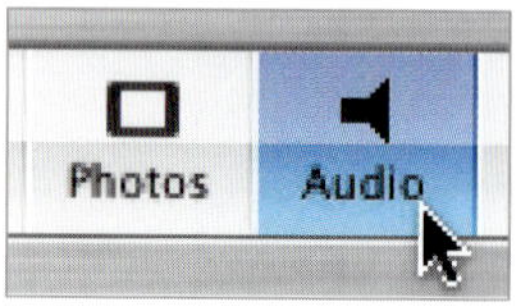

1 Switch to the Audio pane by clicking the Audio button.

Click the popup menu to access your iTunes playlists.

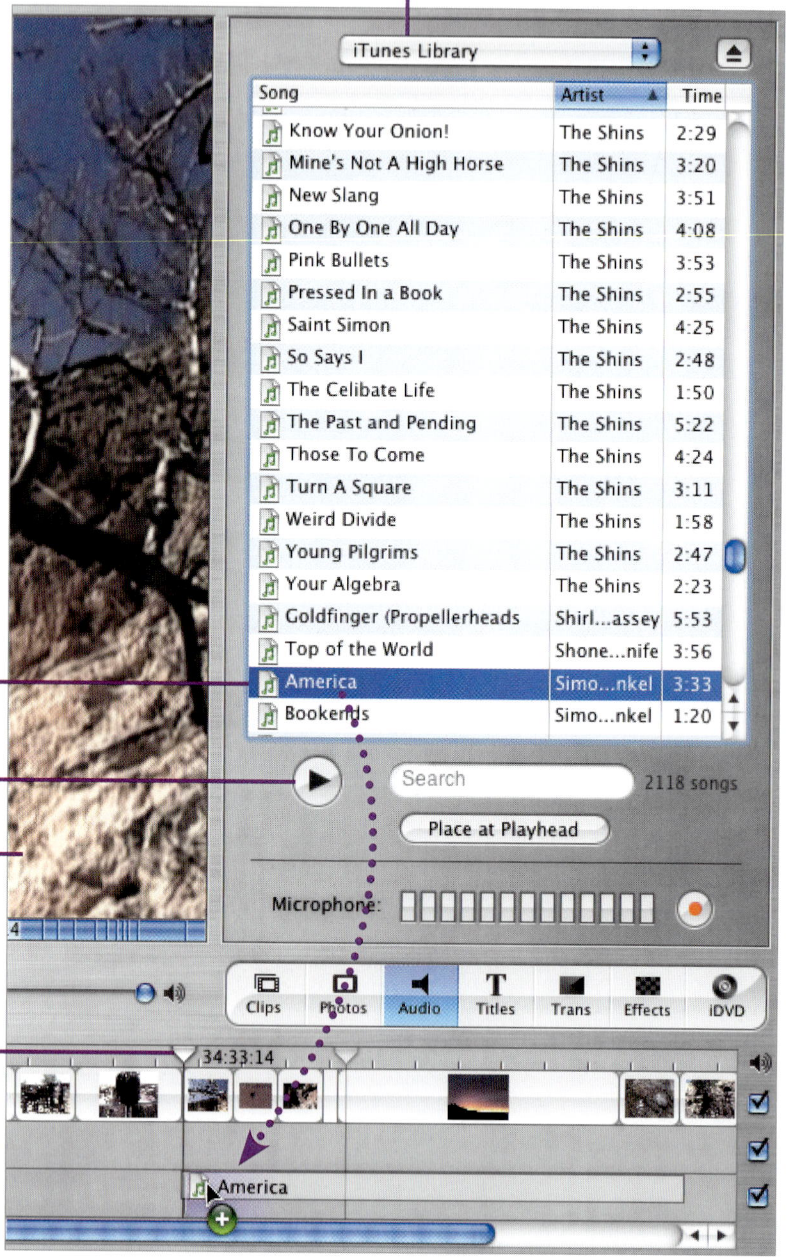

2 Drag a song to the Timeline to add it to the movie.

Click the Play button to listen to a song before adding it.

As you drag, the Monitor displays the current frame under your cursor to help you decide where to place the audio clip.

extra bits

import photos p. 26

- Instead of dragging a photo to the Timeline, you can also click the Apply button, which adds the photo to the end of your movie.
- You can add multiple photos at once. Hold down the [⌘] key and click several photos to select them, then drag them to the Timeline.
- In addition to adding pictures stored in iPhoto, you can drag image files from the Finder directly onto iMovie's Shelf or Timeline.
- If you do drag image files from the Finder, avoid PICT-formatted files—iMovie doesn't display them correctly.
- You can use the Zoom slider to crop still photos, without applying the Ken Burns Effect to them.
- When you import a photo, it's converted to video resolution, and may not look as good onscreen. However, it will look fine when viewed on a television or when exported as a QuickTime file (see Chapter 12).

add motion to photos p. 28

- Click the Reverse button to swap the Start and End states (for example, to zoom out instead of zoom in).
- Decide you want to make a change to your Ken Burns Effect settings? Select the clip in the Timeline, change the settings in the Photos pane, and then click the Update button (which is normally the Apply button).
- Vertical photos appear in iMovie with black bars to their sides (this is known as "pillarboxed"). You could use the Zoom slider to crop the image, but then you're getting only part of the photo. Instead, use the Ken Burns Effect to pan up or down the picture's length.

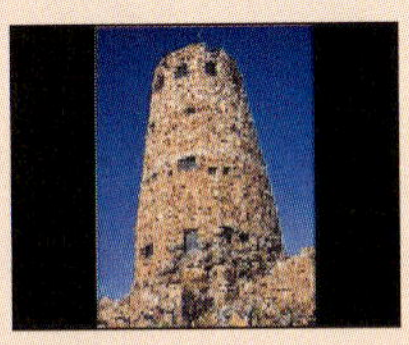

Original

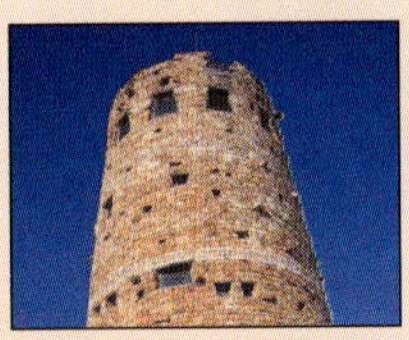

KBE Start

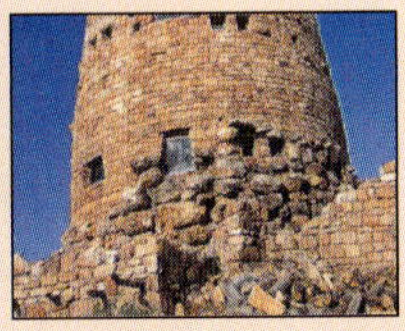

KBE End

extra bits

add music from iTunes p. 30

- If you know the name of a song or artist that you want to use, type it into the Search field to locate it quickly.
- When you drag a song to your movie, the Timeline Viewer automatically appears to display the audio tracks, even if the Clip Viewer was previously active.
- Unlike video clips, which can be stored on the Shelf, audio clips can only appear on the Timeline. As a temporary holding place, put audio clips at the far right edge of the Timeline.
- Can't see the full name of a song or artist? Click and drag the spaces between the column headers to change the column widths.
- Click the Song, Artist, or Time column header to sort the list. Click it again to reverse-sort the list (such as displaying artists' names that begin with Z at the top). I often click the Time column header to see which songs are short when I know I have only a few seconds of time to fill in my movie.
- It doesn't matter into which audio track you place music clips, but I recommend using the lower track; you'll see why in the next chapter.
- GarageBand, which is part of iLife '05, is great for making short segments of background music for your movie. When you export songs from GarageBand, they appear in iTunes—which you can access using the steps outlined in this chapter.
- You can also add music directly from an audio CD. After inserting the CD into your Mac's media drive, switch to the Audio pane, choose the CD from the popup menu, and add songs just as you did from iTunes.
- The Audio pane is also where you can add sound effects. Choose iMovie Sound Effects from the popup menu, then drag an effect to the Timeline.

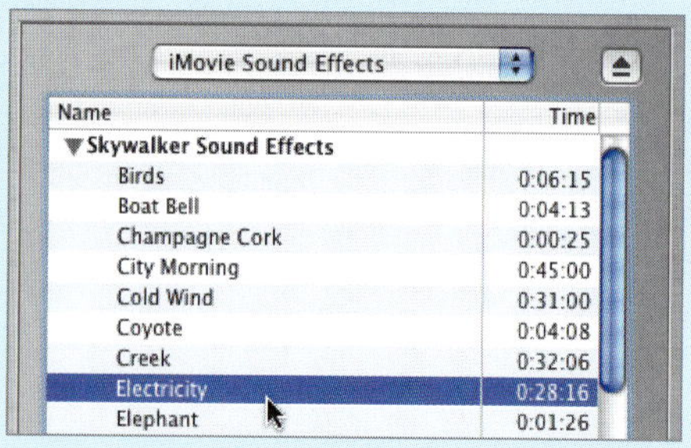

6. edit clips

Now that you've assembled a rough cut of your movie, it's time to start trimming clips and cutting the movie down to make it tight and enjoyable to watch. The editing techniques in this chapter apply to both video and audio clips, including photos (which were rendered as video clips when you added them to the Timeline) and songs you import from iTunes.

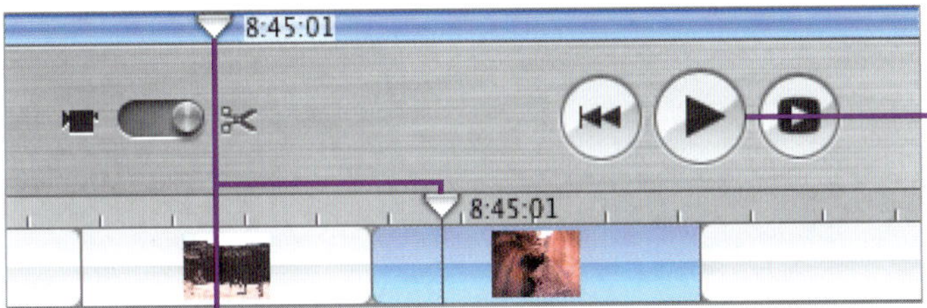

Equally important is seeing how your edits affect clips. The Play button plays your movie in the Monitor starting at the Playhead's location.

However, if a clip is selected, hitting the Play button plays only that clip in the Monitor.

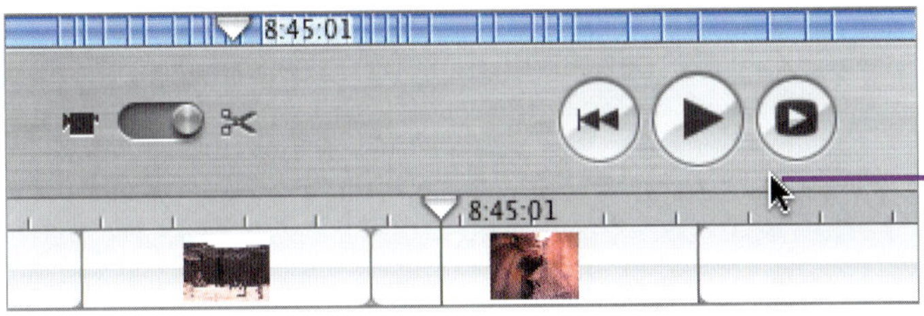

To play the entire movie, deselect the clip by clicking outside the Timeline (such as in the space just above it) and then hit Play.

I want to point out that this chapter differs from the rest in this book because I can't show you how I edit every clip in my movie. Instead, learn about iMovie's different editing techniques from my examples, so that you can apply them to your own footage. View a rough cut of the scene I used while writing this chapter at www.necoffee.com/imovievqs/ (click the Examples link).

direct-trim clips

iMovie uses an intuitive editing style Apple calls Direct Trimming, which lets you hide the frames you don't want to use.

1 Switch to the Timeline Viewer and select a clip.

Timeline Viewer button

Use the Zoom slider to zoom in on the Timeline, enabling you to make finer adjustments to clips.

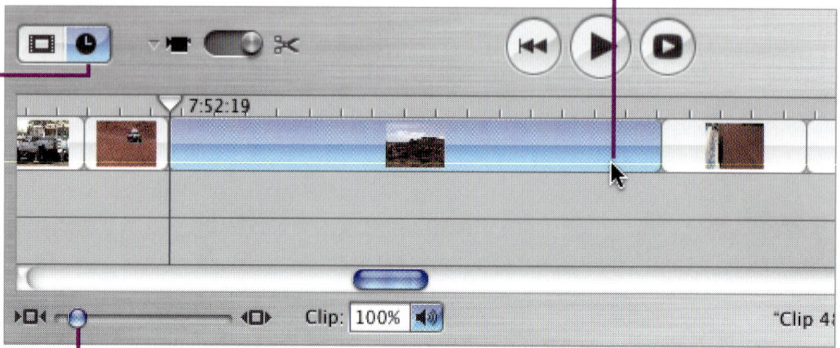

2 Place the mouse pointer at the edge of the clip.

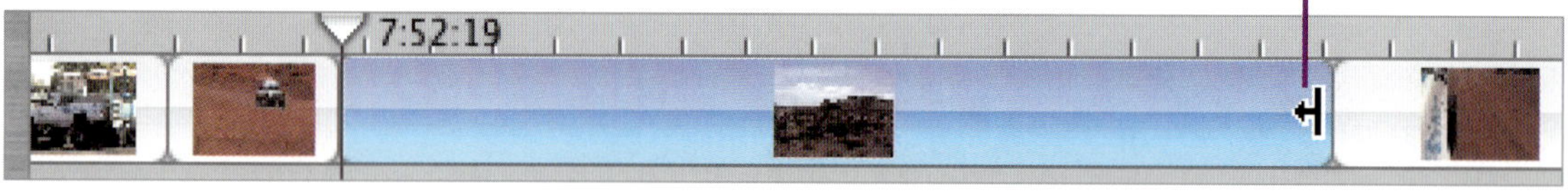

3 Drag to hide frames, then release the mouse button.

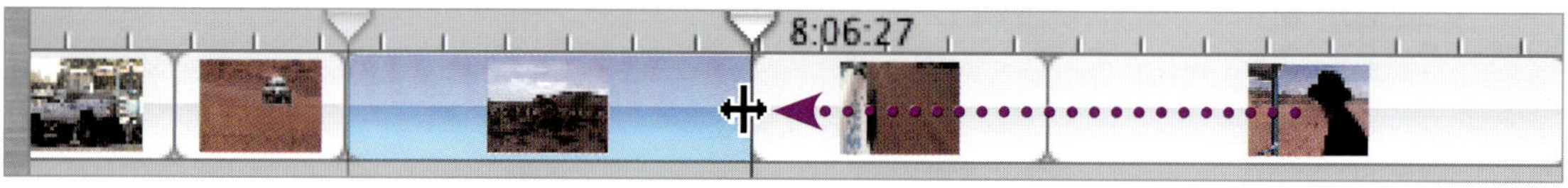

Straight corners indicate direct-trimmed clip.

Rounded corners indicate end of clip media.

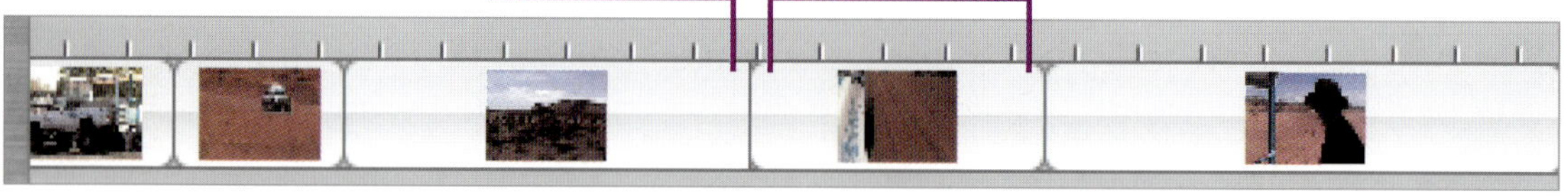

split clips

You can also split clips, just as if you were slicing a strip of film with a razor blade. I often split clips when I know I don't need an entire section, but don't want to click and drag with Direct Trimming.

1 Position the Playhead at the point within a clip where you want to split it.

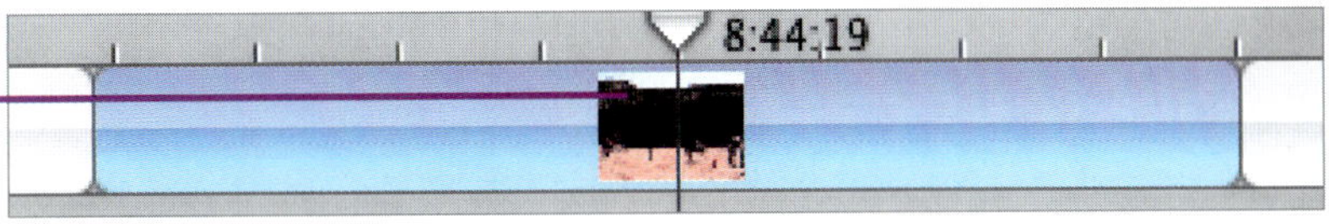

2 Choose Split Video Clip at Playhead from the Edit menu.

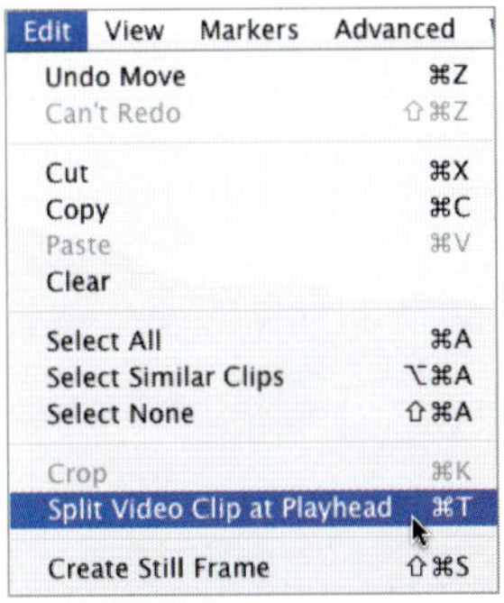

Single clip becomes two separate clips.

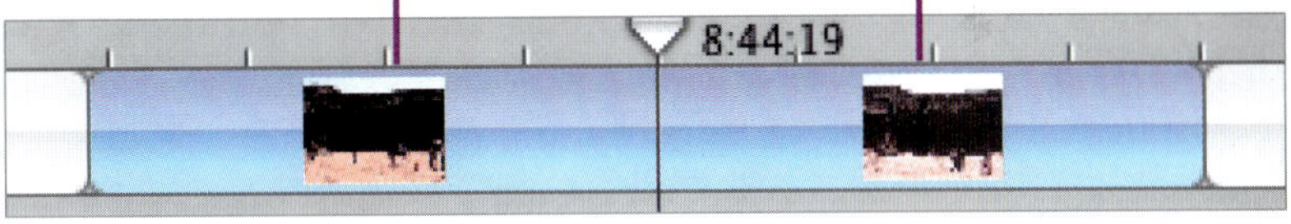

First half of original clip deleted.

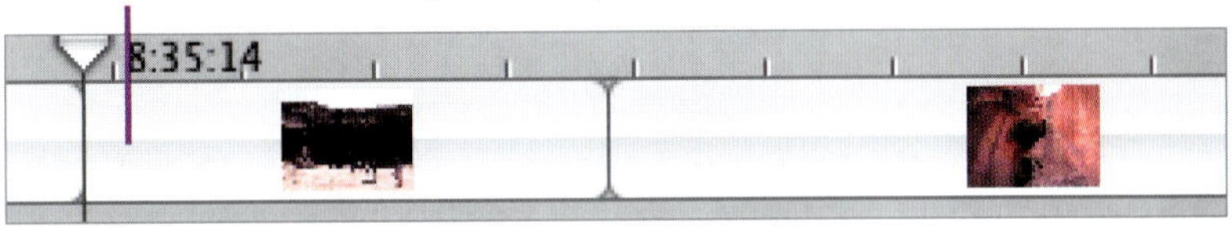

I wanted only the second portion of this clip to appear in my movie, so here I've deleted the first segment. I find that splitting clips and deleting segments (or moving them to the Shelf) is often a faster way of trimming my footage.

crop and trim clips

In addition to editing directly in the Timeline, you can use the Monitor's Scrubber Bar to select a range of frames, then crop or trim the clip. This approach can also be used when editing clips that are still on the Shelf.

1 Select a clip, position the mouse pointer just below the Scrubber Bar, and click to position the crop markers.

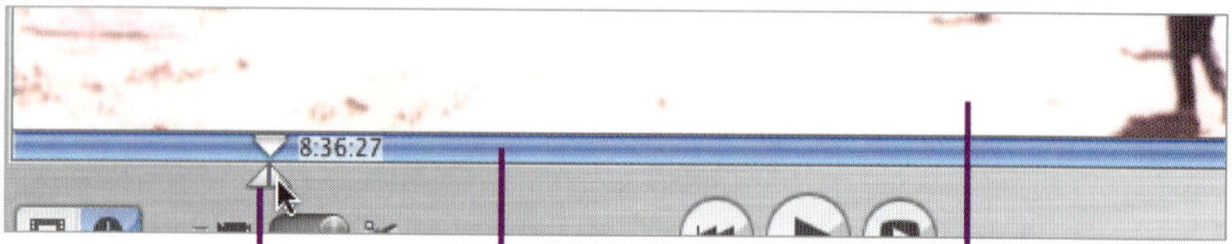

Crop markers Scrubber Bar Monitor

2 While still pressing the mouse button, drag the crop markers to select a range of frames.

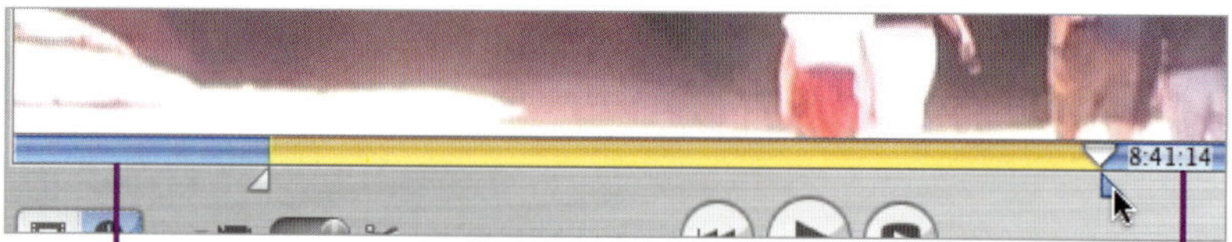

Choose Crop to delete the frames outside the selection.

3 Choose one of the following options from the Edit menu:

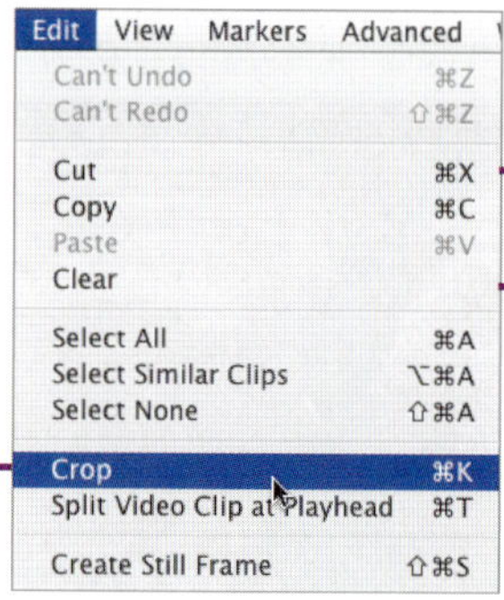

Choose Cut or Clear to delete the selected frames (trim the clip).

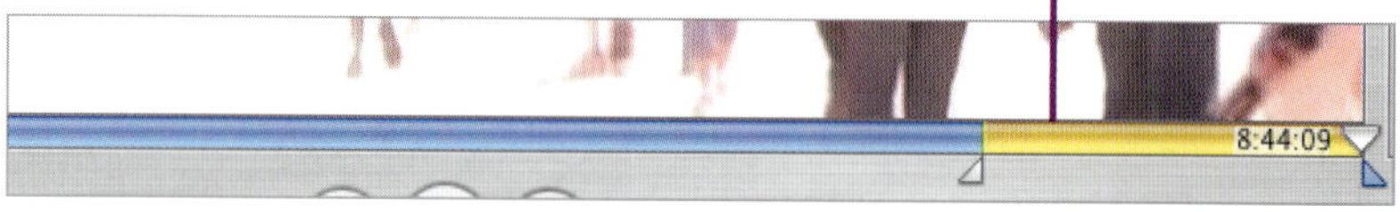

copy and paste

Just like working in a word processor, you can copy and paste frames or entire clips. I use copy and paste when I want to create a new clip out of a selection of frames without breaking up the original clip, in case I want to use the footage somewhere else while I'm editing.

1 Select a range of frames within a clip and choose Copy from the Edit menu.

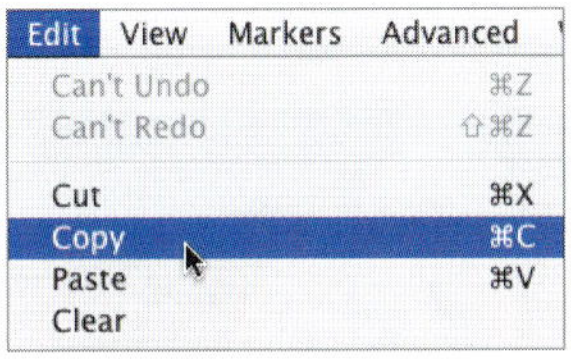

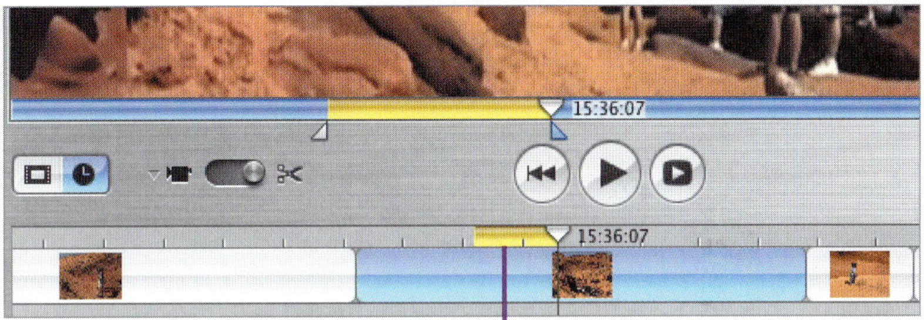

Selection appears in the Monitor and in the Timeline.

2 Select another clip in the Timeline.

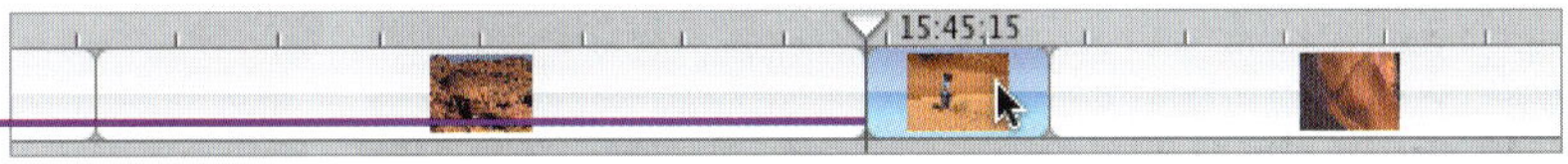

3 Choose Paste from the Edit menu.

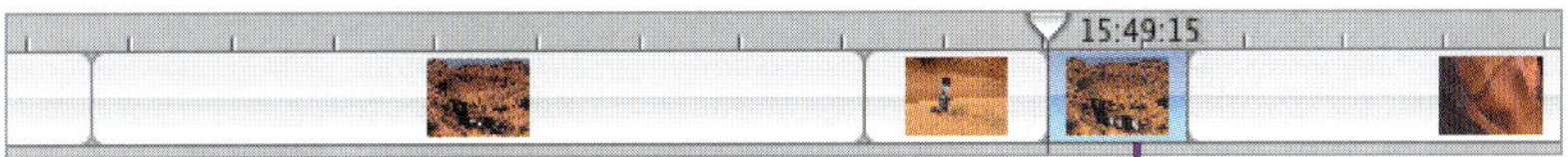

The copied selection appears as a new clip after the one you had selected.

If no clip is selected before pasting, the new clip appears at the Playhead location, even if that's in the middle of another clip.

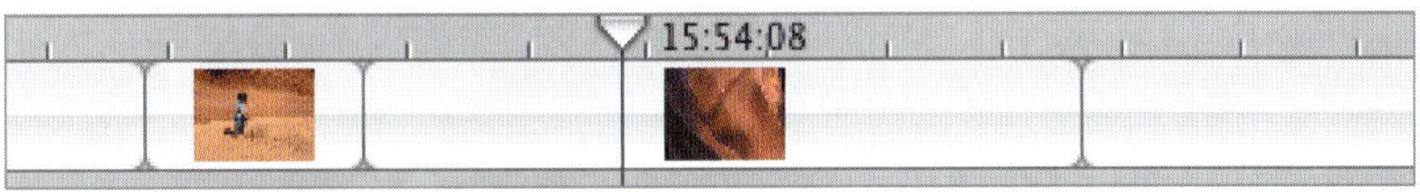

Before pasting

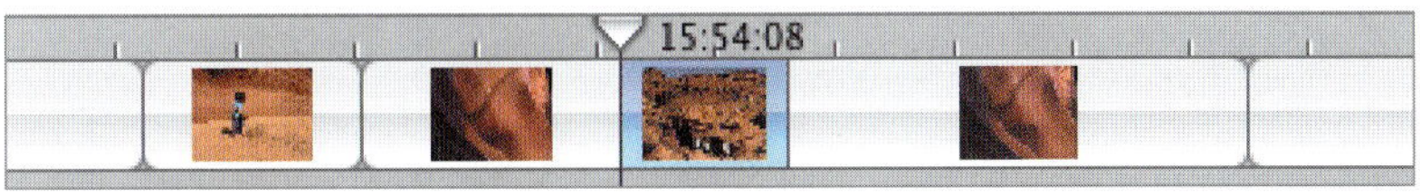

After pasting

paste clips over clips

A common device in movies is to intercut a clip into a scene so that the audio continues to play while the video from a new clip is shown. In iMovie, this is accomplished by pasting a clip over another clip.

1 Open iMovie's preferences and enable this setting (this step is optional, but lets you edit the audio later on).

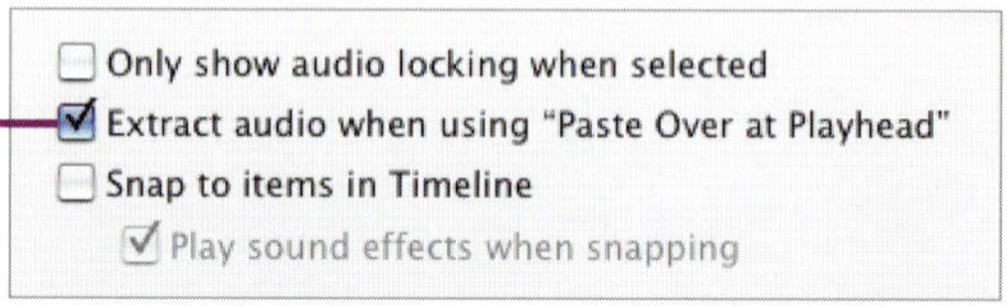

2 Select a range of frames in a clip you want to intercut and copy them.

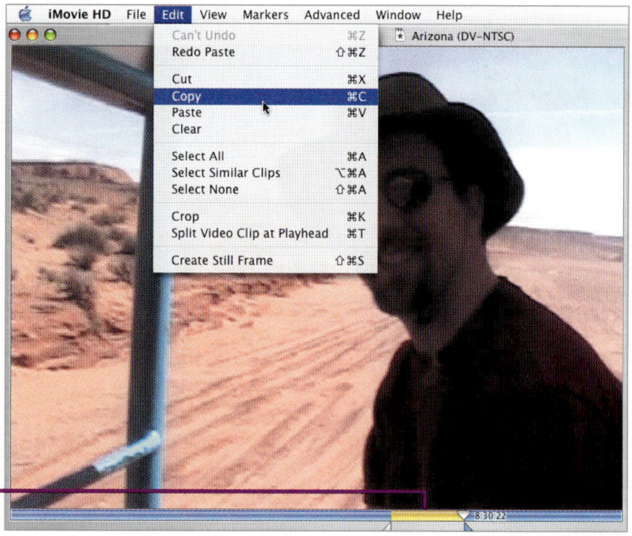

3 Position the Playhead where you want the pasted clip to begin.

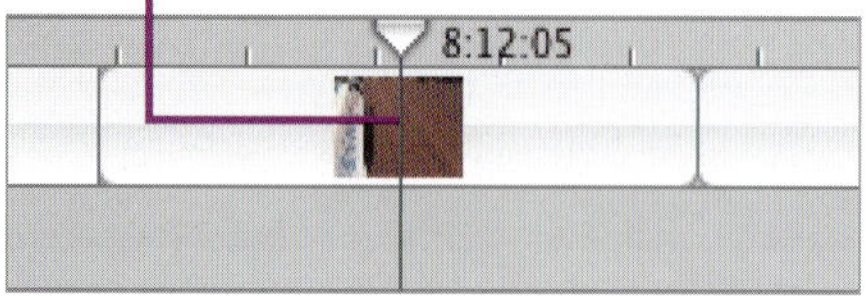

4 Choose Paste Over at Playhead from the Advanced menu. The new clip overwrites the existing one...

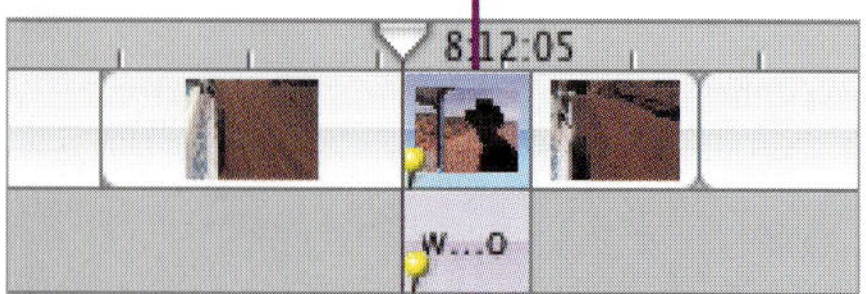

...but plays the original audio.

Original clip

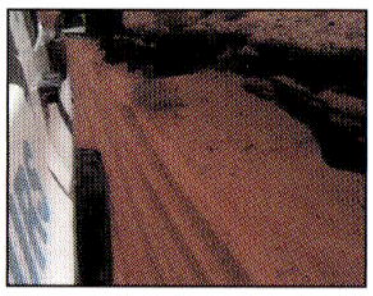

Pasted clip

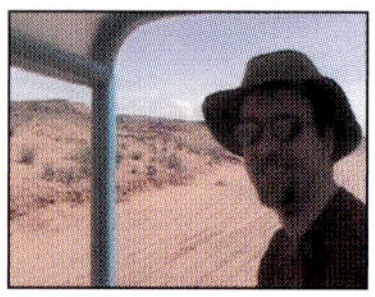

Original clip

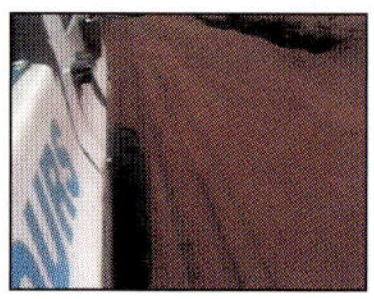

create blank clips

In addition to the footage you imported from your camcorder, and photos you imported from iPhoto, iMovie supports blank clips that can be used as placeholders or just a solid screen of black (or a color you choose; see the extra bits on page 45).

You may not need to use blank clips, but I'm covering them here because you're likely to create one accidentally in the Timeline Viewer: I frequently go to drag the edge of a clip and miss by a few pixels, and accidentally drag the entire clip; I end up with sporadic sections of blank footage in my movie. Here's how to work with (or delete) them.

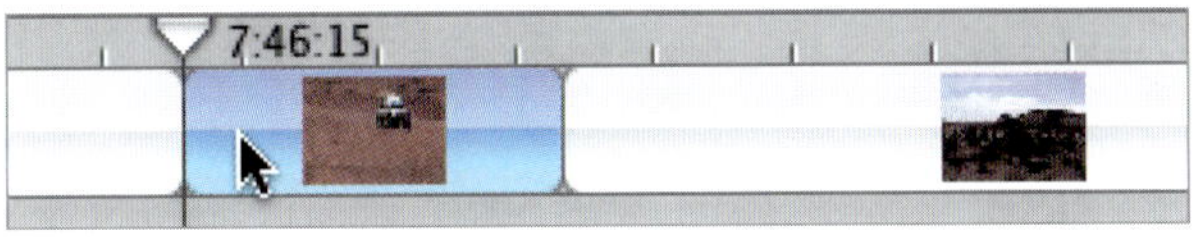

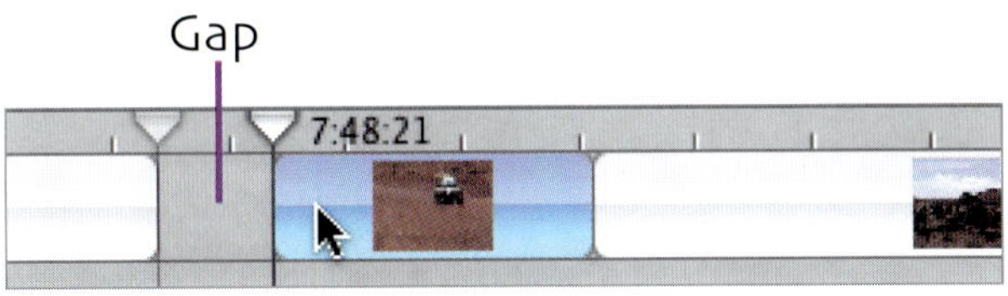

1 In the Timeline Viewer, drag a clip to the right to expose a gap between clips. During playback, the gap appears as solid black footage.

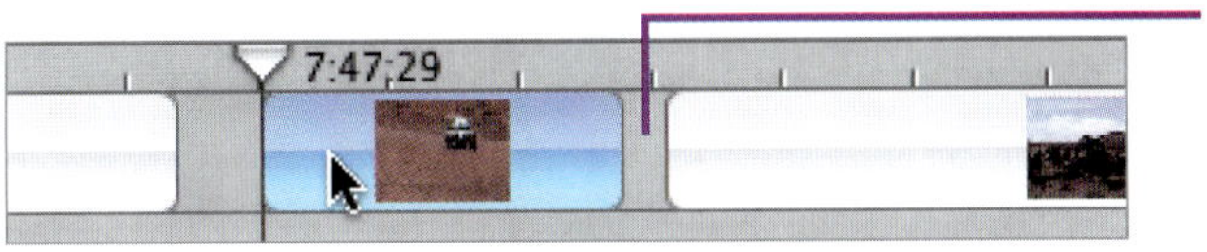

You can't simply drag the clip back into place, because that creates another gap.

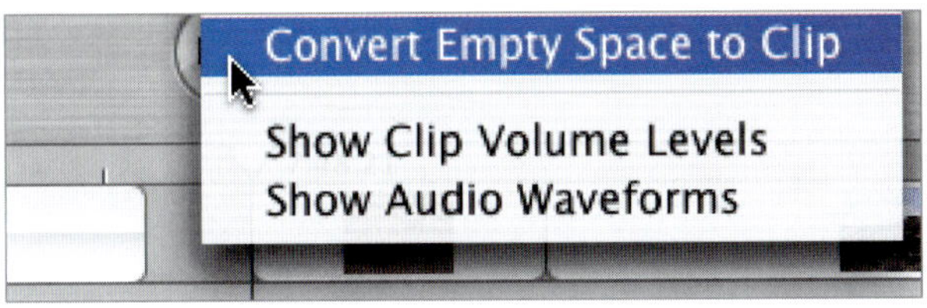

2 Press Control and click the gap to bring up the contextual menu, then choose Convert Empty Space to Clip.

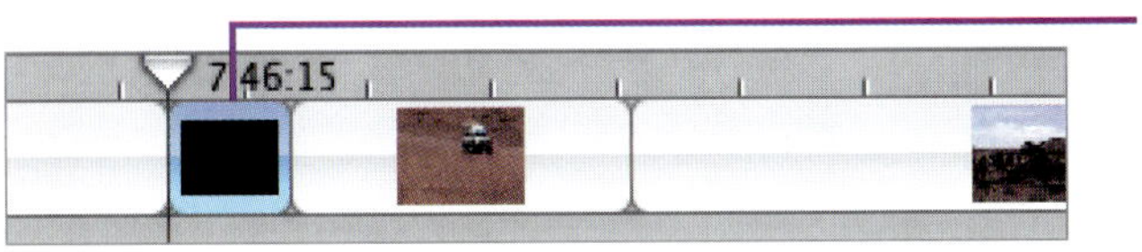

A new blank clip is created to fill the gap. If you made the gap by accident, simply delete the blank clip to remove the gap.

revert clip to original

You've trimmed, split, and cropped a clip to the point where its pieces are strewn all over. Unfortunately, a scene you need is one you had thrown away early in the editing process.

One option is to go digging through the Trash, but it may contain just fragments of your clip that were thrown away. Instead, turn to iMovie's tool of last resort: the Revert Clip to Original command.

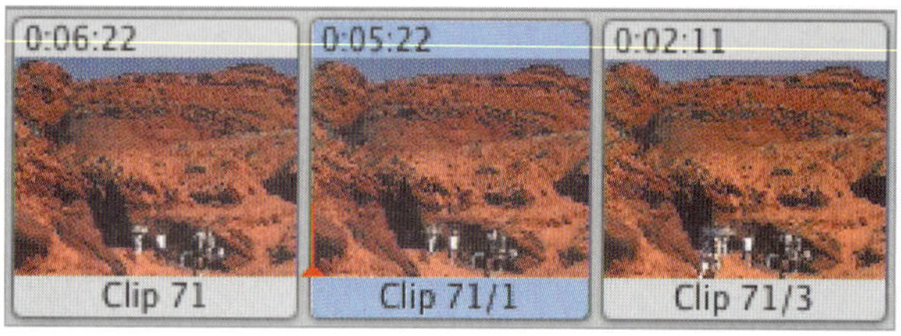

1 Clip 71 was split into multiple pieces, and Clip 71/2 is missing entirely. Select a clip fragment that you want to restore.

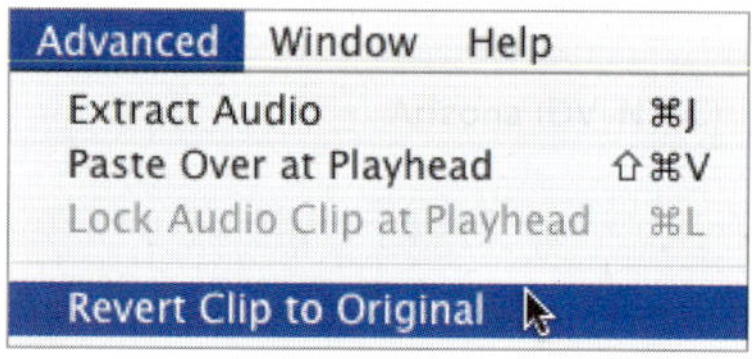

2 Choose Revert Clip to Original from the Advanced menu.

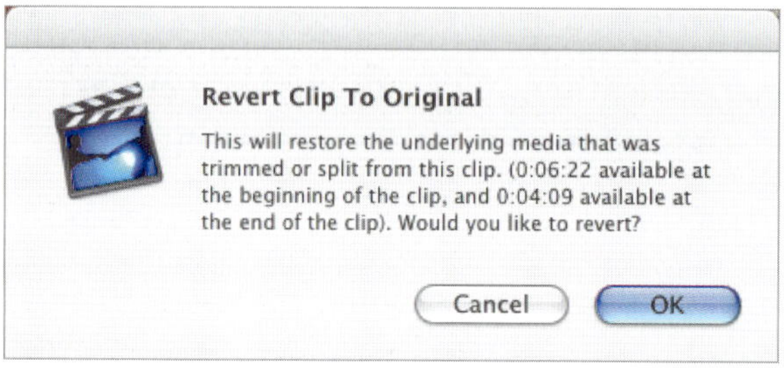

3 iMovie tells you how the clip will be affected. Click OK.

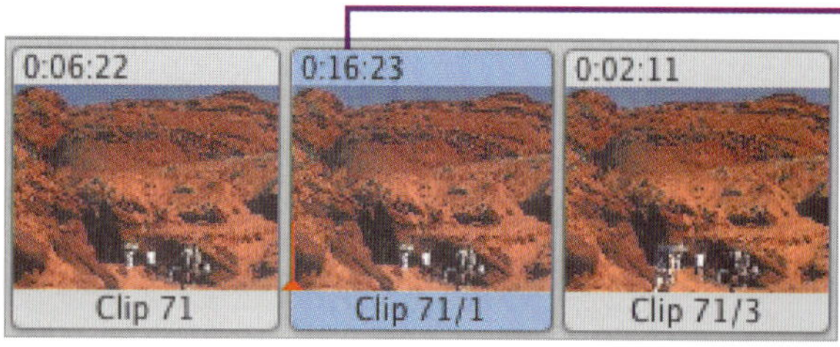

The clip is restored, as you can see by the new duration of 0:16:23.

change clip volume

Do you have a clip whose volume is too loud or faint? You can change the volume for the entire clip, or for sections within the clip.

In this case, the clip includes loud road noise. One option is to decrease the volume for the entire clip (right), but I'd rather fade the volume down at the beginning, then bring it back up at the end of the clip (below).

Video and audio data are combined in the video clip.

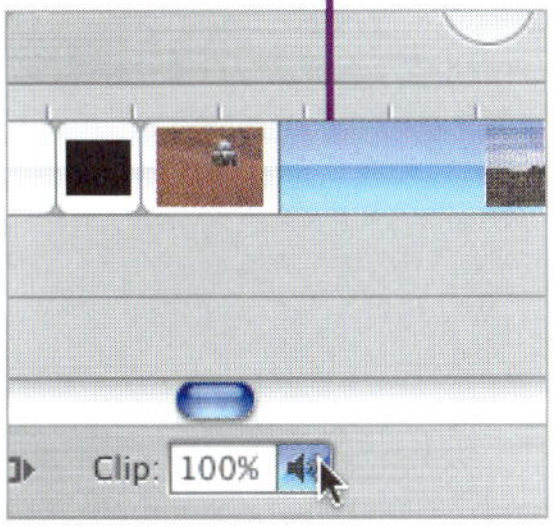

Volume level bar

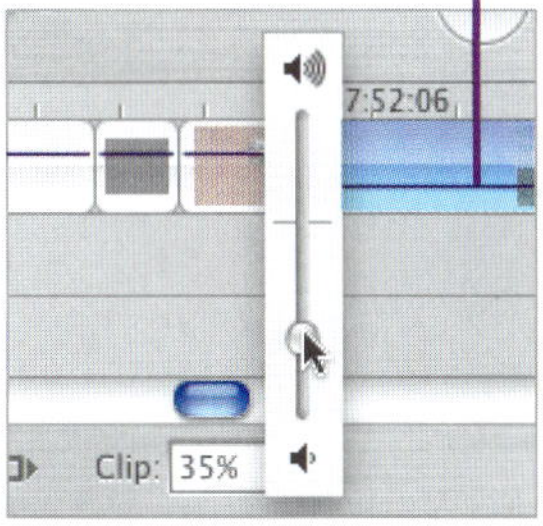

Select a clip, and then drag the Volume slider (or type a number into the field) to change the audio level for the entire clip.

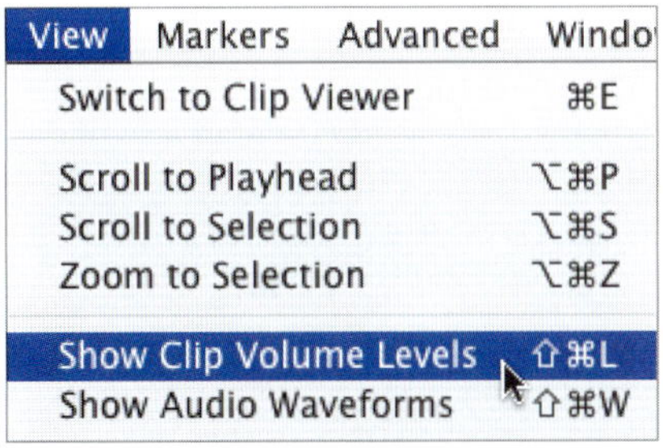

1 To fine tune the volume in a clip, choose Show Clip Volume Levels from the View menu.

Beginning point Volume marker

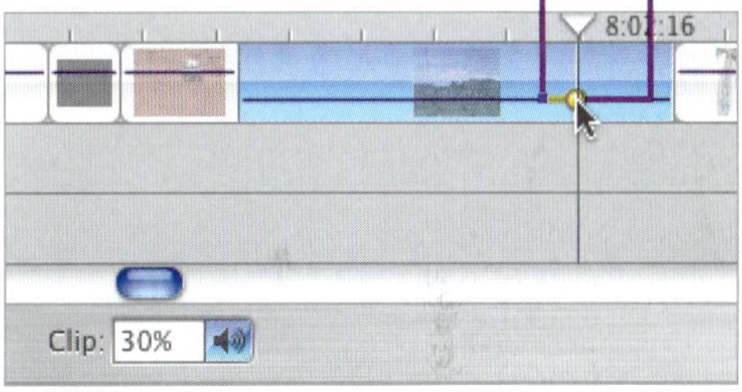

2 Click a point on the volume level bar to set a volume marker.

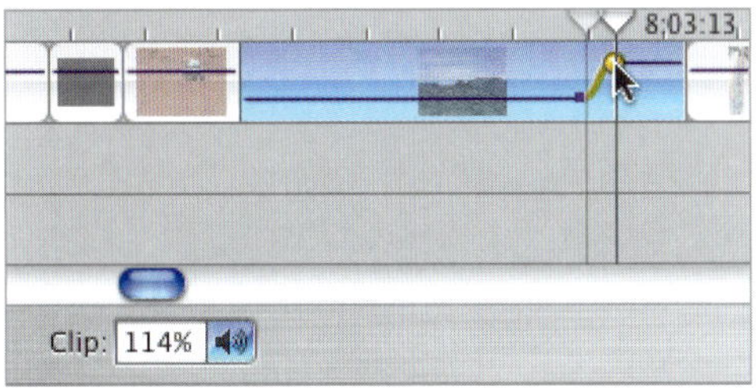

3 Drag the marker to a new level. The curve here indicates a gradual rise in volume.

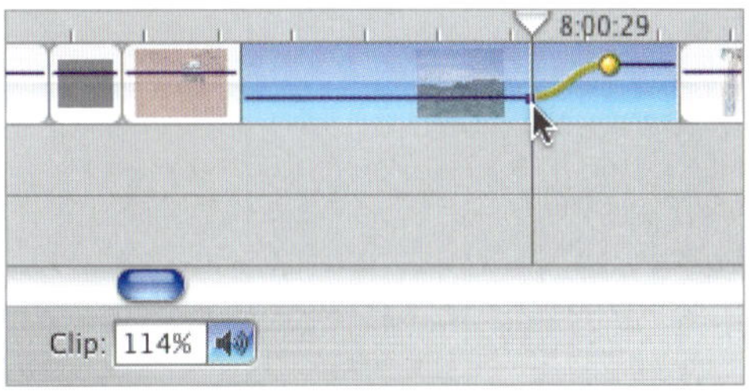

4 Drag the beginning point left or right to set the time it takes for the volume change to occur.

extract audio

For more control when editing audio, extract a clip's audio track.

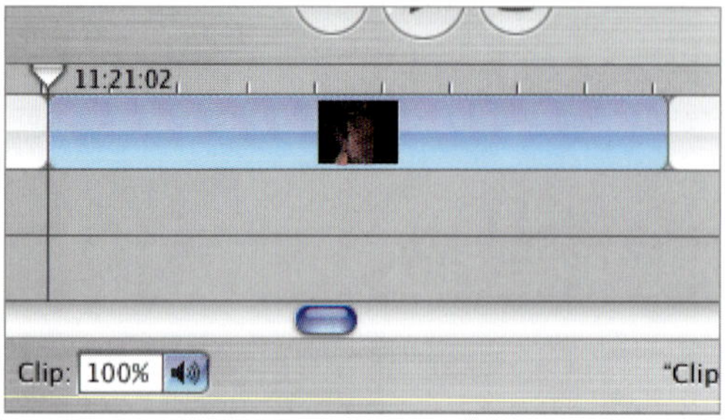

1 Select a video clip.

Extracted audio clip

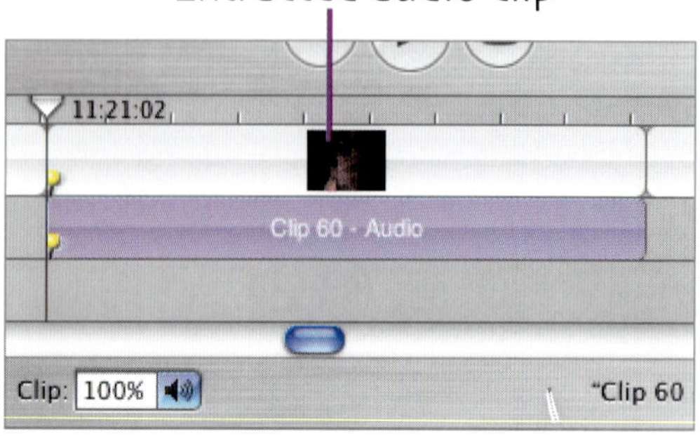

2 Choose Extract Audio from the Advanced menu to create a new clip on the upper audio track.

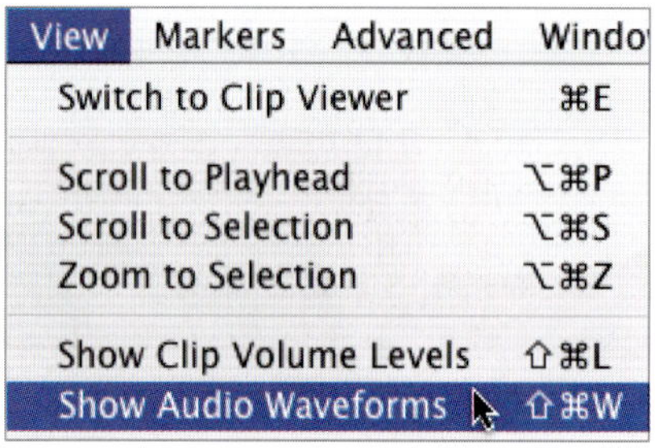

It's easier to edit audio clips when you can see the audio waveforms. Choose Show Audio Waveforms from the View menu.

Audio waveforms

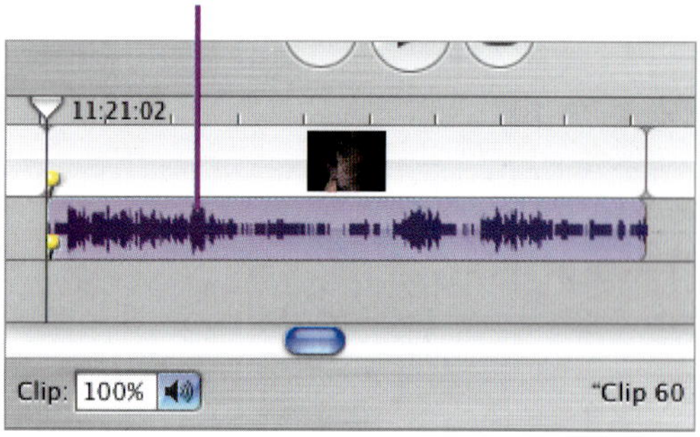

The waveforms display the peaks and valleys of the sound levels, letting you easily split a clip just before someone starts speaking. (This approach is also great for isolating loud, unexpected sounds, such as a cough or sneeze in the background, and editing the volume to minimize the noise.)

lock and unlock audio

Audio lock icons

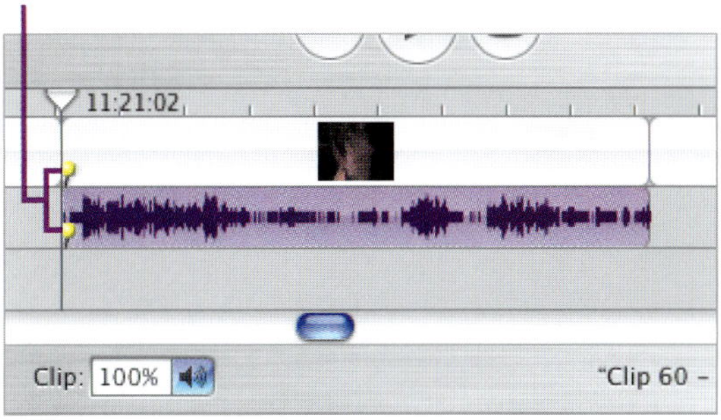

Extracted audio clips automatically lock to their video clips to keep the audio and video synchronized.

Lock icons removed

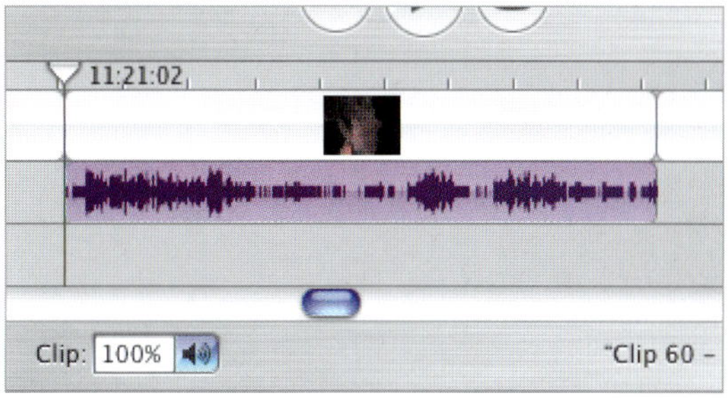

To free the extracted audio, click the audio clip and choose Unlock Audio Clip from the Advanced menu.

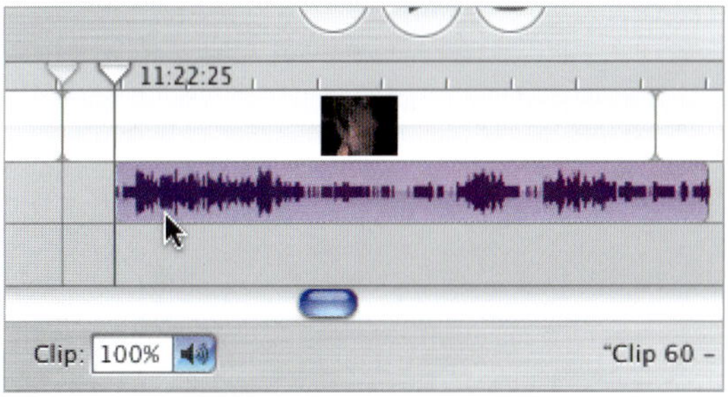

Now you can move the audio clip independently. This is helpful when you want to add the background noise of one video clip to another clip in order to maintain a consistent audio evironment.

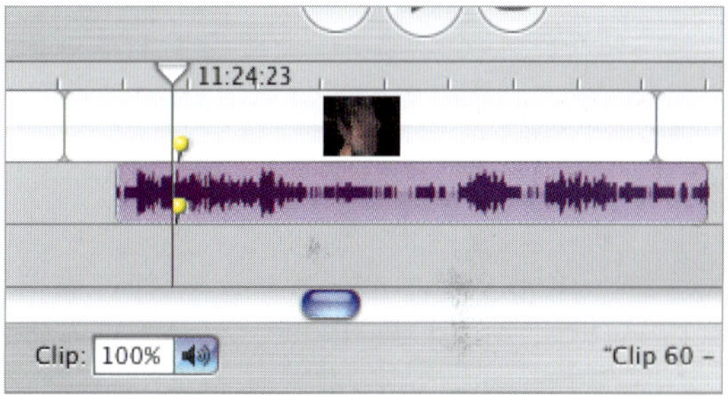

After repositioning the clip, choose Lock Audio Clip at Playhead from the Advanced menu. As you edit other clips in the movie, the audio remains attached to this new position.

extra bits

direct-trim clips p. 34

- One irritating thing about clips edited by Direct Trimming is that sometimes you may want some footage that occurs later in the clip. You could split the clip instead (see page 35), but that doesn't help you if you've already used Direct Trimming. Instead, duplicate the clip by choosing Copy and then Paste from the Edit menu. You can then change the trimming on the duplicate clip to display the other scene.
- As you drag the edge of a clip, the Monitor displays the frame that corresponds to the cursor's location.
- When dragging a clip's edge, look to the information line below the Timeline to see the clip's new length. If I know I want a clip to last exactly 10 seconds, for example, that's where I look; the timecode near the Playhead indicates the time relative to the entire movie.

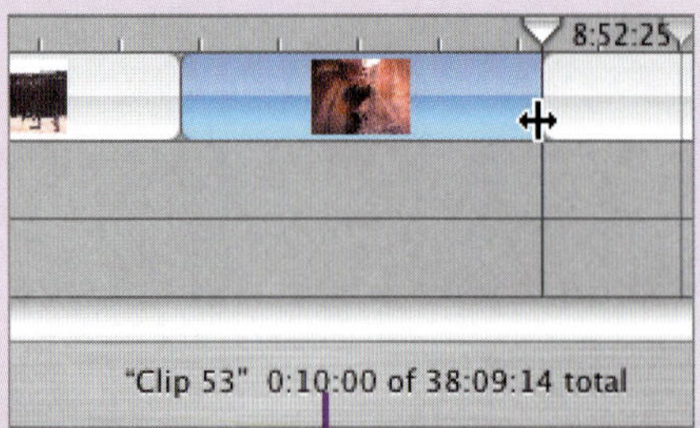

Clip length

split clips p. 35

- After splitting a clip, each section still contains all of the original footage. Use Direct Trimming to reveal it if you need to.
- If no clip is selected and you choose Split Video Clip at Playhead, only the video clip under the Playhead gets split; audio clips not selected remain intact.

crop and trim clips p. 36

- Initially, the crop markers appear at the far left edge of the Scrubber Bar. Click and drag anywhere under the bar to activate the crop markers; you don't have to drag them from the left side.
- To deselect frames without applying any edit to them, click another clip or click at the top of the Timeline. You can also choose Select None from the Edit menu.

copy and paste p. 37

- Consider renaming your newly pasted clip, since it will share the original clip's name.

extra bits

create blank clips p. 39

- Although a blank clip is normally black, you can change its color easily. Double-click a blank clip to bring up the Clip Info dialog, click the Color field, and choose a new color in the Colors palette.

revert clip to original p. 40

- I mentioned this in Chapter 4, but it's worth repeating: don't empty iMovie's Trash until you've finished your project. This ensures that you won't permanently delete a clip you might need later.
- iMovie HD features unlimited undos, which means you can experiment with edits and then go back several steps.
- Another way to encourage experimentation is the Save Project As command, located under the File menu. This creates a duplicate of your iMovie project; if you don't like the direction the duplicate is taking you, simply delete it and return to the original project. Be aware, however, that each saved copy of your iMovie project takes up as much hard drive space as the original.

change clip volume p. 41

- To remove a volume marker, click it and then press Delete.
- You can have as many audio edits as will fit within the clip.
- When Show Clip Volume Levels is enabled and you want to select a clip, be sure to click somewhere other than the volume level line to prevent adding an unintended volume marker.

extract audio p. 42

- Audio waveforms appear only on audio clips, not on video clips. Sometimes it's worth extracting the audio to use the waveforms as guides while editing.
- Use the Zoom slider to zoom in on a clip in the Timeline Viewer to see more waveform detail. For an even closer look, select the audio clip and press the ↑ or ↓ key to temporarily enlarge or diminish the waveforms.
- If you delete an extracted audio clip, the sound isn't gone forever. The original audio is still embedded in the video track, but it's set to zero. Select the video clip and increase the volume level. You can then extract the audio again later, if you wish.

7. add transitions

As your movie currently stands, each clip is separated by a jump cut, an abrupt switch to the next clip. If you watch movies or television, most shots are separated by jump cuts because they involve no extra work by the editor and because we, as viewers, subconsciously stitch cuts together to form scenes without losing track of what's going on.

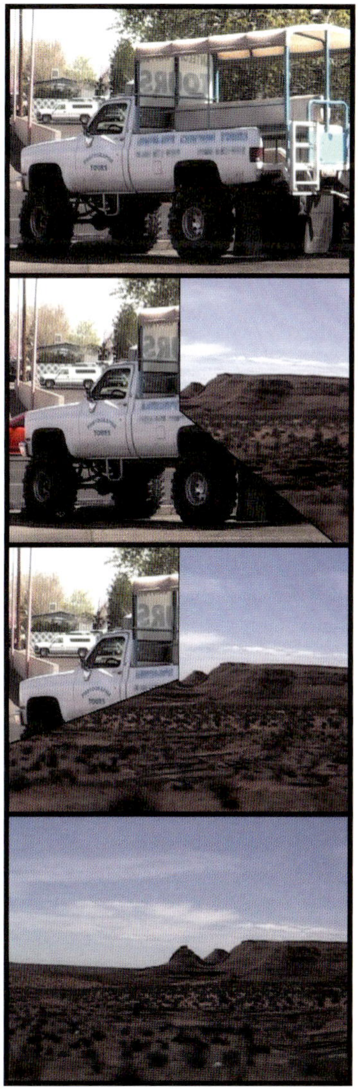

However, too many jump cuts can be visually jarring, and sometimes it's more appropriate to add some sort of transition that ties two clips together. iMovie includes 16 transitions that will help give your movie a bit more polish.

edit settings

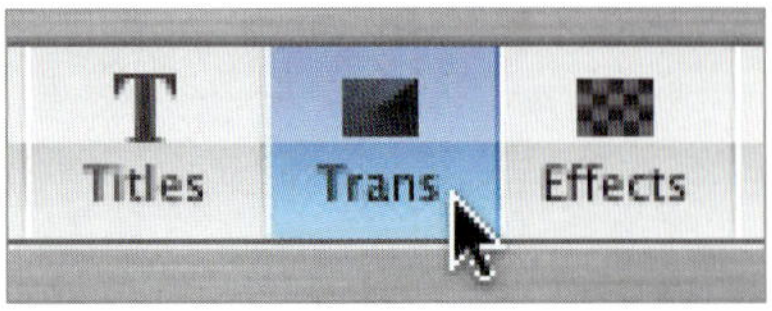

1 Click the Trans button to view the Transitions pane.

2 Position the Playhead near the break between two clips.

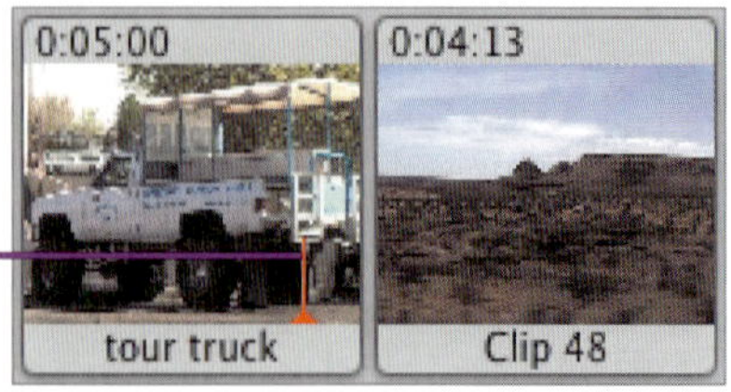

3 Click a transition type from the list.

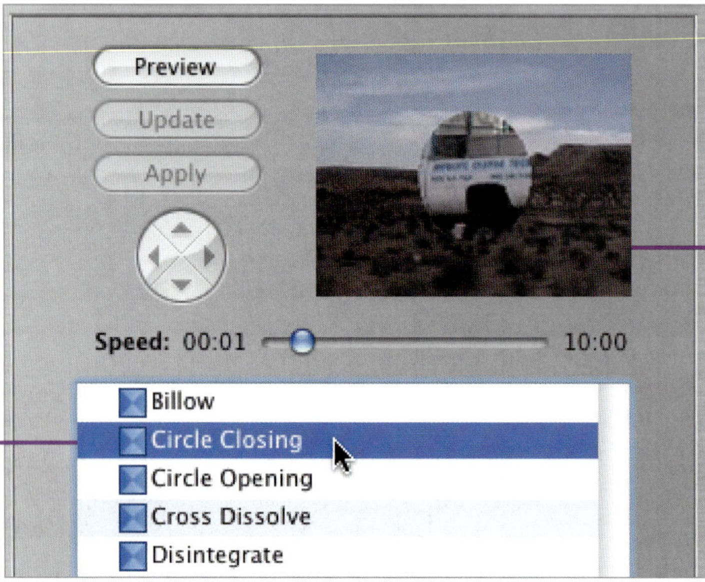

A small preview appears when you click a transition.

4 Change duration using the Speed slider.

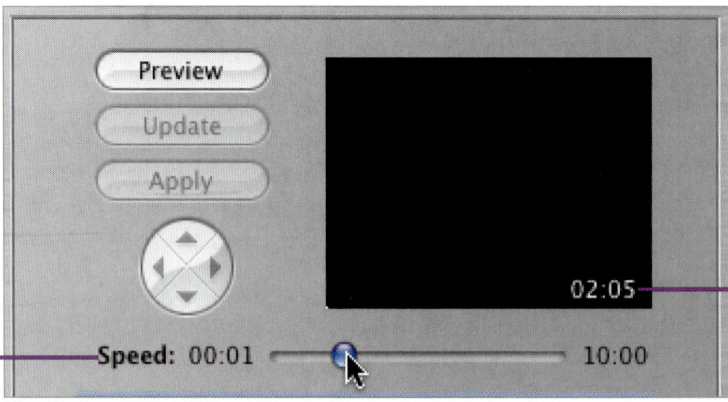

Duration amount

5 If you selected the Billow or Push transition, click a direction button to determine from which side the next clip appears.

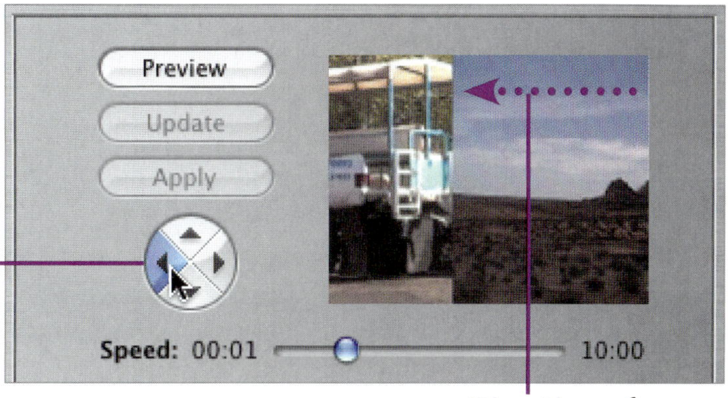

Direction of Push transition

6 For a better idea of how the transition will appear, click the Preview button to play a rough version in the Monitor.

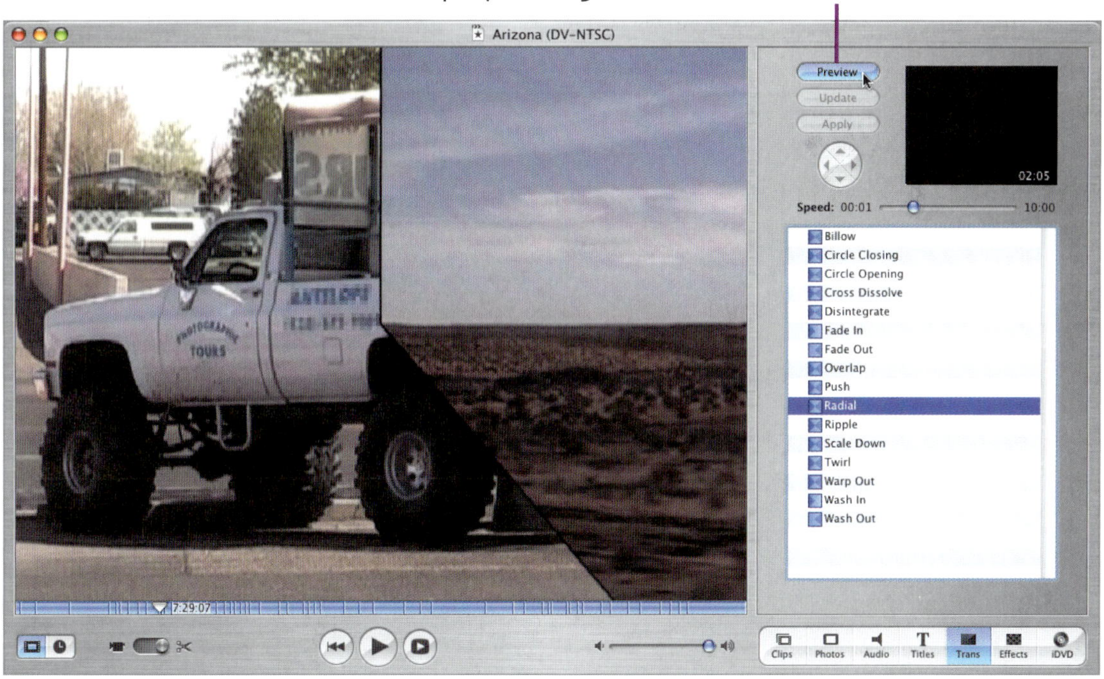

add the transition

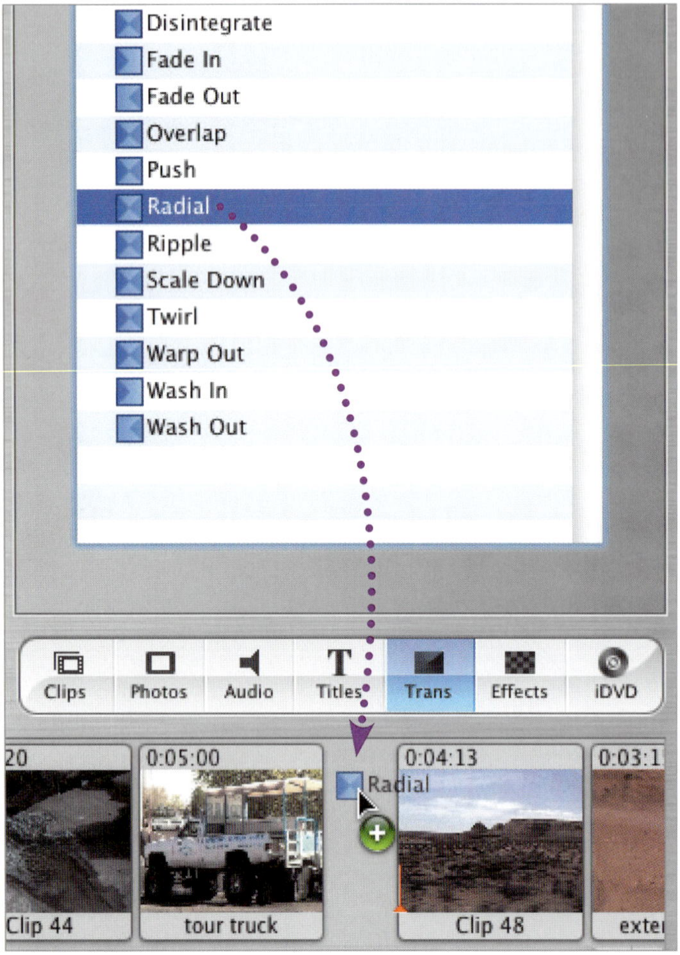

When you've arrived at the settings you want, drag the transition to the Timeline (either the Clip Viewer or Timeline Viewer).

A red bar indicates the rendering progress.

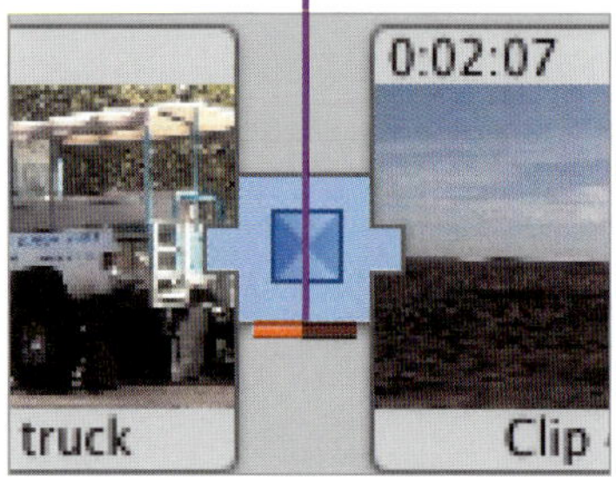

Transition in Clip Viewer

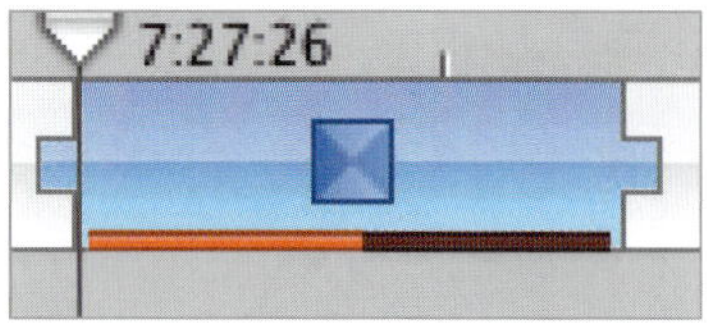

Transition rendering in Timeline Viewer

Is the transition not quite what you expected? You can tweak the behavior at any time by selecting the clip in the Timeline, making adjustments to its settings in the Transitions pane (even changing the type of transition), and then clicking the Update button.

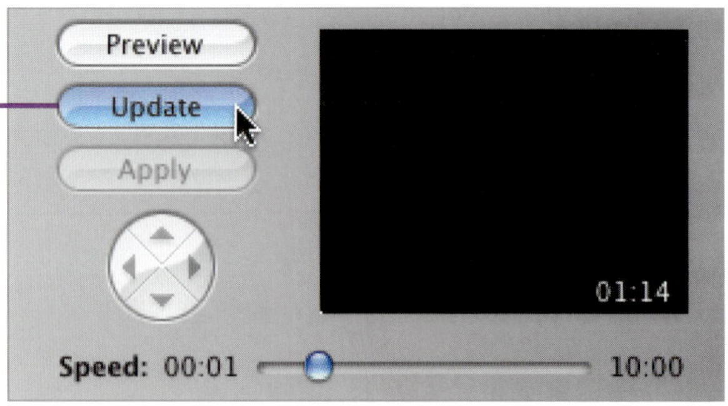

extra bits

edit settings p. 48

- iMovie creates transition previews based on the location of the Playhead. If it's near the beginning of a clip, the transition starts with the previous clip; if it's near the end, the transition starts with the current clip and ends with the next one.
- Several third-party developers have released packages of transitions you can add to iMovie. See Appendix B.

add the transition p. 50

- After adding a transition, you can't use Direct Trimming to edit a clip in the Timeline Viewer. Delete the transition, make your edits to the clip, and then add a new transition.
- You can't move transitions like regular clips. Instead, create a new one for the new location in your movie.
- If you decide you don't want a transition just after you've added it, press [⌘]-[.] (period) to cancel the rendering process.
- To delete a transition from your movie, simply click it and press [Delete].
- During one sequence of my movie, I wanted to use a simple Cross Dissolve transition between several clips. Instead of creating each one individually, I selected the range of clips (hold [⌘] and click them), chose and configured the transition, and then clicked the Apply button to add them all at once.
- You can edit volume levels within transitions (see Chapter 6). Some transitions, such as Fade In and Fade Out, automatically adjust the audio levels to fade the sound in or out in tandem with the video.

8. add titles

Movie titles weren't always easy to create, which is probably why a movie with a title looks more polished than plain video footage. iMovie gives you several options for adding titles that can appear anywhere within your movie.

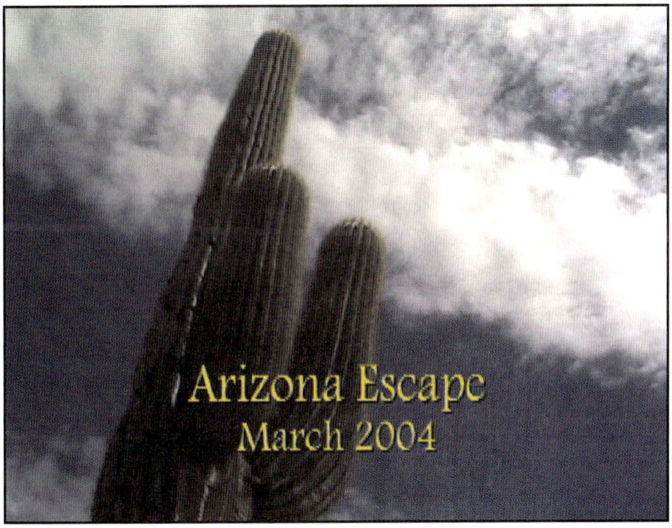

create a title

1 Click the Titles button to view the Titles pane.

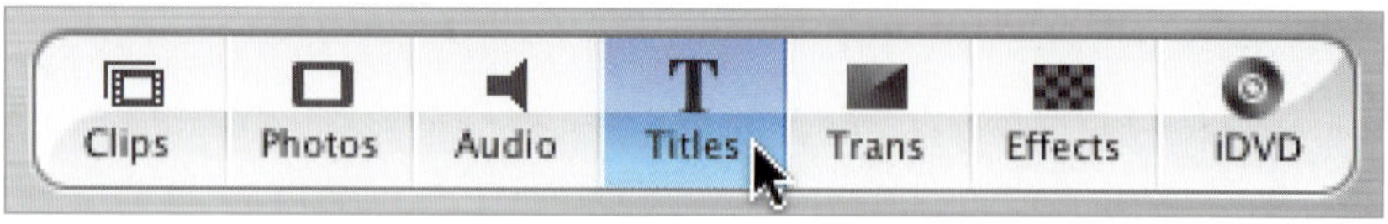

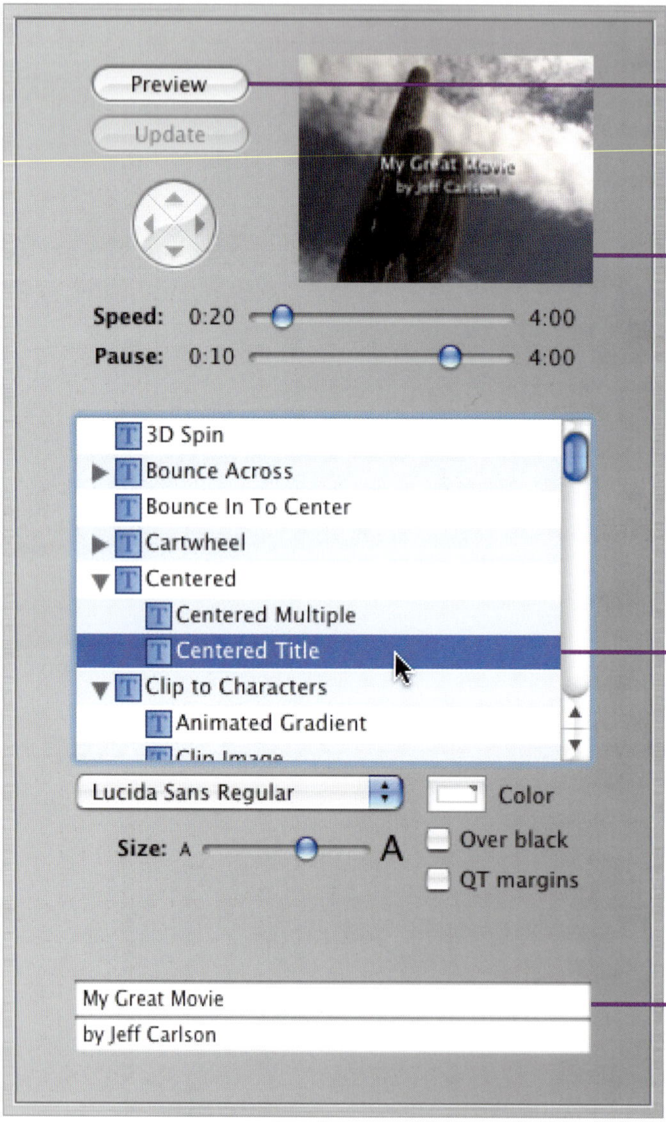

Clicking Preview displays a full-size preview in the Monitor.

A small preview of the title appears over the clip at the current location of the Playhead.

2 Click a title name to select it. Clicking any title displays how the title effect will appear in the small preview window.

3 Type a title into the fields provided. Text in the top field will show up slightly larger than text in the bottom field.

iMovie's titles come in three varieties:

Single shows two lines of text at once.

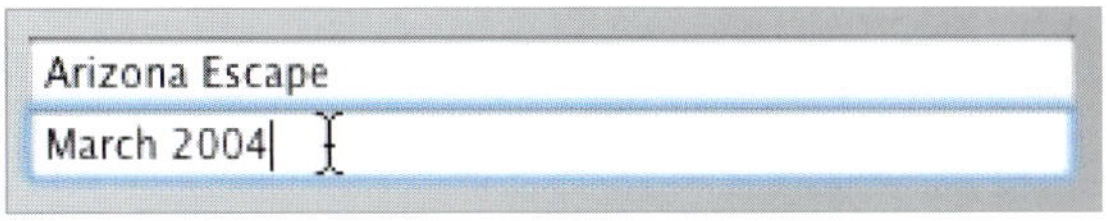

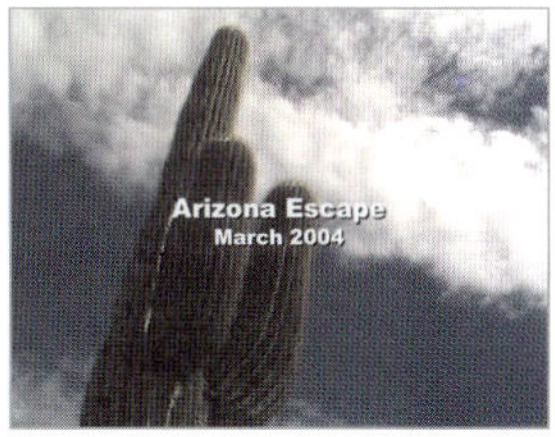

Multiple shows one text pair, then another.

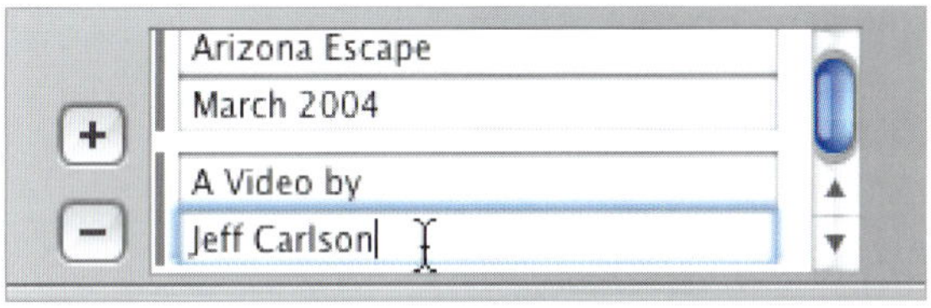

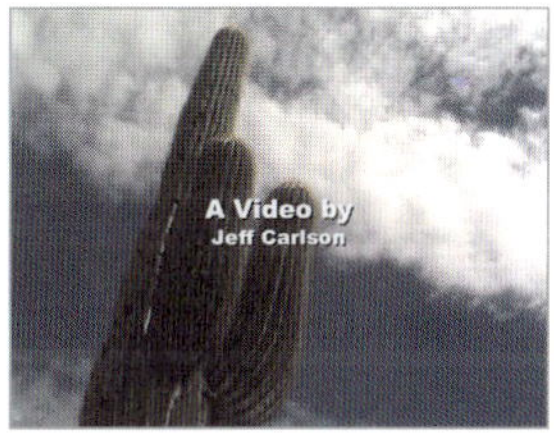

Text block is used for longer titles.

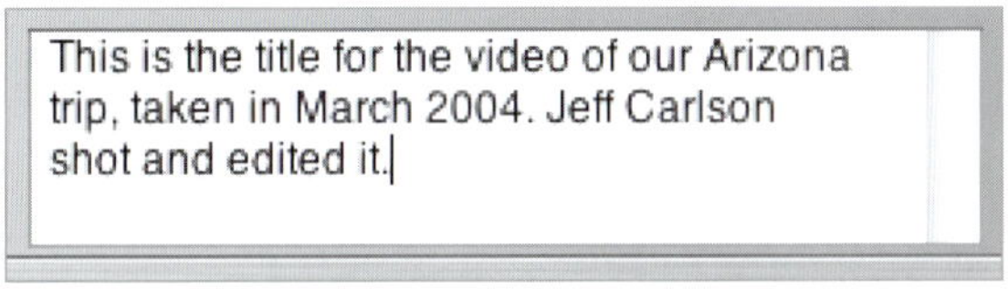

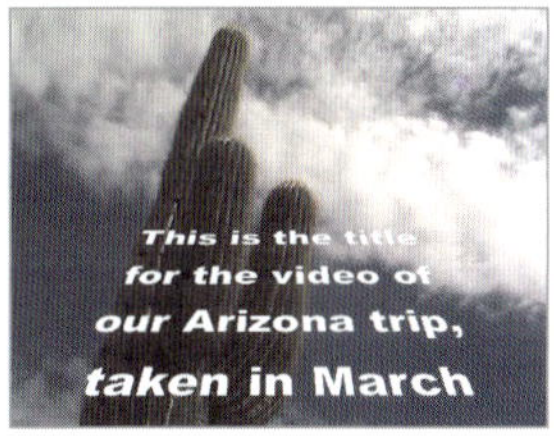

4 Use the duration sliders to set the time that the title will appear onscreen.

Speed is the time it takes for the title to appear; Pause is how long it stays before disappearing.

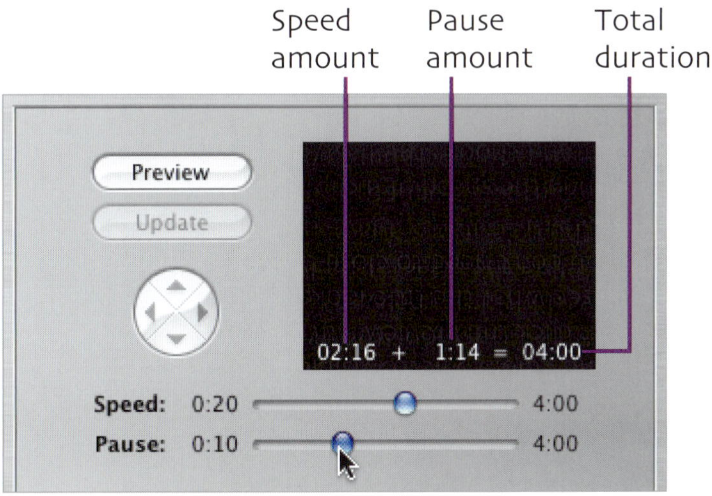

style the text

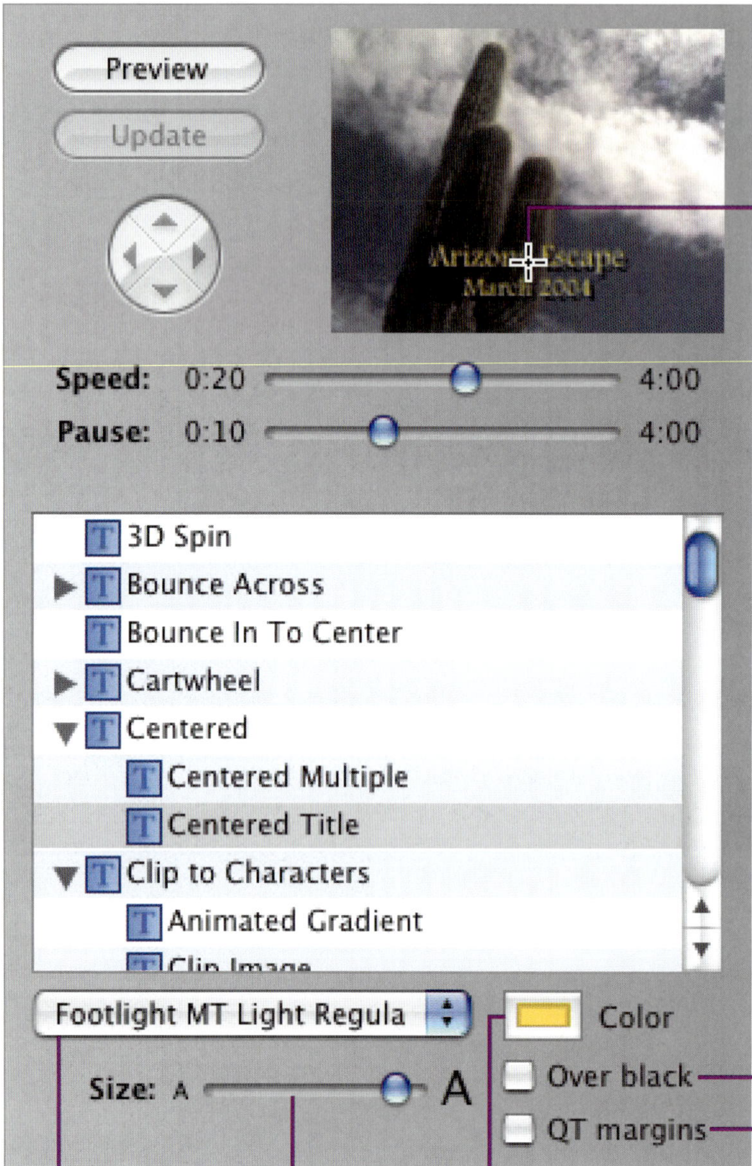

With some titles, you can click the preview window to position the text horizontally. Look for your pointer to change to this icon, then click to position the title.

Click here to create the title on a black background instead of superimposed on a video clip.

To ensure that words don't get cut off when played back on a television, iMovie limits the size of titles. If you know you're going to view your movie only in QuickTime format, click the QT margins box to use the entire frame for titles.

Choose a font from the popup menu.

Drag the Size slider to change the size of the text.

To change the text color, click the Color field to bring up the Colors palette.

add the title

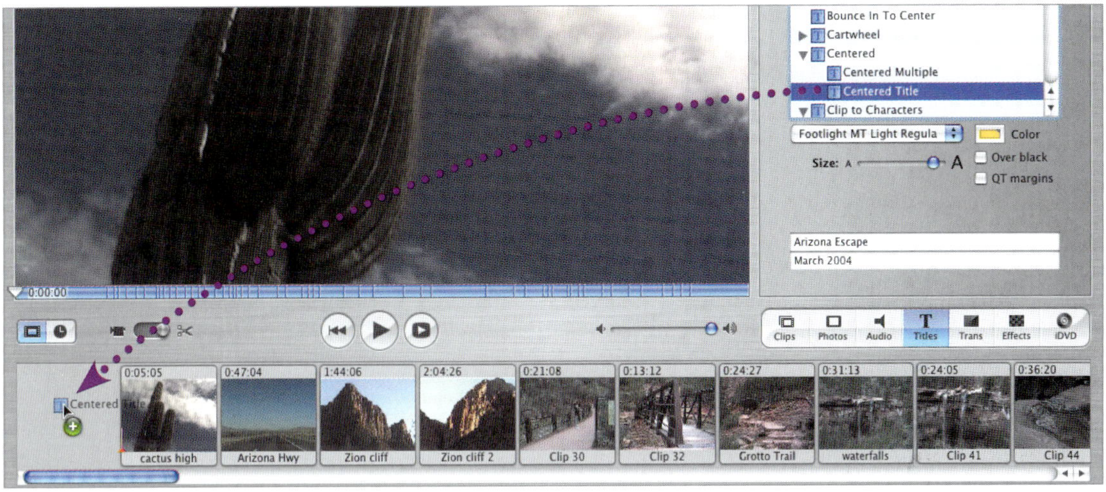

When the title looks as you want it to, drag the title's name from the list to the Timeline (either the Clip Viewer or Timeline Viewer).

Before

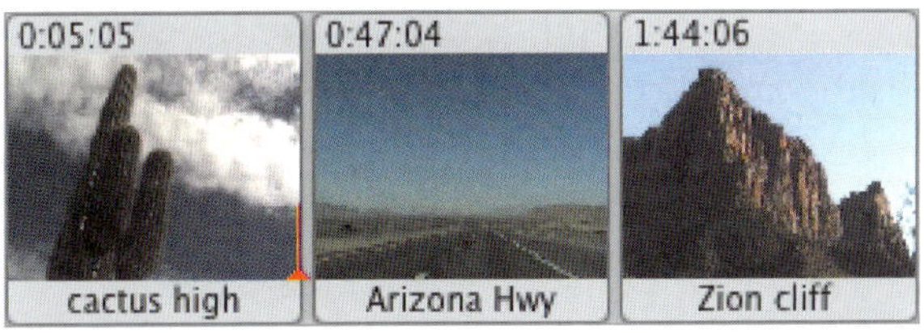

Titles work a bit differently than regular video clips. Think of a title as a clip that's been laid on top of its source clip. Deleting a title restores the original video clip.

After

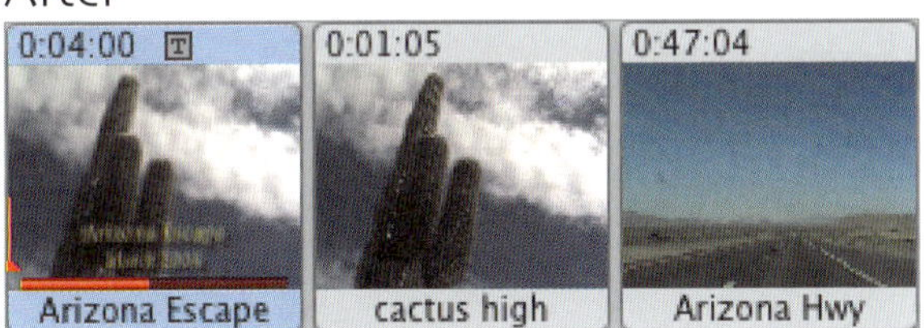

This title occupied only part of the clip below it, so a new clip with the remaining footage was created.

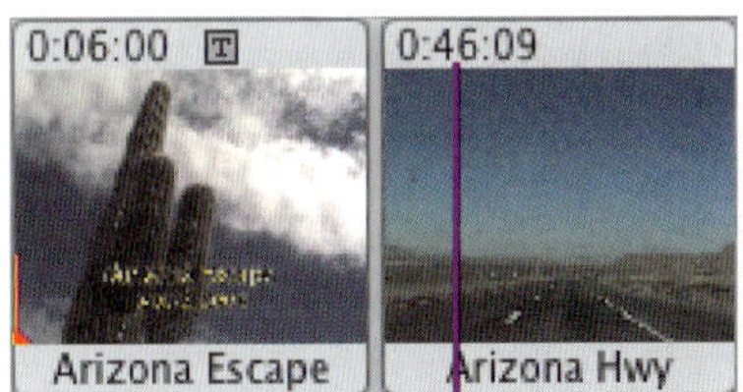

If a title is longer than the clip it appears on, the title bleeds over into the next clip and steals some of its footage.

extra bits

create a title p. 54

- iMovie remembers the last text you entered, so if you click another title name, you don't have to re-enter your text.
- When working with titles that feature multiple text pairs, click and drag the pairs to rearrange the order in which they appear.
- Some titles include additional controls. For example, Bounce Across features a Wave slider to control how bouncy the text is. Feel free to experiment with the settings.
- Several third-party companies have developed other titles that you can add to iMovie. See Appendix B.

style the text p. 56

- The size of the title depends on the font you use and the number of words you type. A title of "Star Wars" will appear larger than "The Empire Strikes Back," even if both are set to the same size.
- With the Colors palette visible, you can click the Preview button to see what the title looks like; you don't need to close the palette.

add the title p. 57

- After adding a title to the Timeline, don't be surprised if the text looks jagged. When viewed on a television, the letters look better.
- You can overlap more than one title if you want. For example, suppose you want a timestamp in the lower-right corner of the screen (using the Music Video title) and a main title in the center (using Centered Title).
- As with transitions (described in Chapter 7), you can change the settings of an existing title. Click the title in the Timeline, make your adjustments in the Titles pane, and then click the Update button.
- To delete a title, select it in the Timeline and press Delete. The title clip is removed, leaving the original clip(s) it overlapped in the same condition as before the

9. add effects

iMovie's effects aren't used as frequently as transitions and titles, mainly because they offer a specific look or action—you just won't have that many occasions to use Fairy Dust. However, some effects are more subtle, such as adjusting a clip's color balance, or applying sepia or black-and-white tone to the footage.

One exception, however, is a new effect in iMovie HD: Fast/Slow/Reverse. Previous versions of iMovie featured a Clip Speed slider below the Timeline that let you speed up or slow down a clip. Now, you use this effect to make those changes; it also reverses the clip to play from the last frame to the first. See page 62 for more information.

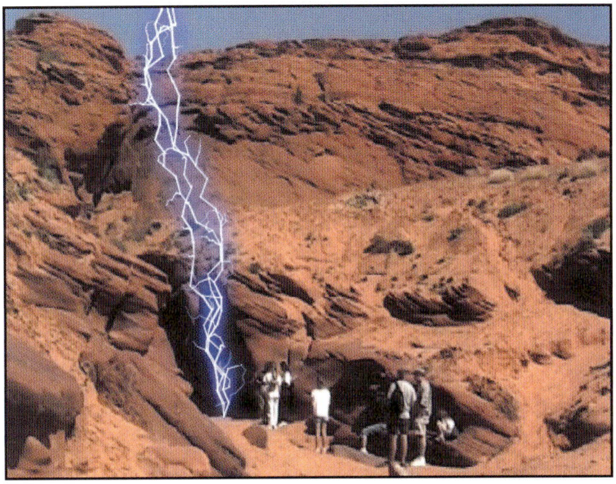

Is it a Star Trek episode, or just iMovie? You can bet I wouldn't put this effect in a vacation movie (but you can view it at www.necoffee.com/imovievqs/; I just couldn't help myself).

edit effect settings

1 Click the Effects button to view the Effects pane.

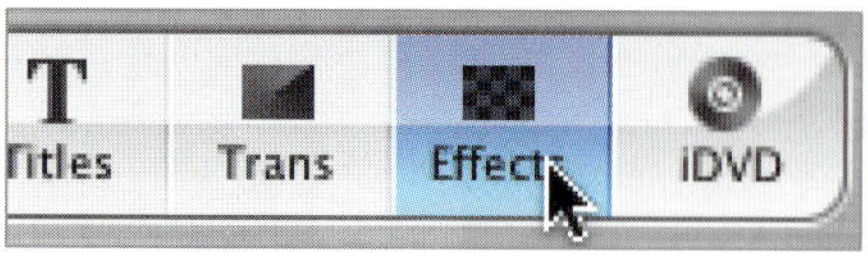

2 Select a clip in the Timeline (using either viewer).

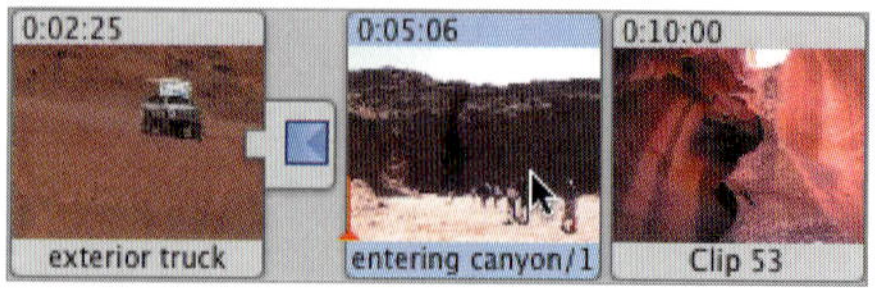

Clicking Preview displays a full-size preview in the Monitor.

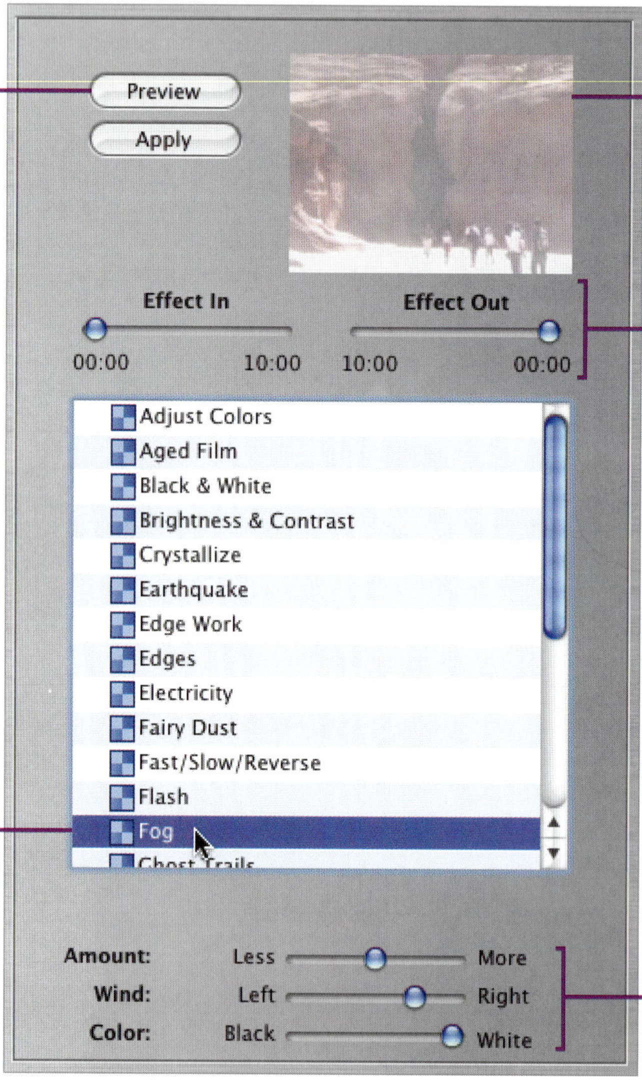

The small preview window shows the effect when you click an effect name.

These sliders make the effect appear or disappear gradually (such as blending from Aged Film to normal footage.

3 Click an effect's name to access its controls.

4 Use the sliders to control aspects of each effect.

apply the effect

Click Apply to add the effect to your selected clip. You cannot drag an effect name to the Timeline as you can with titles and transitions.

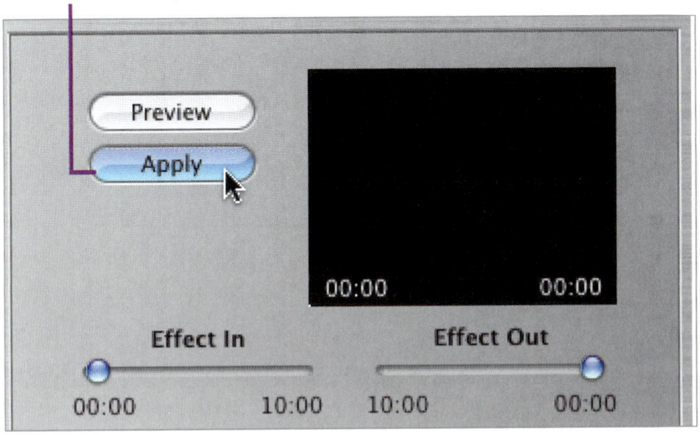

This icon indicates that an effect is applied to the clip.

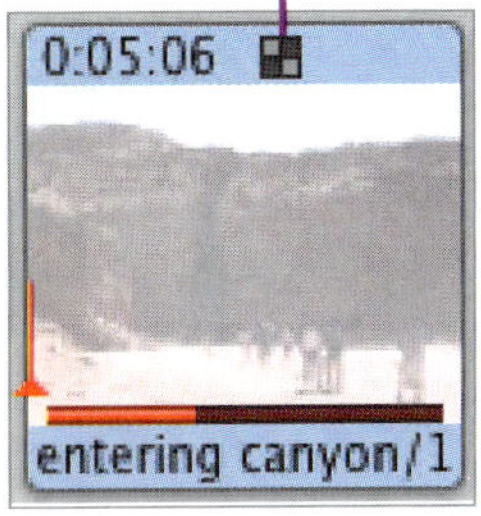

Multiple effects can be layered upon the same clip. In the clip below, I added Aged Film to Fog to give the scene an old 1930s explorer feel; the graininess accentuates the Fog effect well here (view samples at www.necoffee.com/imovievqs/).

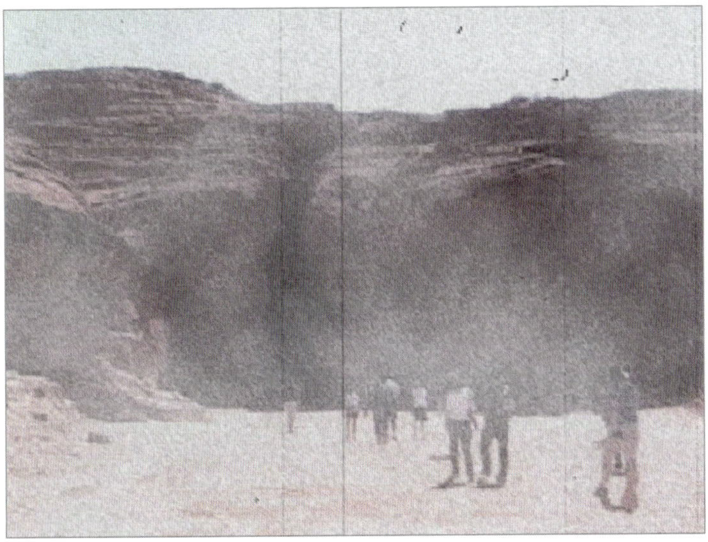

The number tells you how many effects are applied.

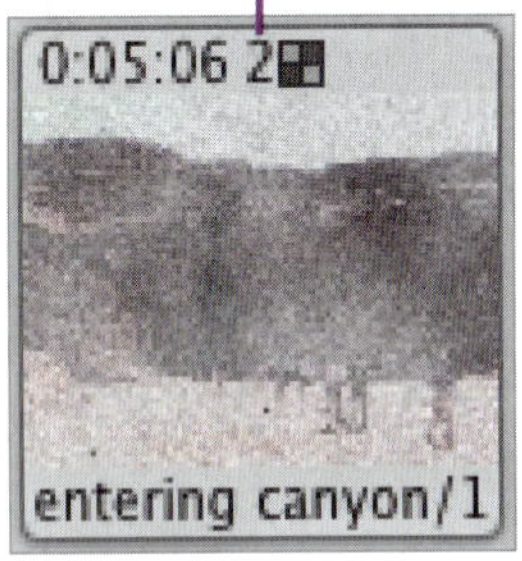

To remove an effect, click the clip to which it's applied and press Delete. The original clip remains intact.

extra bits

edit effect settings p. 60

- If the clip you want to use for an effect has transitions attached to it, applying the effect may remove the transitions (iMovie warns you if this is the case). After adding the effect, simply create the transitions again.
- To change the speed of a clip, select it and choose the Fast/Slow/Reverse effect.

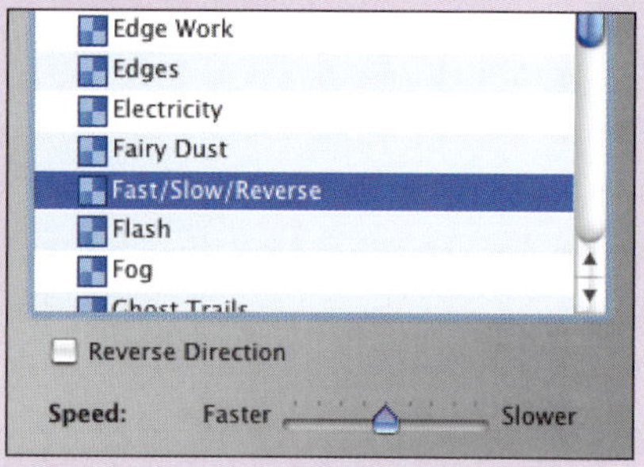

- Some effects, such as Fairy Dust, feature controls in the small preview window. Click within the preview area to determine the angle of the light burst, as in this example (ouch).

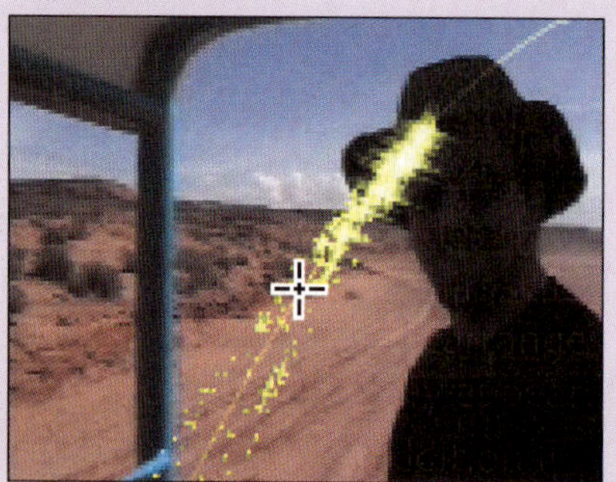

apply the effect p. 61

- You can't change an effect's settings once the effect has been applied like you can with titles and transitions. Instead, you must delete the effect, make your changes, and then re-apply the effect.
- To stop the effect from rendering, press [⌘] - [.] (period), or choose Undo from the Edit menu.
- When you delete an effect from a clip that contains multiple effects, you delete only the most recently applied effect, not all effects on that clip.
- If you apply some effect types to a still photo, the image needs to be converted to a regular video clip. iMovie warns you if this is about to happen, and gives you the option to cancel.
- Effects cannot be applied to clips on the Shelf. However, you can add an effect to a clip in the Timeline and then move it to the Shelf for later use.
- You can apply transitions and titles to clips that incorporate effects.

10. share your movie

Let's recap our progress so far.

By this point, you've imported your footage from the camera, added any songs and still photos, and assembled the clips in the Timeline. You've also edited the clips and incorporated transitions, titles, and effects.

Before you proceed, make sure any final polishing work has been done on your movie (such as adding other music, trimming clips to tighten the movie's timing, etc.).

In this chapter, you'll share the movie with the rest of the world by emailing it to someone, building a .Mac HomePage (if you're a .Mac subscriber; if not, see the extra bits section on page 69), creating a QuickTime file, and finally creating an iDVD project in preparation for burning the movie to a DVD.

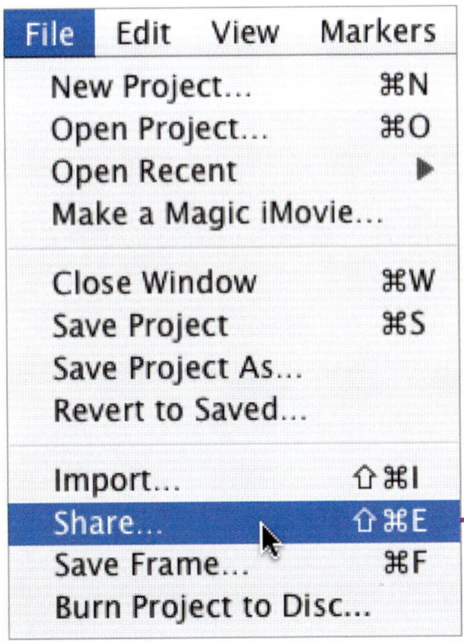

To share a movie, choose Share from the File menu to display the Share dialog, then follow the instructions in the rest of this chapter.

If you want to share only a section of your movie, select the clips in the Timeline before choosing the Share command.

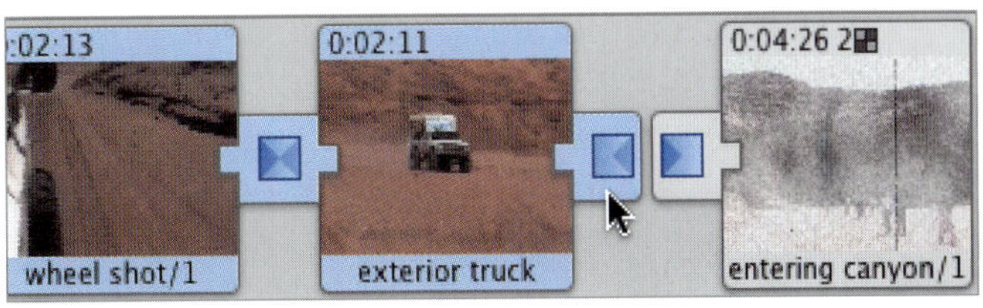

share via email

1 In the Share dialog, click the Email button.

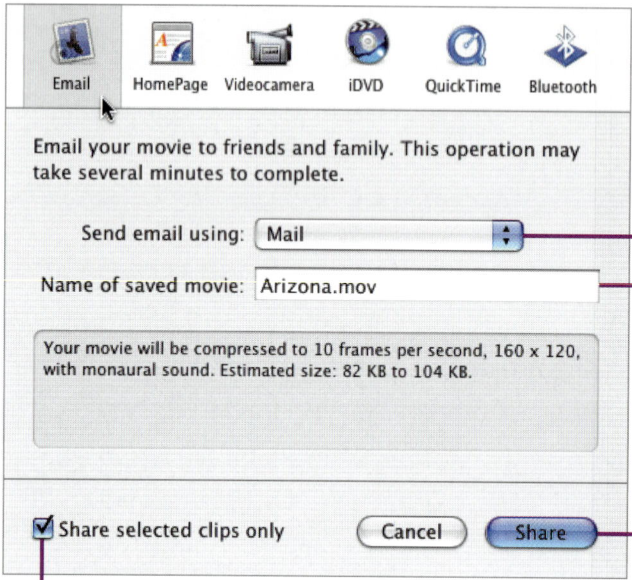

If you're sending just a section of your movie, click this box.

2 Choose your email program from the popup menu.

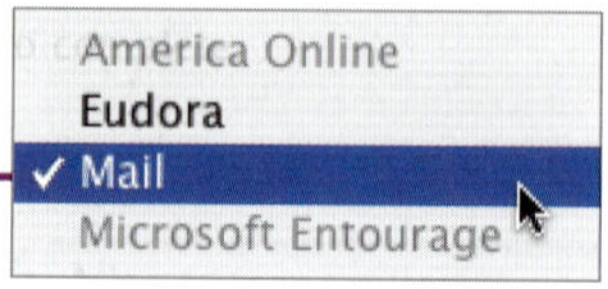

3 Enter a name for the movie file that will be sent.

4 Click here to share the movie. iMovie compresses it to an appropriate size.

5 iMovie launches your email program and creates a new outgoing message with the movie attached (Apple Mail shown here). Enter a recipient, write a brief note, and hit Send to zing it on its way.

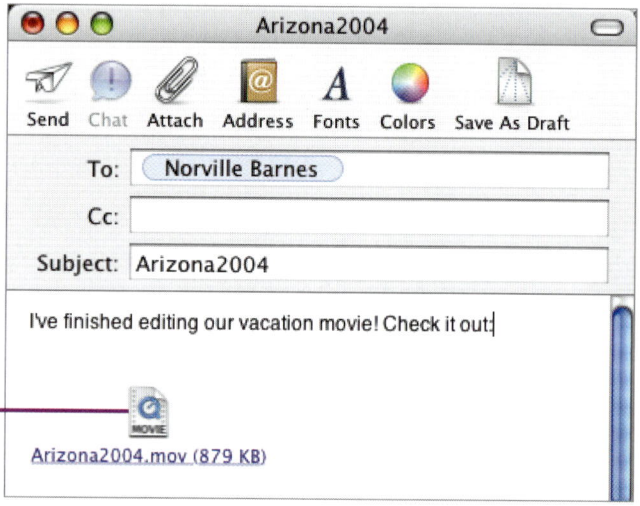

Movie attachment

share via a web page

1 In the Share dialog, click the HomePage button.

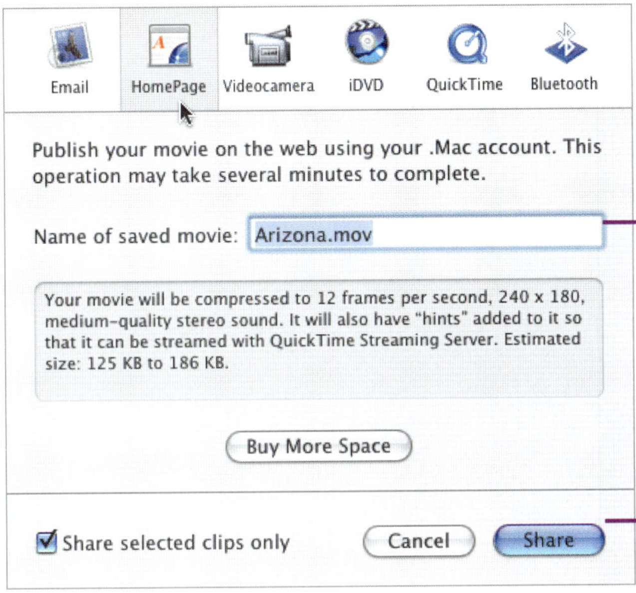

2 Enter a name for the movie file that will appear on the Web.

3 Click Share. iMovie compresses the movie and automatically copies it to your iDisk, then loads the .Mac Web site into your browser. (See extra bits on page 69 if you don't currently have a .Mac account.)

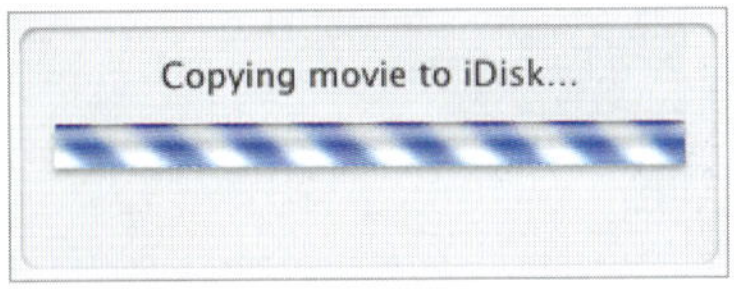

4 After signing into your account, choose a section of your HomePage site, and click an iMovie theme.

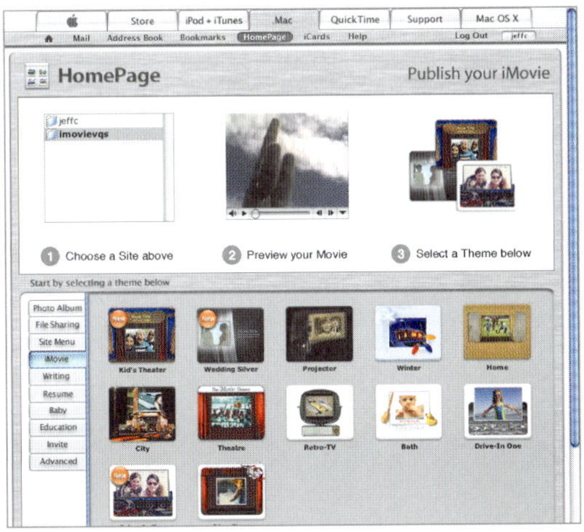

5 Type a page title, movie title, and description into the fields, then click Publish to make the page live.

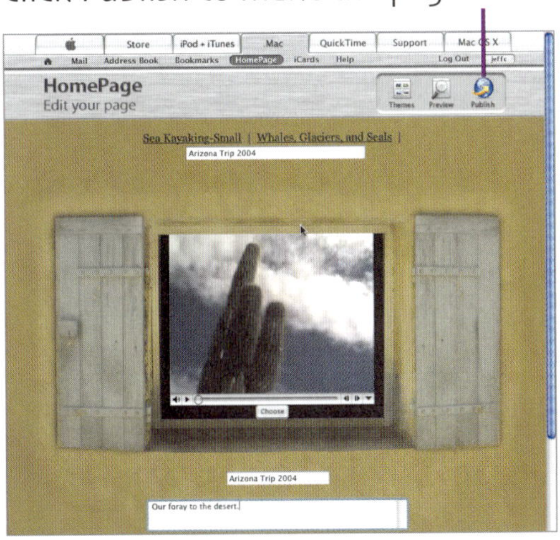

share via QuickTime

1 In the Share dialog, click the QuickTime button.

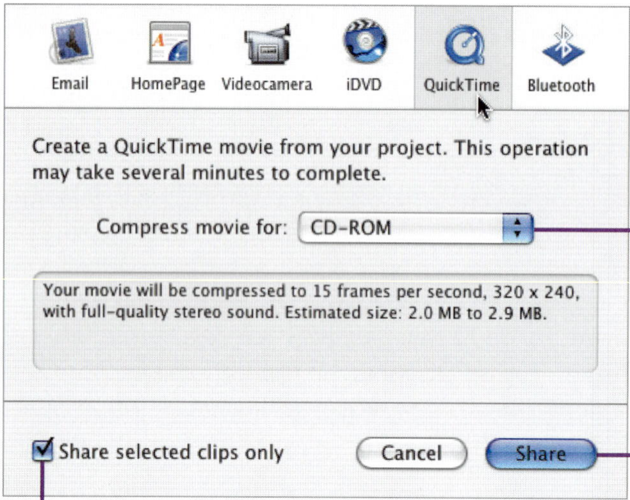

If you're sending just a section of your movie, click this box.

2 Choose a compression setting from the popup menu (see the next page).

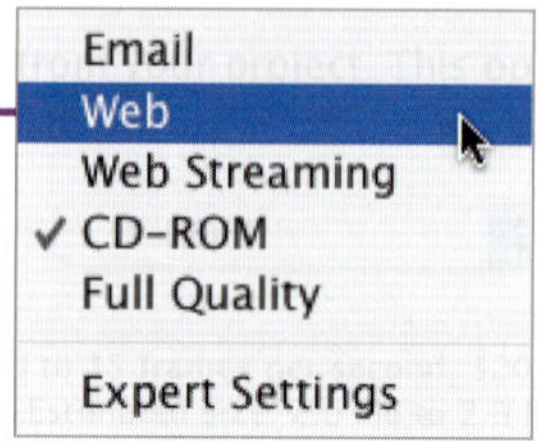

3 Click here to share the movie.

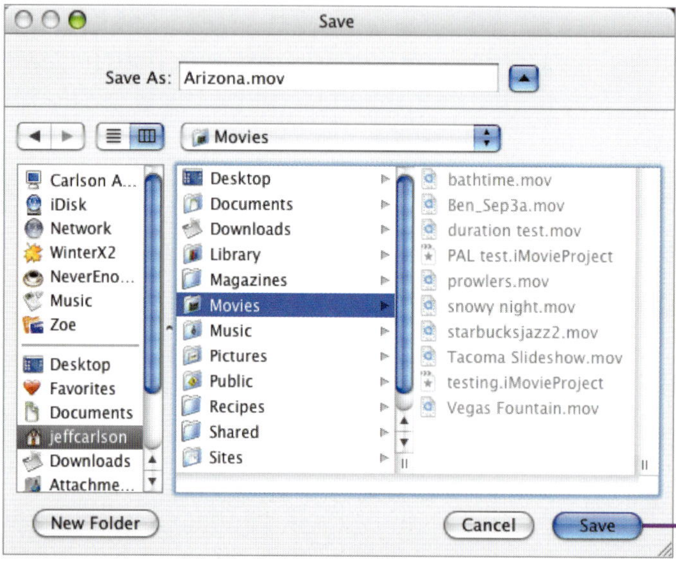

4 In the Save dialog that appears, choose a location on your hard disk.

5 Click Save to compress and save the QuickTime movie file.

You can burn that file to a CD-ROM, upload it to a Web site, or use it for whatever you see fit for a self-contained movie file.

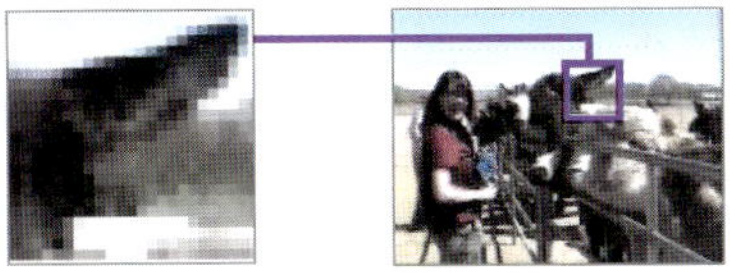

Email

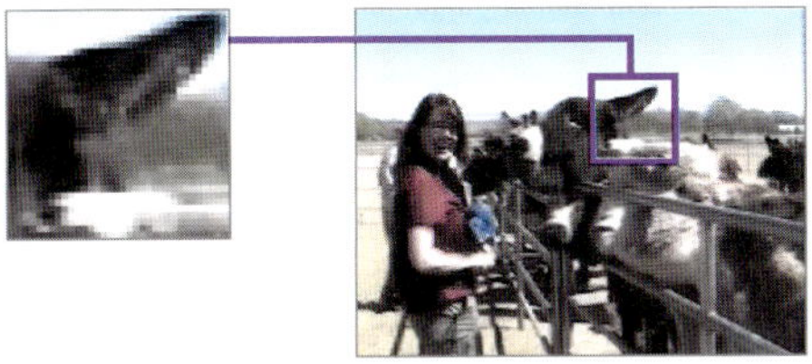

Web,
Web Streaming

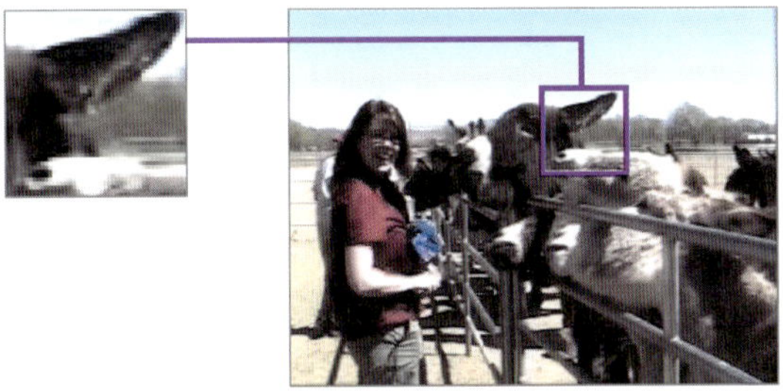

CD-ROM

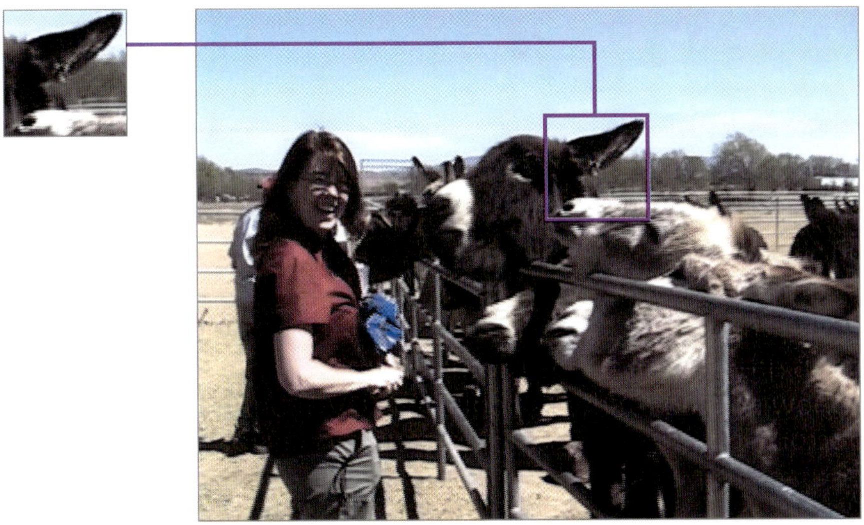

Full Quality DV

The preset QuickTime settings are scaled and compressed for their intended medium, so, for example, the Email version is smaller in dimension and is more compressed to reduce the file size significantly.

Full Quality DV is not compressed at all, leading to huge file sizes, but the best image quality.

create an iDVD project

One advantage of DVDs in general is the capability to jump to specific scenes within a movie, instead of fast-forwarding through the entire movie. You set up these scenes, called chapters, in iMovie before creating the iDVD project.

1 Click the iDVD button.

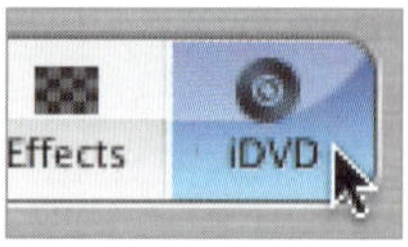

2 Position the Playhead where you want a chapter to begin.

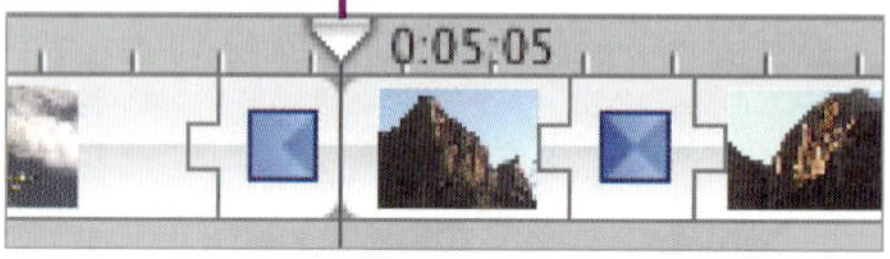

3 Click the Add Chapter button.

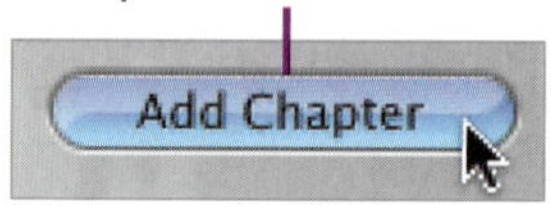

A new chapter is added in the iDVD pane.

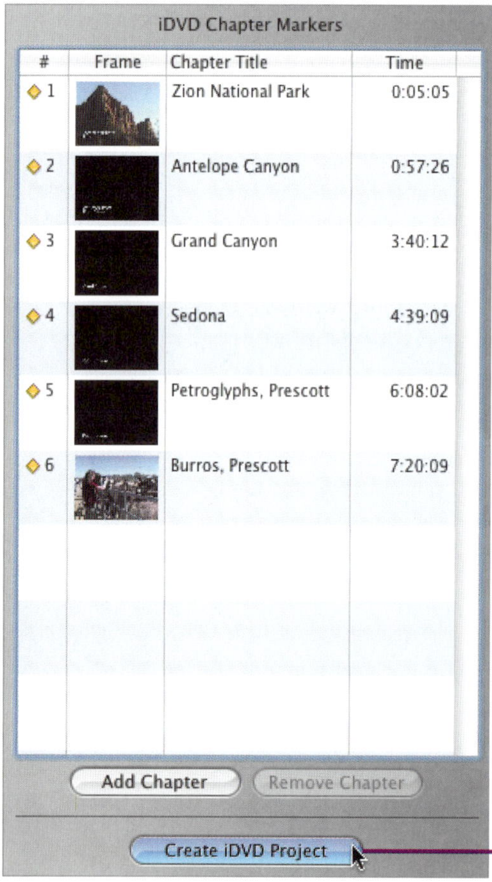

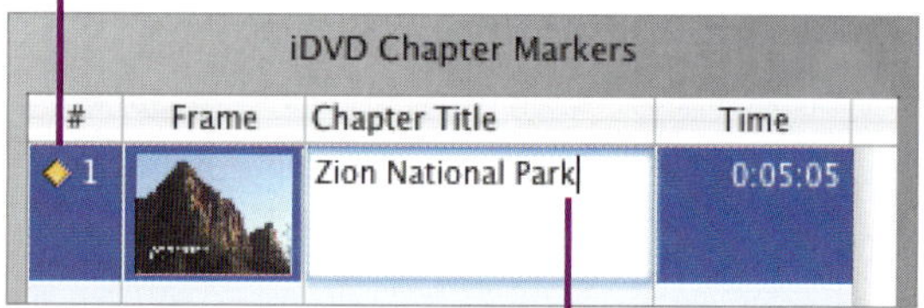

4 Type a name for the chapter as it will appear in iDVD.

5 After adding all your chapters, click the Create iDVD Project button.

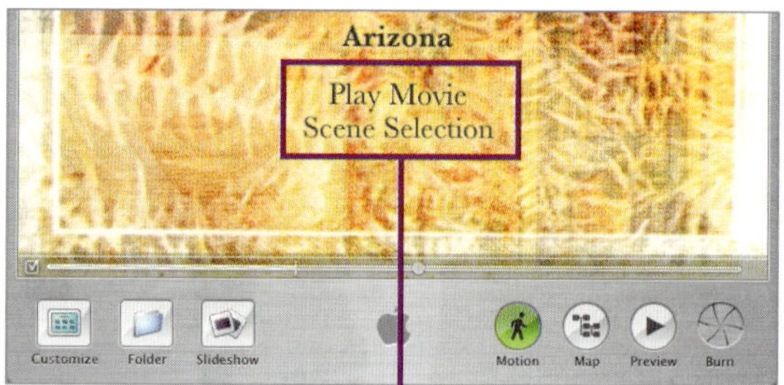

6 iDVD launches automatically, with your movie already set up in iDVD's main menu screen. You're now done with iMovie, and ready to tackle iDVD in Chapter 11!

extra bits

share your movie p. 63

- When sharing just a range of clips, the selection must be contiguous—they all need to connect to each other. Otherwise, the "Share selected clips only" option is disabled.
- You can share video clips that are on the Shelf, too. If you select more than one, iMovie assembles them in the order they were originally imported, not their order on the Shelf.

share via email p. 64

- iMovie warns you if the movie's expected file size is too large to send via email. Look in the summary below the file name field.
- Be a responsible Internet citizen: refrain from sending large files (2 MB or larger) via email. A copy of the movie must be stored on every email server between you and your recipient's computer; combined with spam and malicious email attachments floating around out there, this puts a strain on Internet service providers, who may in turn restrict your capability to successfully send large attachments.

share via a web page p. 65

- If you're not a .Mac member, go to www.mac.com to sign up. A one-year membership costs $100, but you can try the service free for 60 days. (Even if you don't choose to pay, you get to keep your .Mac screen name, which is used by iChat AV.)
- At this writing, the .Mac service includes 125 MB of hard disk space. If you find yourself filling that up with movies (or photos or other files), Apple is happy to sell you more space—up to 1 GB of storage (at $50 per year).
- iMovie reads your .Mac membership information when it launches. If you want to publish to another person's account, you need to quit iMovie, make the change in the .Mac pane of the Mac OS X System Preferences, and then relaunch iMovie.
- You can also publish movies to a .Mac HomePage without doing it directly from iMovie (if you've created a QuickTime movie using custom settings). Copy the movie file to your iDisk, log on to .Mac, click the HomePage icon, and follow the instructions.

extra bits

share via QuickTime p. 66

- iMovie's default QuickTime settings offer decent image quality and file sizes, but you can do better. Choose Expert Settings from the popup menu, then specify another type of video compression, such as Sorenson Video 3. Apple has more information on its support Web site: http://docs.info.apple.com/article.html?artnum=165371.
- You'll notice that the frame size for Full Quality DV is 720 x 480 pixels, which is a wider screen size than the Monitor's size of 640 x 480. What's going on?

  Although each frame is made up of pixels, the pixels in video are rectangular, not square (taller than they are wide). When you view it in iMovie or iDVD, the size is converted to prevent video from looking squished.

create an iDVD project p. 68

- Clicking a chapter marker in the iDVD pane moves the Playhead to that point in the Timeline.
- You can't move chapter markers. Instead, select a marker in the iDVD pane, click the Remove Chapter button, and then create a new marker in the new location.
- Instead of going to the iDVD pane, use the Add Chapter Marker (or press [⌘]-[Shift]-[M]) or Delete Chapter Marker ([Option]-[Shift]-[M]) items in the Advanced menu.
- Another way to share is to record your movie back to a MiniDV tape in your camcorder, using the Videocamera option in the Share dialog. If you aren't able to burn DVDs, you can connect your camcorder to your television to view the movie.
- If your Mac supports Bluetooth (a short-range wireless network protocol) and you own a Bluetooth-enabled cellular phone, you can share your movie via Bluetooth in the Share dialog.

11. explore iDVD

Now that you've created an iDVD project (thanks to the tight relationship between iMovie and iDVD), let's look at what you'll be working with.

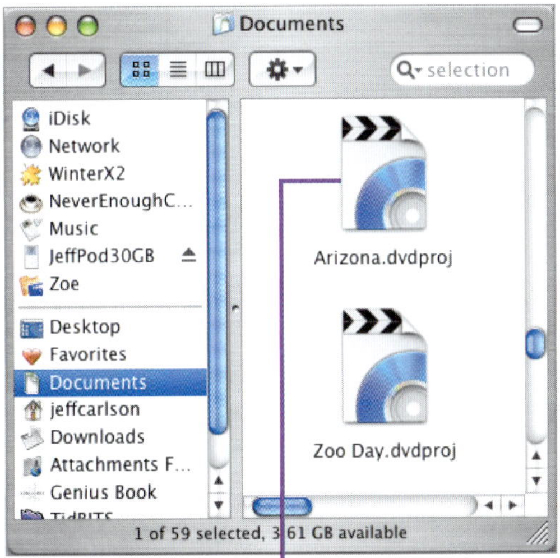

The project file is automatically saved in the Documents folder within your Home directory, with a filename ending in .dvdproj.

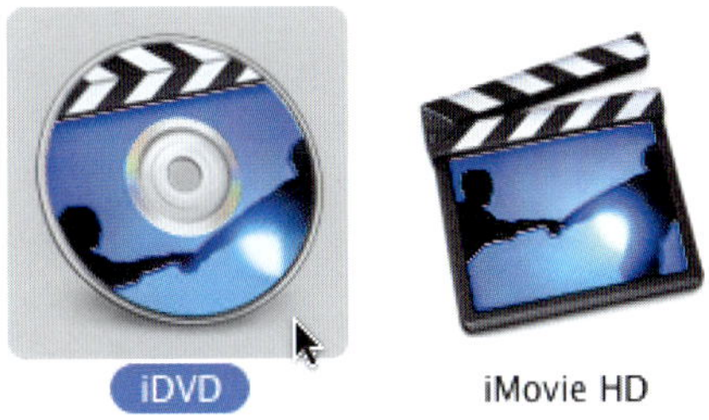

In Chapter 10, iDVD launched when you created the project in the iDVD pane. I should point out that you can also launch iDVD by double-clicking its application icon or the project file. Like iMovie, iDVD opens the last project that was active.

the iDVD interface

Some themes contain one or more drop zones, where you can drag photos or movies to customize the menu.

Each screen is known as a menu, an editable preview of the finished DVD.

The title is the name of the project. A menu can have only one title.

A button is an interactive element on the menu. Each theme draws buttons differently; in this theme, a button is just a text block. When clicked, this button plays the movie from start to finish.

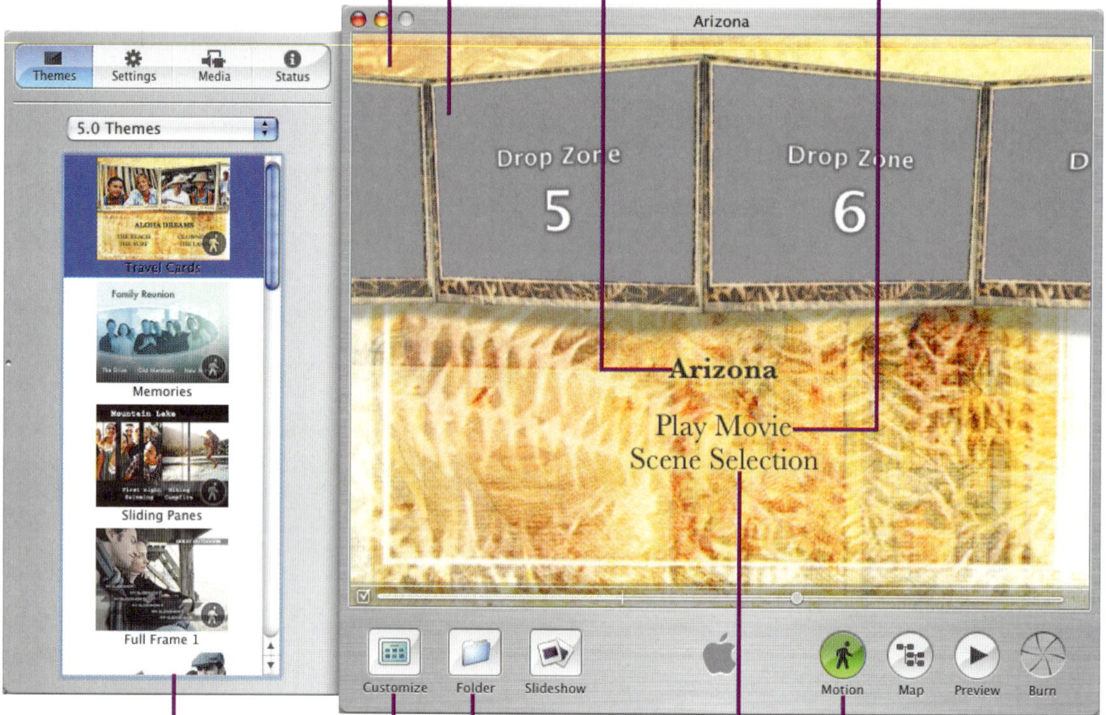

Click the Customize button to view the Customize panel, where you access themes, settings, and media, such as photos or music.

The Folder button creates a submenu, which looks like a text block here, but appears differently in other themes (you'll see in Chapter 12).

The Motion button activates a theme's animated elements, such as the moving collection of travel note cards (which contain drop zones) shown here.

Click the Map button to switch to iDVD's Map view (below) which displays your project's structure; click it again to return to the menu. Double-clicking an icon takes you to that menu or movie (except for the AutoPlay well, which works differently; see Chapter 13).

The AutoPlay well lets you play content before the DVD's main menu loads.

Main menu

Button

Submenu

Video chapter

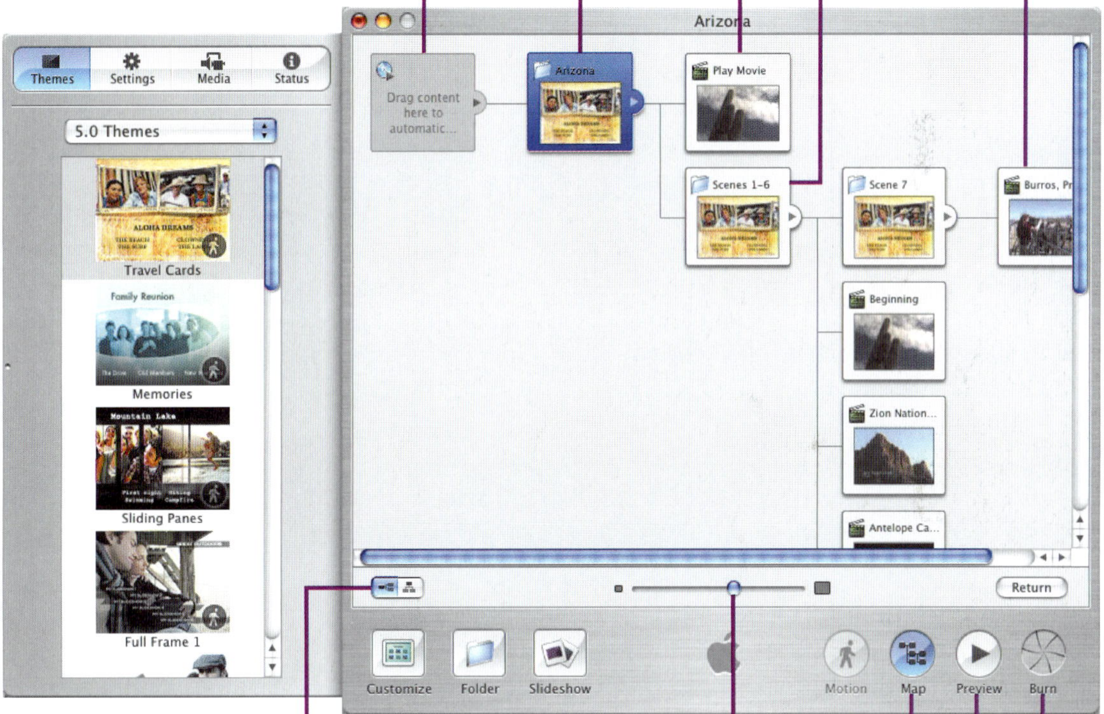

Map button

View the map horizontally (shown here) or vertically by clicking these buttons.

Use the Size slider to view more objects in the Map view.

Click the Preview button (in the Map view or the editing view) to experience the project as if you were viewing it on a DVD player.

When you're ready to create a DVD disc, click the Burn button (asbestos suit not required).

extra bits

explore iDVD p. 71

- If you should happen to rename the iDVD project file, be sure to keep the .dvdproj extension; if you don't, iDVD won't recognize the file, and the Finder displays it as a folder.
- iDVD 5 offers a new feature, OneStep DVD, that automatically imports video from a camcorder and burns it to a DVD disc. This is good if you need a plain DVD copy of your footage, but it won't give you a menu or interface of any kind—the video just begins to play immediately after you insert the disc into a DVD player. Since we're creating a DVD with menus and other elements, we don't need to use OneStep DVD.

the iDVD interface p. 72

- You cannot resize the iDVD window.
- In the Map view, clicking the triangles on each menu icon hides objects farther down in the hierarchy. This is useful if you're navigating a complicated project and don't need to see all of the branches on screen at once. Clicking the triangle again reveals objects that were hidden.
- iDVD uses a lot of your computer's processing power to display motion elements, so unless you're actively working on motion (or you have a wicked-fast Power Mac G5), I recommend turning Motion off while editing your iDVD menus.

12. choose and customize a theme

Instead of starting off with a blank slate, iDVD offers a selection of professionally designed themes to enhance your DVD menus. You can stick with one of Apple's creations, or customize the look by changing elements of the interface. Either way, you end up with a DVD that looks good, no matter how talented you are in the design department.

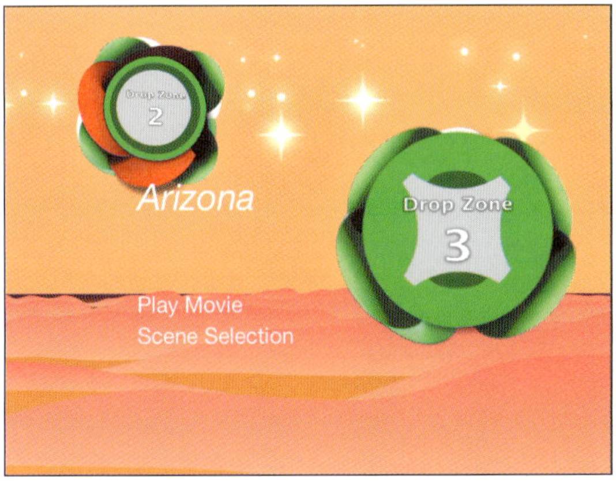

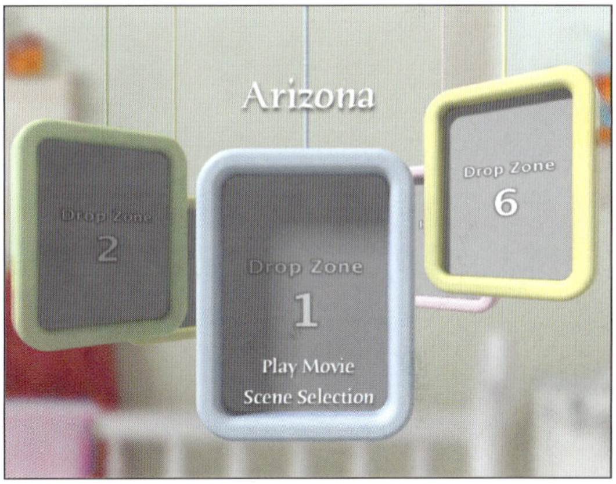

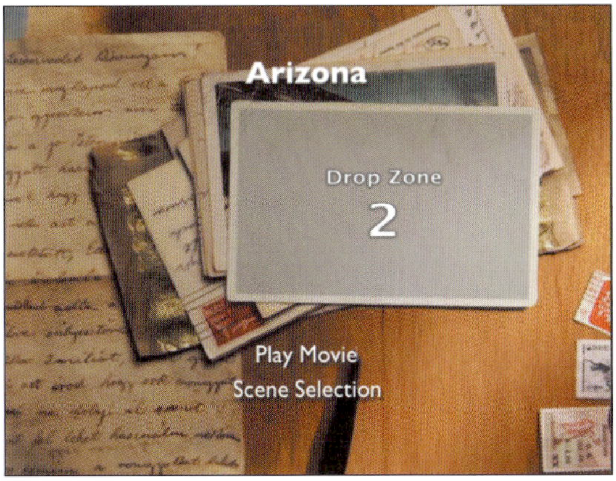

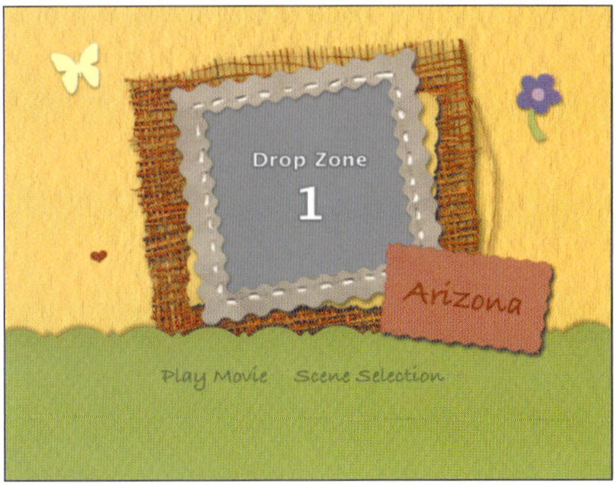

apply a theme

iDVD includes 73 pre-designed themes, ranging from specific topics such as Anime Pop to general imagery like Portfolio. I'll choose Travel 1 to match my vacation theme and express a world-traveler feel.

1 Click the Themes pane if it's not already visible.

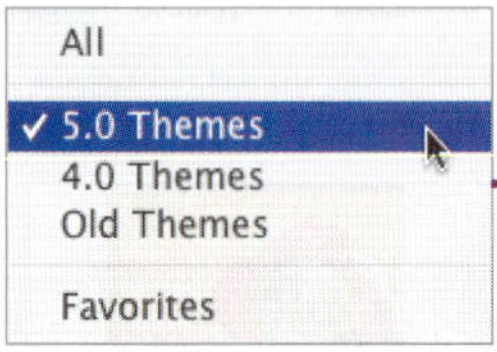

To view more theme groups (listed by previous versions of iDVD), choose one from the popup menu.

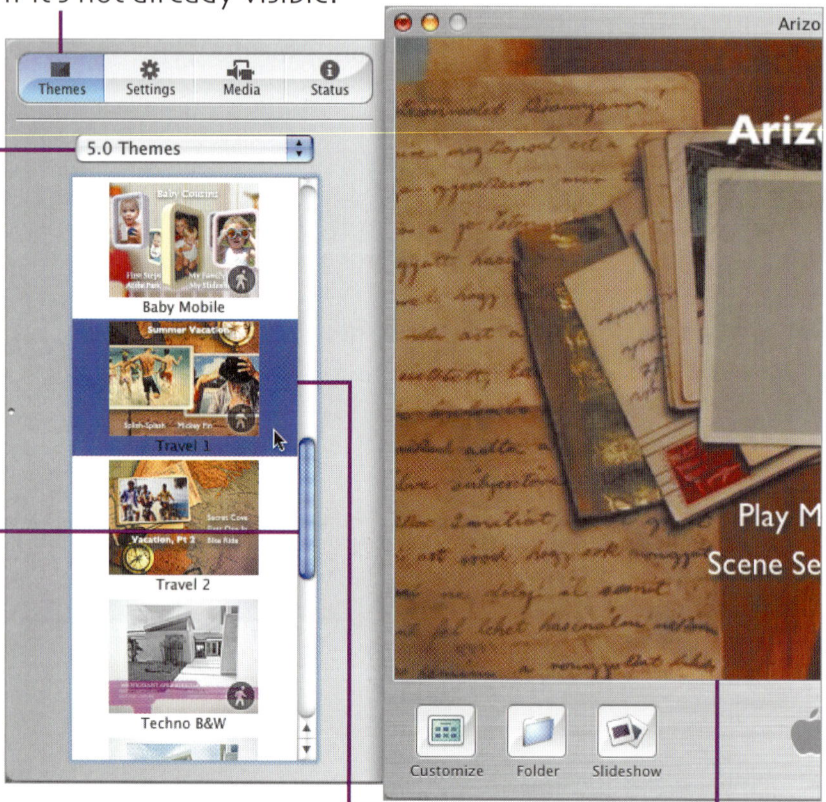

Scroll to find the theme you want.

2 Click a theme icon to apply it to the menu.

The theme changes appearance, but the buttons and submenus remain intact.

edit the title

You can have only one title in a menu, and it behaves a bit differently than other text, depending on the theme. You don't need to select the title to edit its formatting.

1 Click the Settings pane.

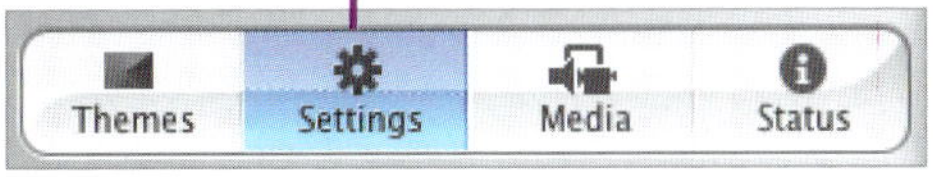

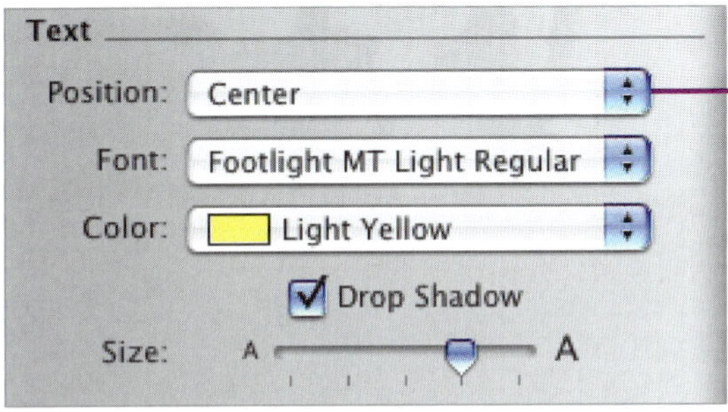

2 Customize the text's appearance by choosing Font, Color, and Size, and whether it should include a drop shadow.

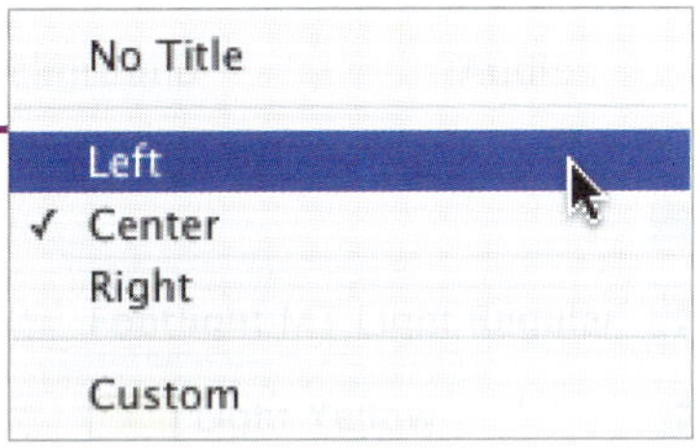

3 Choose a position for the title. The Left, Center, and Right options align the title to a specific area based on the theme. Choose Custom to drag the title anywhere onscreen.

Before changing formatting settings

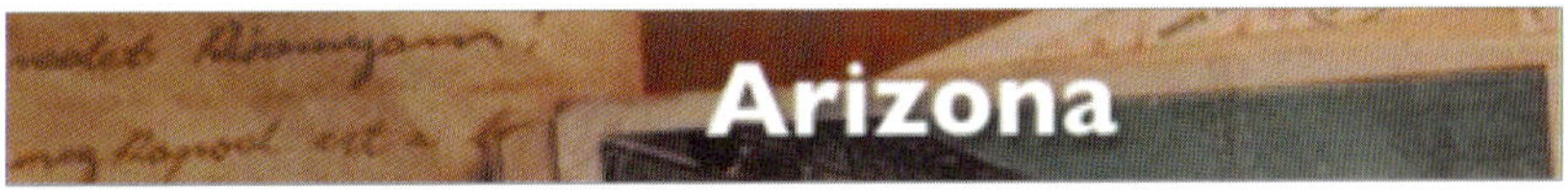

After changing formatting settings

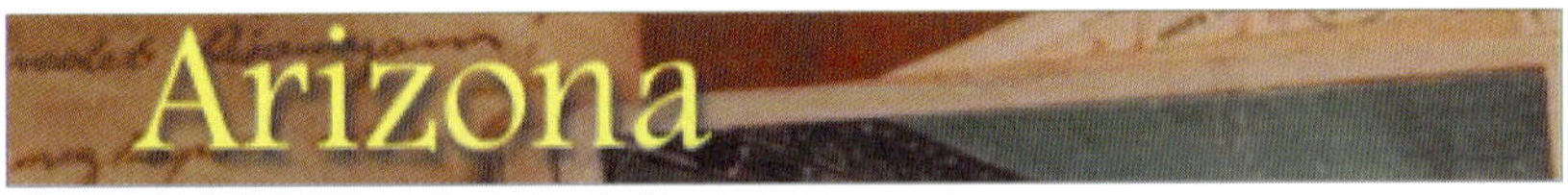

4 If you want to change the title's wording, double-click it to make the text field editable.

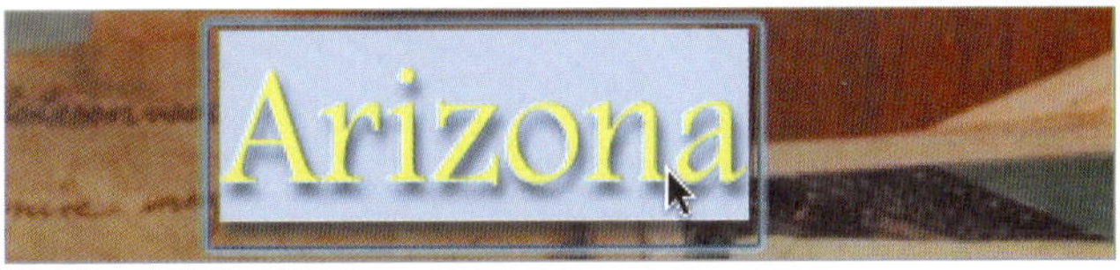

5 Type your new title, and then click outside the box to apply the change.

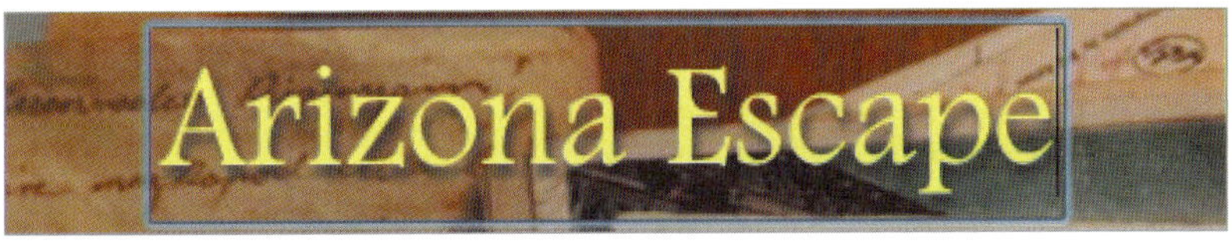

edit the buttons

Formatting buttons involves two components: the buttons' text (if there is any), and the buttons' shape. When editing buttons, the settings apply to all buttons and submenus on the page. These controls are also found in the Settings pane.

1 Click a button once to select it (if you double-click, it's action will engage, such as playing the movie or opening a submenu).

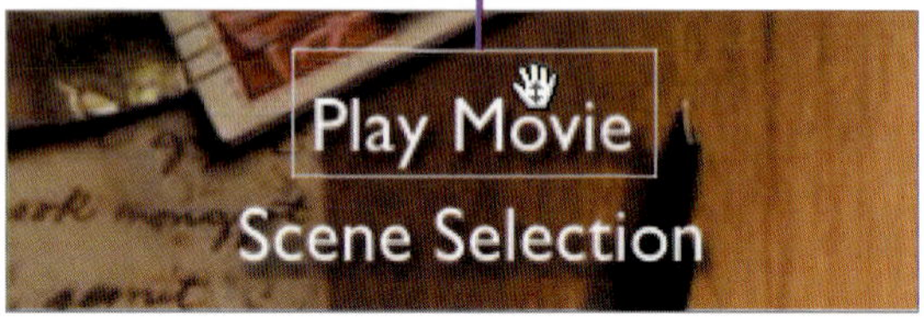

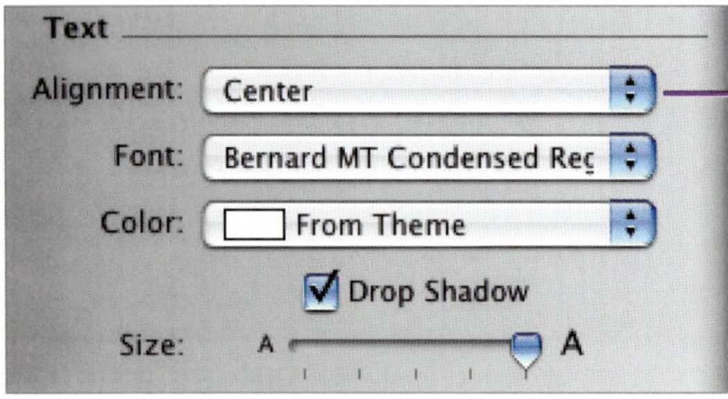

2 Customize the text's appearance by choosing Font, Color, and Size, and whether it should include a drop shadow.

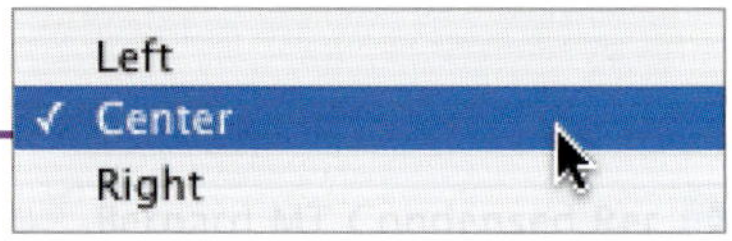

3 Choose an alignment for the button's text. For buttons that are just text, the alignment dictates how the buttons line up in relation to one another.

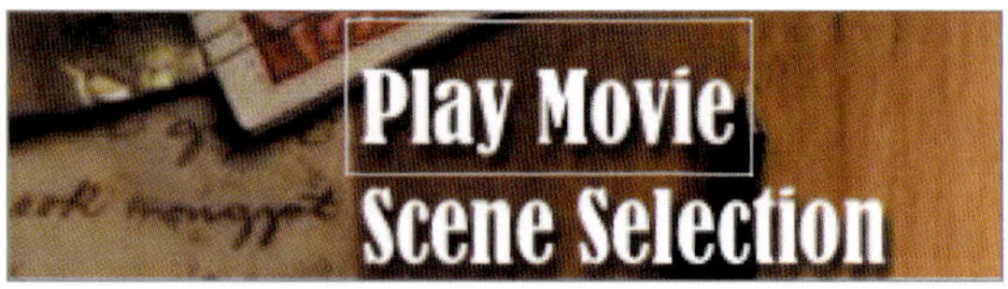

Aligned left

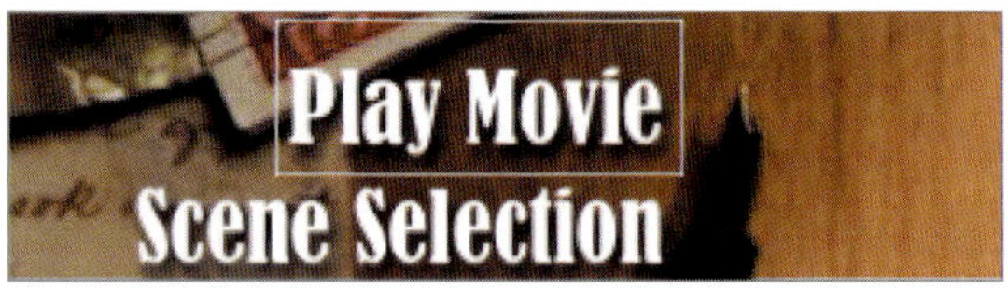

Aligned right

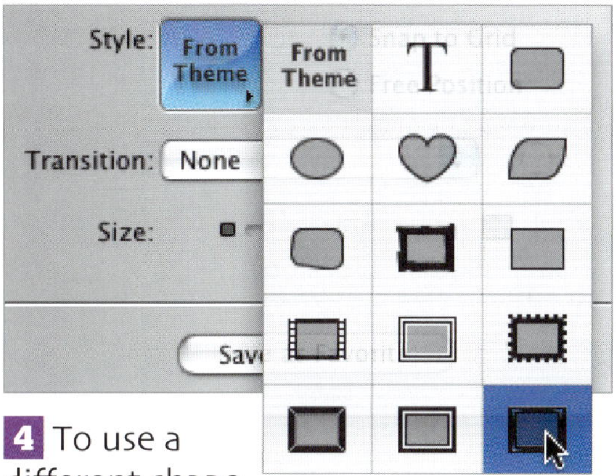

4 To use a different shape (or in this case, to use a button shape in addition to the text), click the Style popup menu.

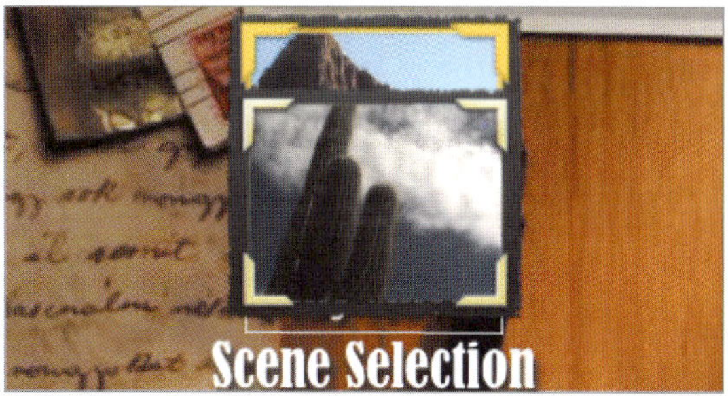

The buttons are currently snapped to the underlying grid, which is why they're overlapping.

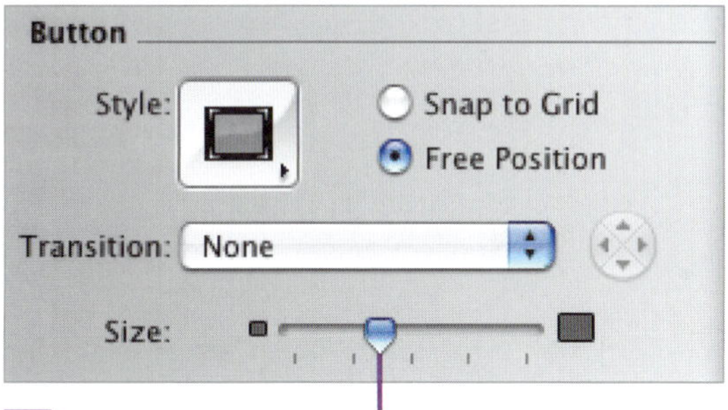

5 If you want to adjust the button sizes, drag the Size slider.

6 Click the Free Position button to liberate the buttons, then drag them into your preferred locations.

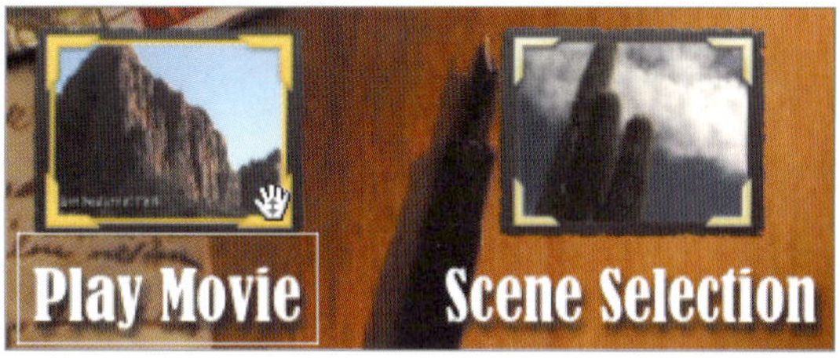

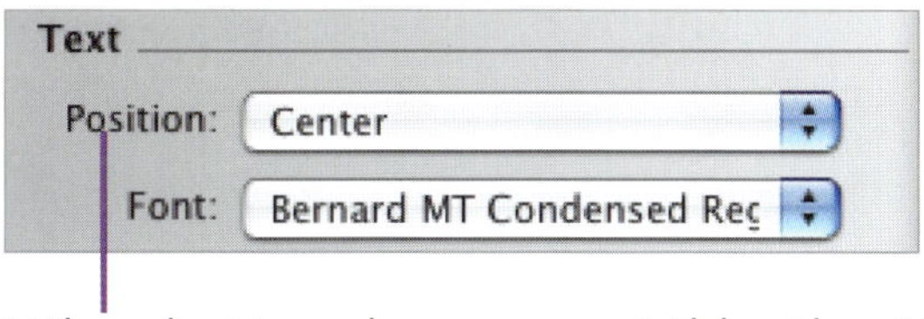

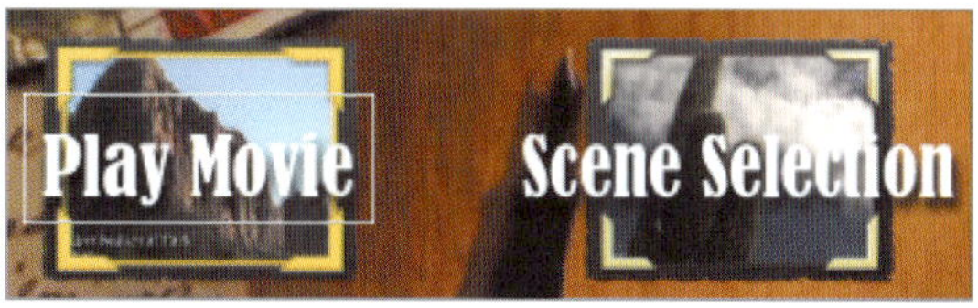

When button shapes are visible, the Alignment popup menu becomes the Position menu, which controls the position of text relative to the button.

edit motion buttons

Buttons don't have to be static pictures. Part of iDVD's Motion features are motion buttons. A button that links to a movie can play a portion of the movie in the button's thumbnail image. If the button leads to a submenu containing movie clips, you can choose which clip's starting frame appears in place of the generic folder icon.

If you don't want the movie to play in the button's shape, deselect this checkbox. You can still choose a starting frame to use as an icon.

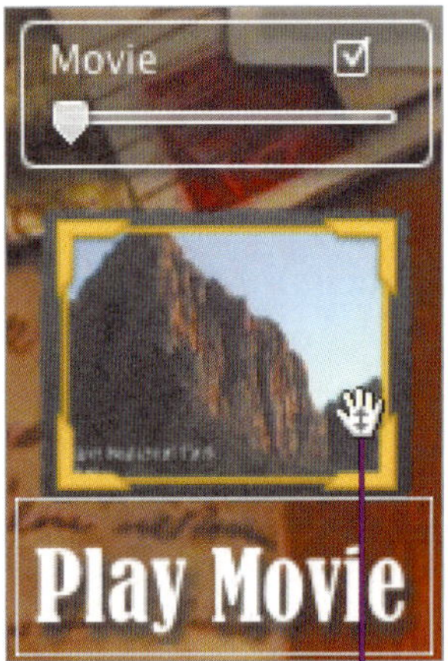

1 Click a button once to select it.

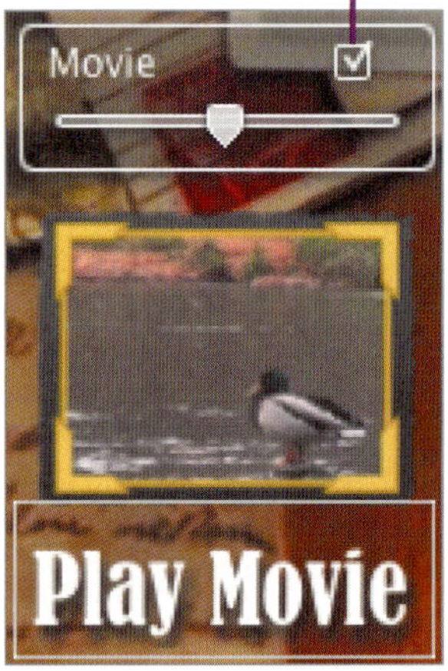

2 Drag the Movie slider to locate the frame you wish to use as the starting point.

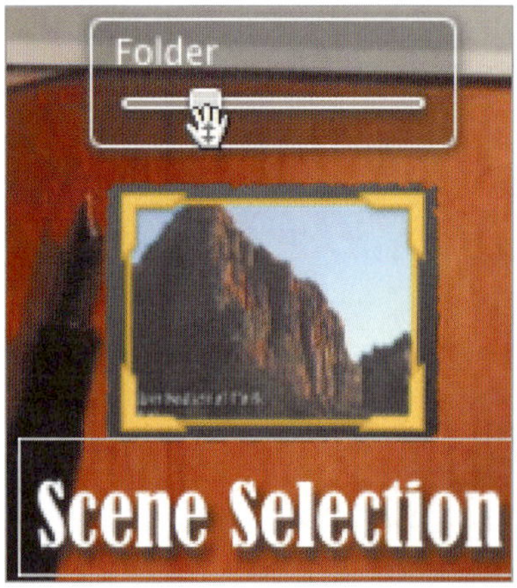

Submenu buttons work the same way: drag the Folder slider to locate an image to use as the button's icon.

3 To see how the button plays back, click the Motion button. Click it again to turn motion off.

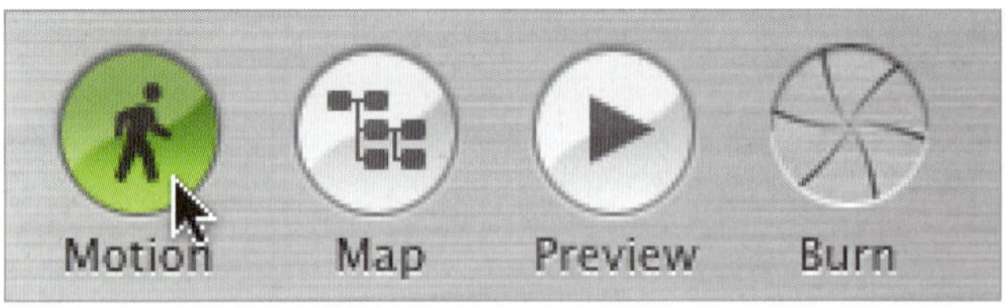

set background audio

DVD isn't just a visual medium—you can add your own music that will play while the menu is onscreen. Some themes already include background music, which you can easily change.

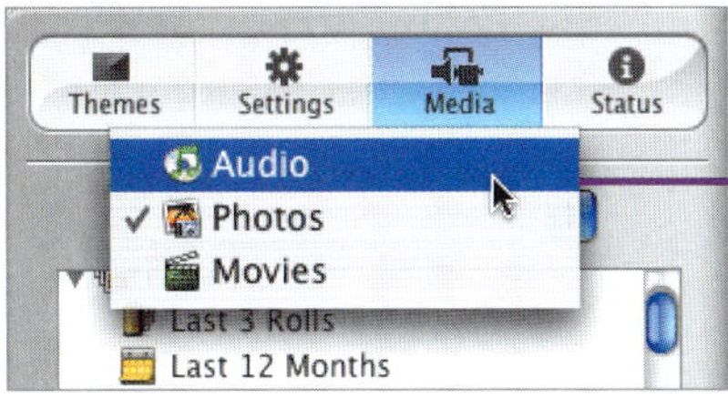

1 In the Media pane, choose Audio from the popup menu.

2 Locate the song you want to use.

3 Drag the song to the menu's background. It will play while Motion is enabled.

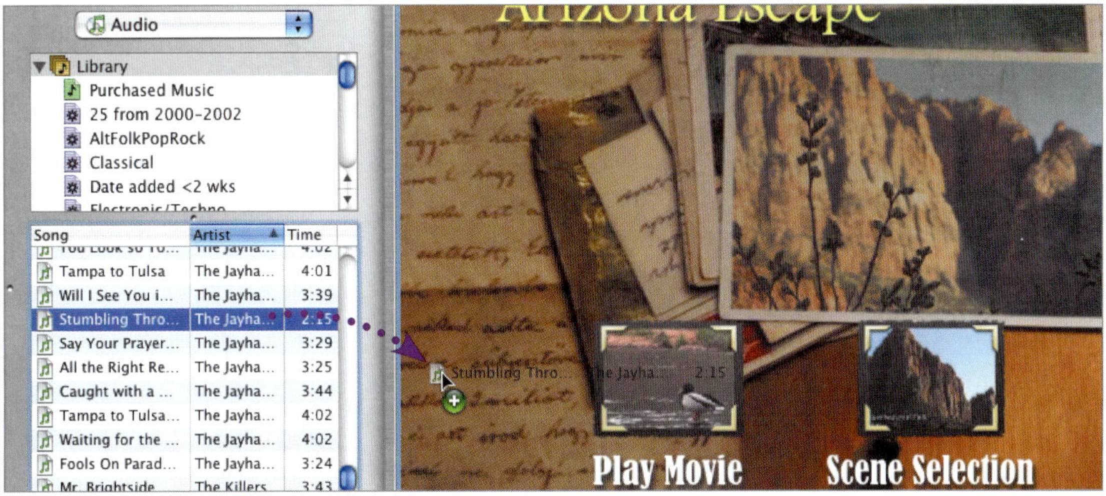

Removing a song is as easy as dragging it out of the Audio well, where it disappears in a puff of smoke.

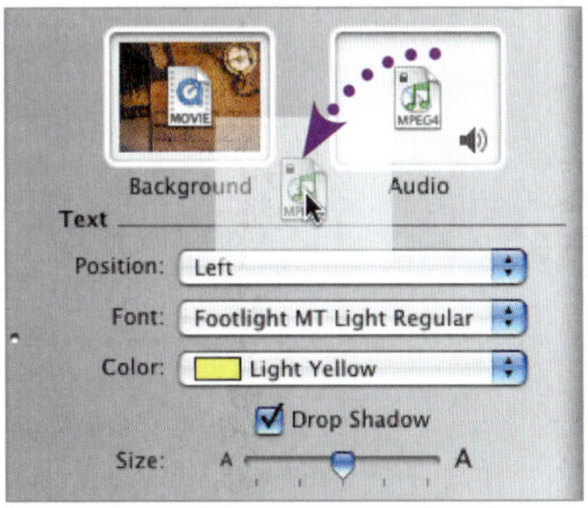

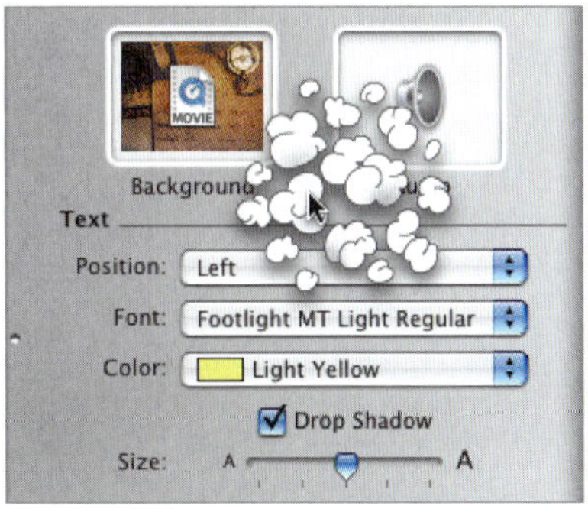

add drop zone media

Several iDVD themes include one or more drop zones, areas that can accept video or image files to add more visual interest. You can add multiple photos or single video files to drop zones. For this example, I'm adding pictures to a zone.

1 Click the Media pane.

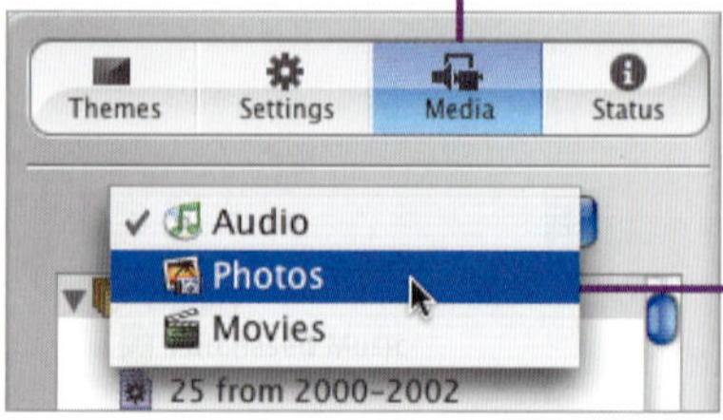

2 Choose Photos from the popup menu.

3 Select one or more photos from the list.

iDVD tells you how many pictures are being added.

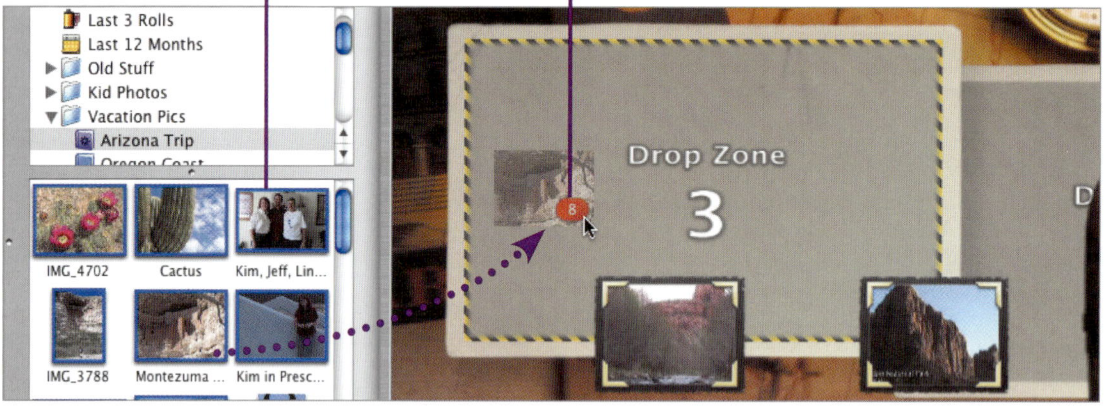

4 Drag the selected photos to the drop zone to add them.

5 Click the drop zone, and use the Photos slider to choose which photo appears first in the slideshow.

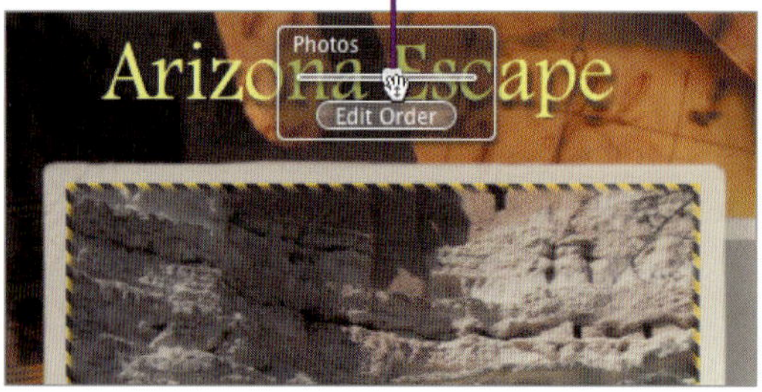

6 Click and drag within the drop zone to reposition the photo. Be careful not to drag outside the zone.

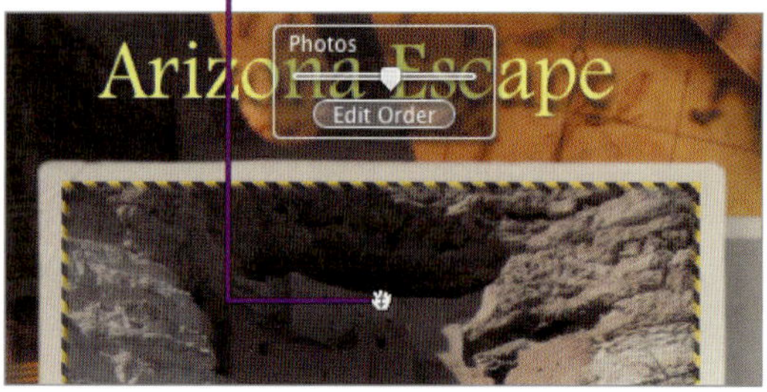

7 Would you like to rearrange the order in which the photos appear? Click the Edit Order button to bring up the Drop Zone Editor.

To delete a photo, select it and press Delete.

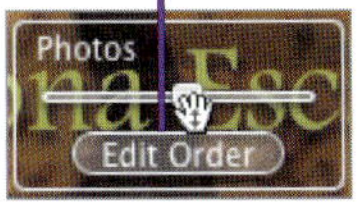

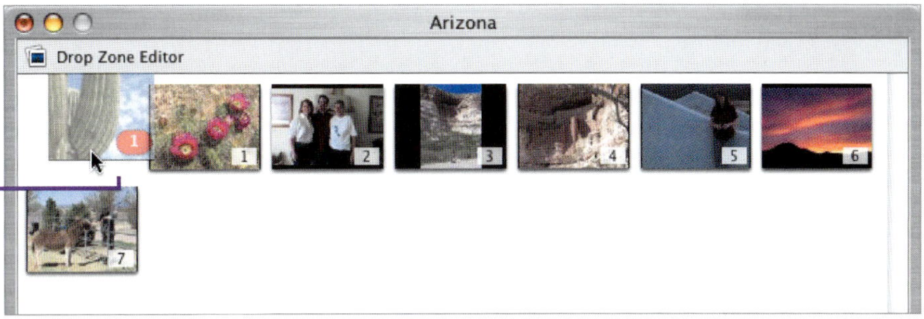

8 Drag the thumbnails to change the order.

You can also drag more photos (up to 30) from the Media pane to the Drop Zone Editor to add them to the slideshow.

9 When you're finished, press the Return button in the lower-right corner of the Drop Zone Editor to go back to the menu.

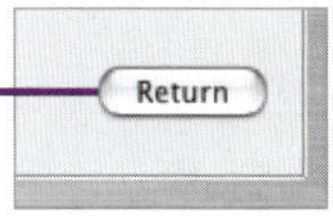

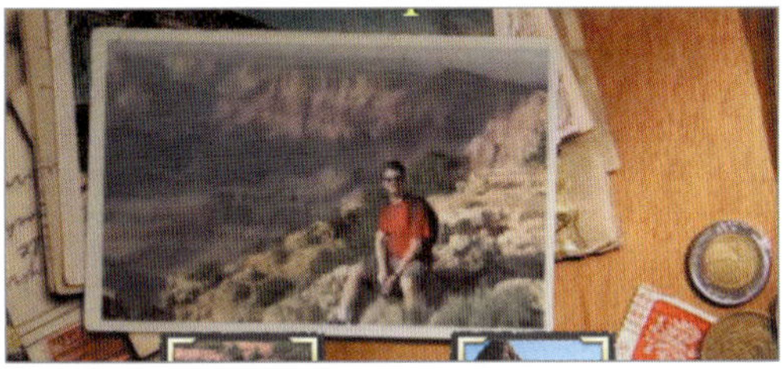

If you added a movie to the drop zone, the movie plays back when Motion is enabled. In this example, I exported a section of my movie to a QuickTime file (see Chapter 10).

To remove drop zone video or photos, click and drag the contents out of the zone.

The media disappears in a puff of smoke.

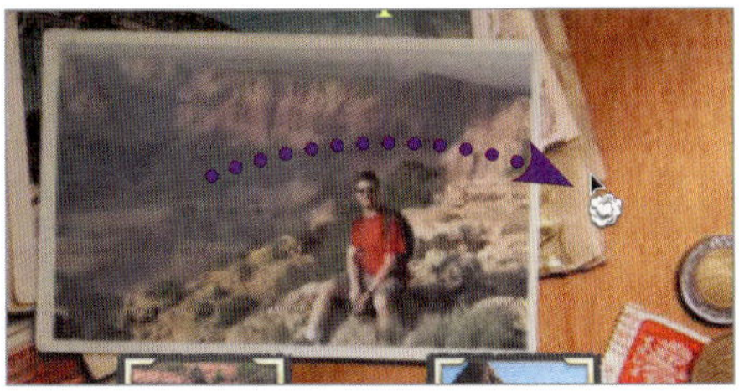

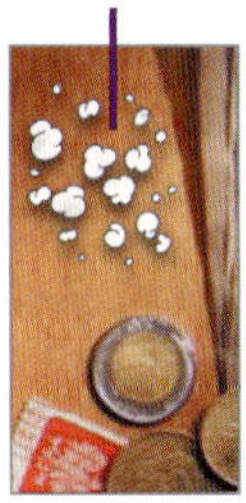

use animated drop zones

Most of the new themes introduced in iDVD 5 feature animated drop zones. Instead of having one drop zone area in the menu, these themes offer several drop zones that move. In my project, the Travel 1 theme features drop zones moving right to left across the screen while other travel-related items (a globe, suitcases) whiz past the screen.

You work with animated drop zones just as with the drop zones found on the previous two pages. If Motion is turned on, however, you'll be trying to drag media files onto moving targets. Instead, follow these steps.

Introductory animation; the rest of the animation starts over at the break. Click the checkbox to remove this section.

1 Turn Motion off.

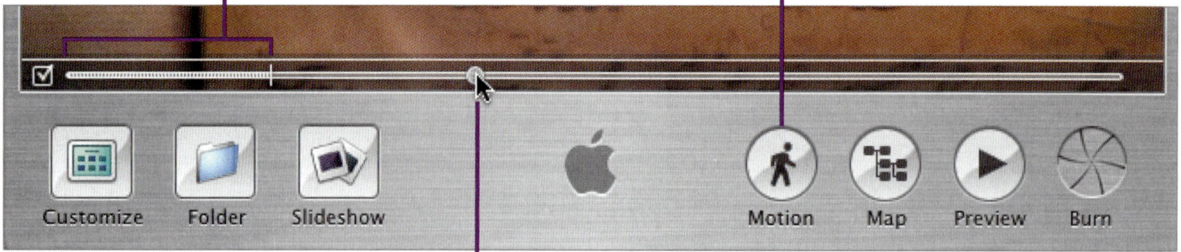

2 Drag the Motion Playhead to the right to advance the animation and expose more drop zones, then add media to them.

3 You can also double-click a drop zone to bring up a special Drop Zone Editor made for the animated drop zone themes. Drag photos or movie files to the empty slots to populate the drop zones.

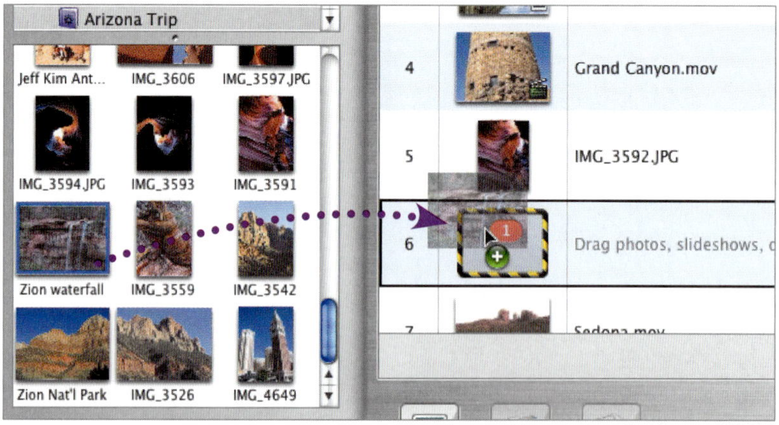

change background

A dramatic way to customize your menu is to replace a theme's background image with one of your own, either a photo or a movie.

Drag a photo from the Media pane to the menu's background.

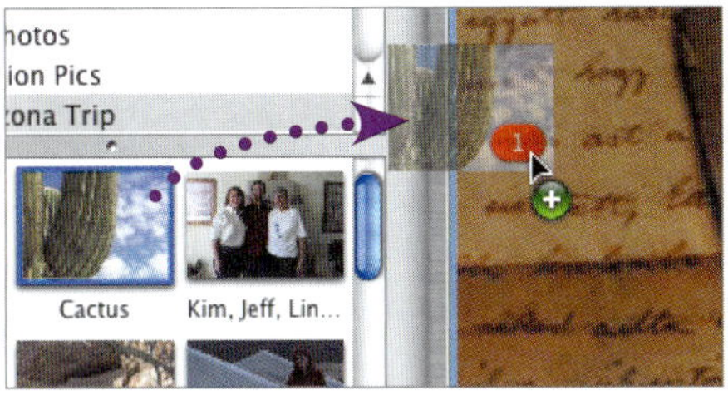

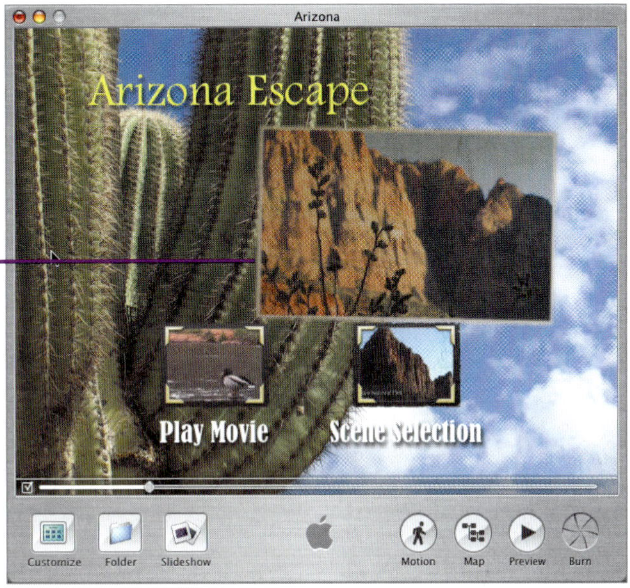

Changing the background with this technique retains the drop zone, which may not be ideal in your design (but may work with other themes).

Another method is to drag a media file to the Settings tab...

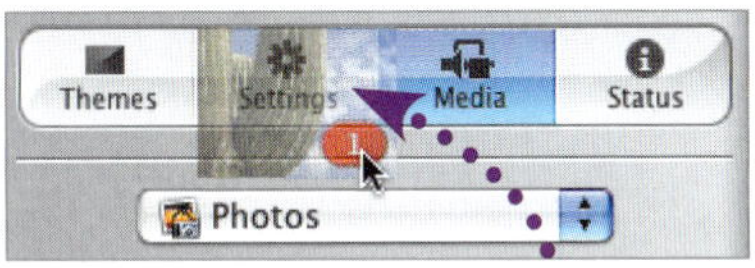

...and, after the Settings pane appears (without releasing the mouse button), drag the file to the Background well.

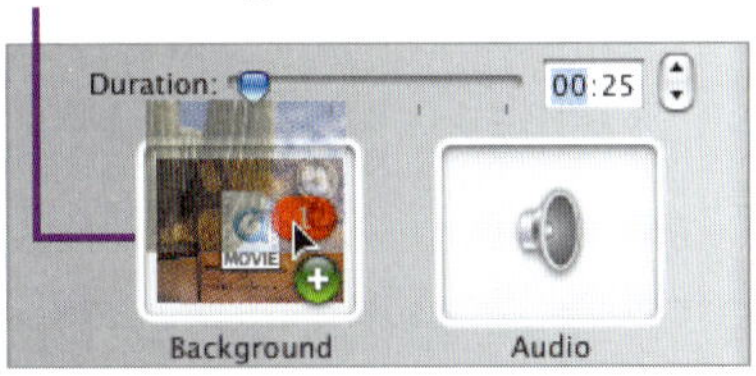

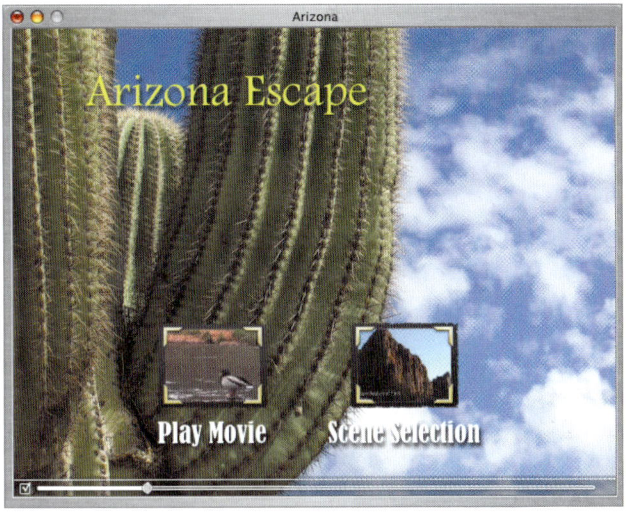

With this approach, however, the drop zone is hidden by the background image.

apply submenu theme

Your main menu is now done, so it's time to turn to the submenu that iDVD automatically created to access the chapters you set up in iMovie.

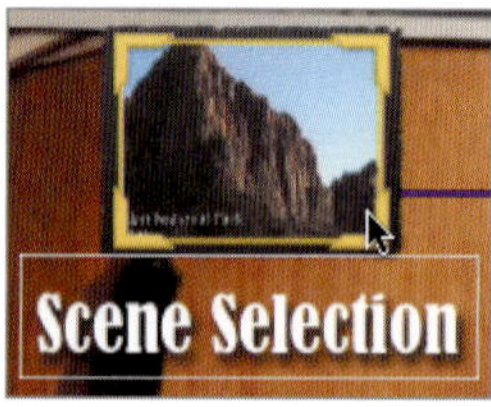

1 Double-click the icon for the submenu to load it into the editing screen.

Buttons access the movie chapters.

iDVD assigns a default theme to the submenu.

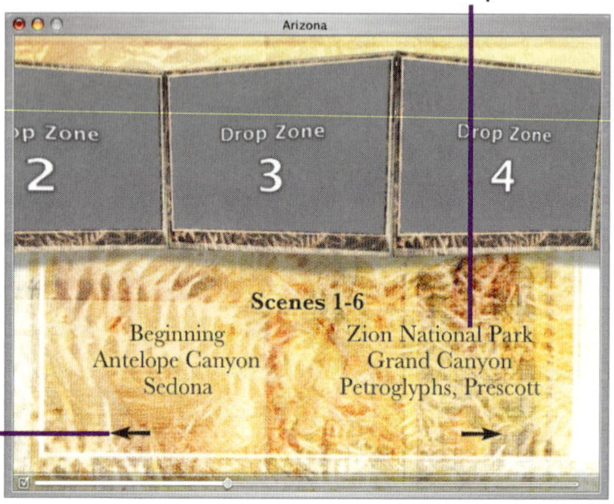

Navigation arrow takes you to the main menu.

2 Choose a new theme in the Themes pane.

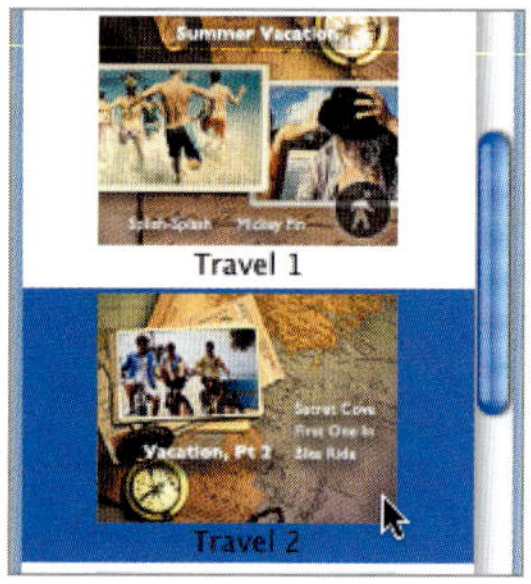

3 You can also apply themes in the Map view. Simply click a menu, and then choose a theme from the Themes pane.

4 Using the steps you learned in this chapter, customize the buttons and other elements of the submenu.

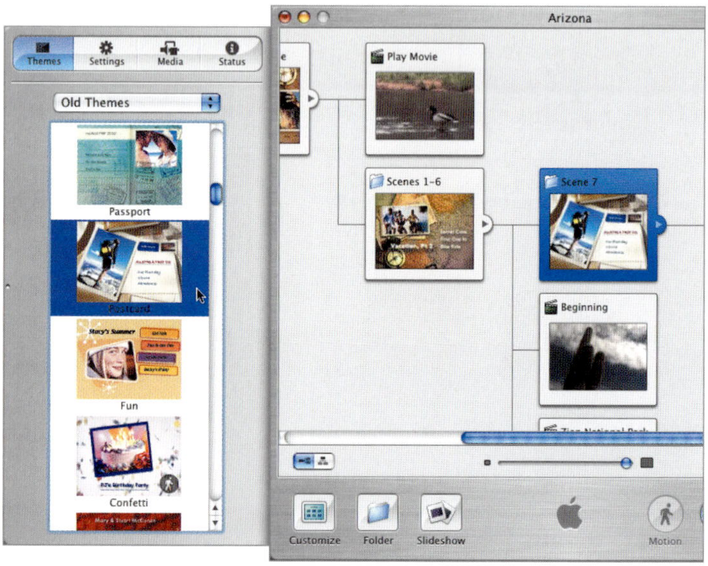

extra bits

apply a theme p. 76

- If 73 built-in themes aren't enough for you, consider buying themes from other developers. See Appendix B.
- Some themes include background music when the Motion button is enabled. That's fine for playing the DVD on a television, but can be grating while editing. I usually activate Motion only when I need to view animated elements.

edit the title p. 77

- When using the Custom position for the title, remember that most television screens cut off part of the visible image. Choose Show TV Safe Area from the Advanced menu to view recommended boundaries marked in red.

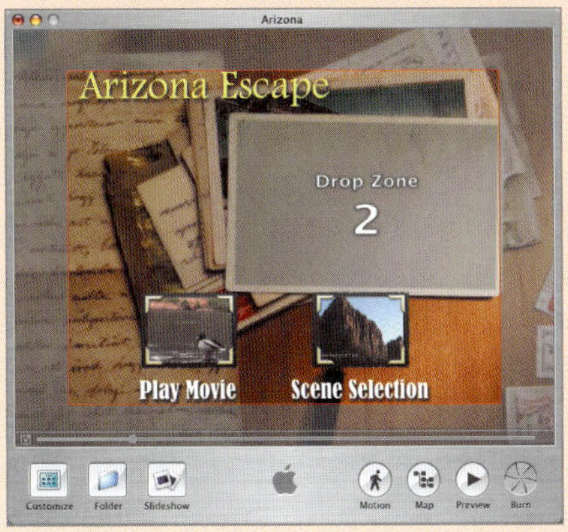

edit the buttons p. 78

- To make multiple-line button titles, simply hit Return between words.

edit motion buttons p. 80

- Is nothing happening when you click the Motion button? Go to the Settings pane, and check the Duration slider—it may have gotten set to zero. Duration controls how much of the menu's motion plays before starting over. Typically, this amount is the menu's longest background movie or audio, but you can set it lower.

set background audio p. 81

- You can drag a QuickTime movie to the Audio well, which will use only its audio track.
- The music loops created in GarageBand make for great background music on a DVD.
- When you drag a song onto the Audio well in a theme that already has background music, your song takes precedence. If you remove your song from the well, the theme's song is still there—you need to delete that, too, for no background audio.

extra bits

add drop zone media p. 82

- If you'd rather not see the drop zone text ("Drag photos..."), go to iDVD's preferences and uncheck Show Drop Zones. The zones are still there, just not explicitly marked.
- Go to iDVD's preferences if you want to turn off the Apple logo watermark.
- You can also drag image and video files from the Finder to a drop zone, instead of using the Media pane.
- The length of time each photo appears onscreen depends on how many photos you've added, and the Duration amount. The fewer the photos, the longer each will be visible.
- It's not possible to resize or crop drop zone photos within iDVD.
- If you've already added photos to a drop zone, dragging more to the zone replaces the ones you have. To add more photos and retain the existing ones, use the Drop Zone Editor instead of dragging them in the menu.
- In the Drop Zone Editor, view the photos in a list by clicking the view preference buttons in the lower-left corner of the screen.
- A drop zone video plays back from the beginning of the clip; you can't choose a starting frame like you can with motion buttons.

change background p. 85

- If you want to use a movie as a background image (also known as a motion menu), you need to drop it on the Background well—otherwise, the movie becomes a button. Also, export it from iMovie as a Full Quality DV QuickTime movie to get the best image quality.
- If you switch to a new theme, your custom background is deleted; you'll have to add it again to the new theme.

apply submenu theme p. 86

- For a little more visual snazz, apply a transition between menus. Choose one from the Transition menu in the Settings pane. Also note that transitions play only when going to a submenu, not when returning to the previous menu.
- In the Map view, Shift-click multiple submenus to select them, and then click a theme to apply it to them all at once.

13. add more content to the DVD

The iDVD project has been pretty straightforward so far: you've added chapters to an edited iMovie video, tossed it into iDVD, and edited the project's theme to make it look slick and polished. In this chapter, you'll add a few more things to the project: an additional submenu, other movies, a photo slideshow, and DVD-ROM data that is stored on the disc and accessible to people using computers instead of commercial DVD players.

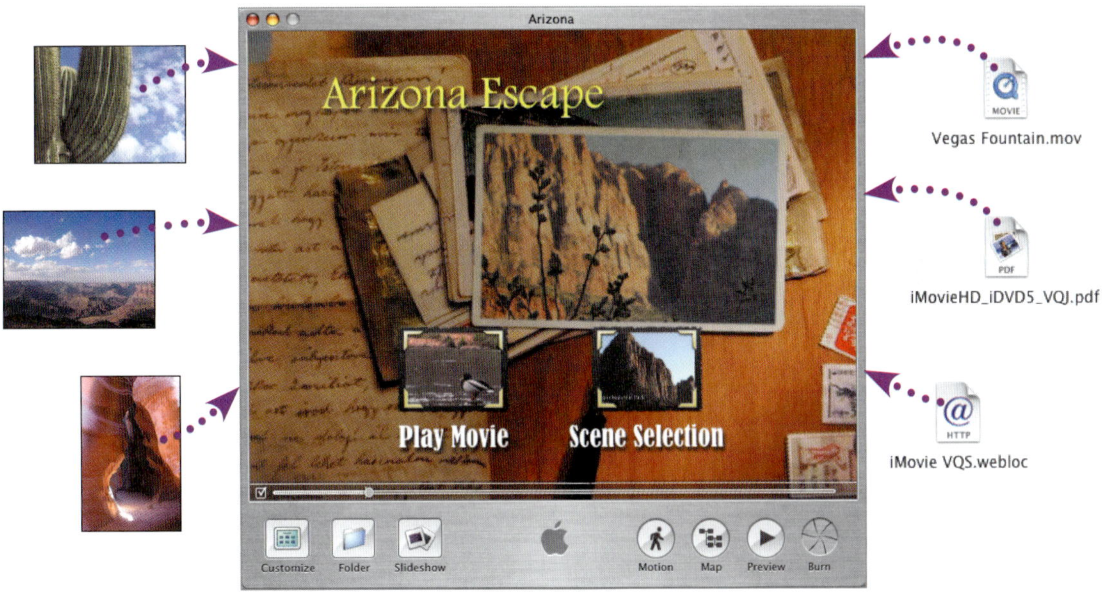

create a submenu

You already have one submenu in your project—the Scene Selection folder that contains each chapter of your movie. However, since you'll be adding more content in this chapter, let's create a new submenu to store it.

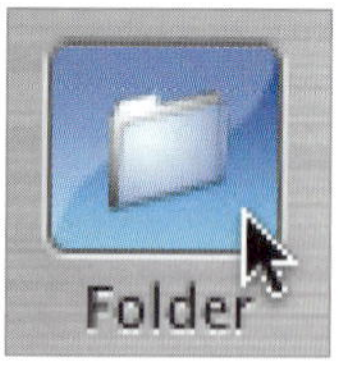

1 Click the Folder icon to create a new submenu.

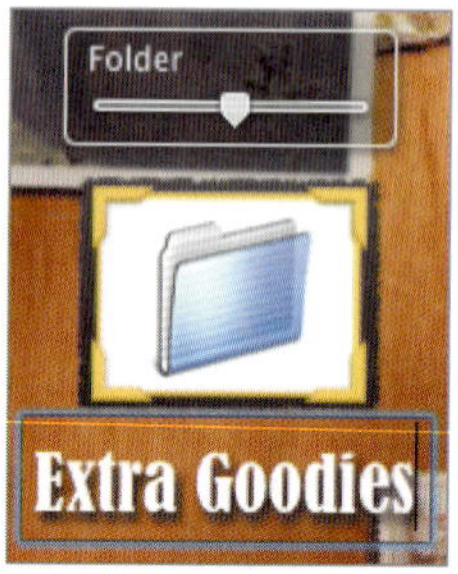

2 Enter a custom title (instead of "My Folder"), and double-click its icon to open it.

iDVD retains the drop zone content you added to the previous menu.

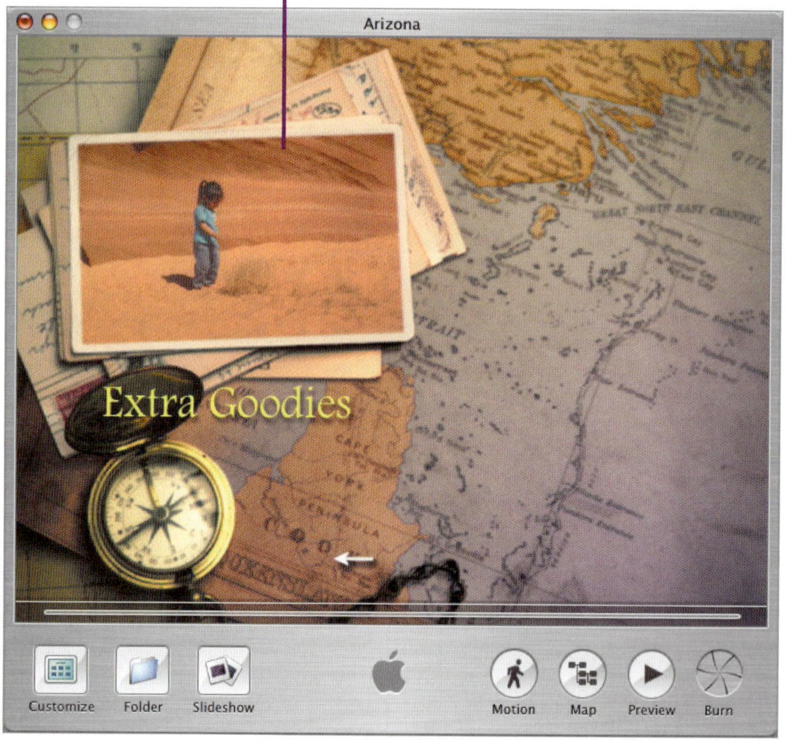

3 Apply a theme and edit the text as you did in the last chapter.

Here's a simplified map showing where the submenu fits in:

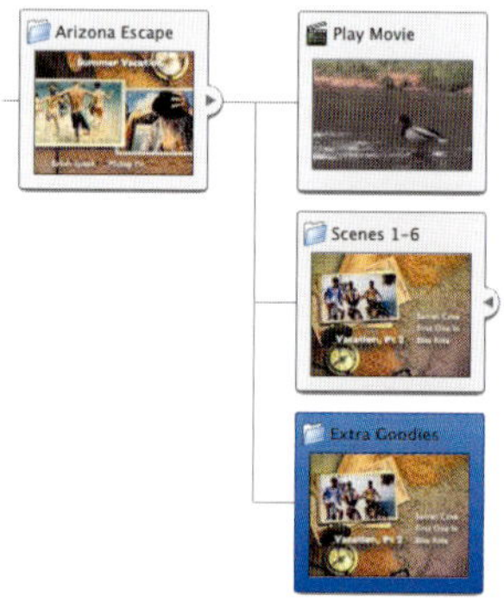

add movies

I wanted to share a clip that didn't make it into my final edited movie. I used iMovie's Share feature to save it as a QuickTime file (see Chapter 10), which I can now bring into iDVD.

1 Click the Media pane.

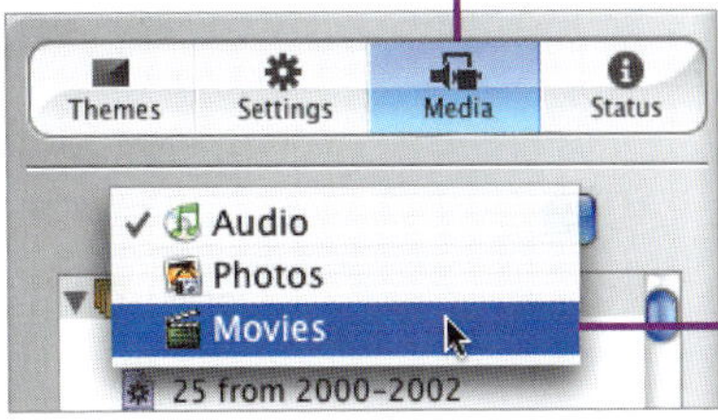

2 Choose Movies from the popup menu.

3 Drag a movie clip to the menu.

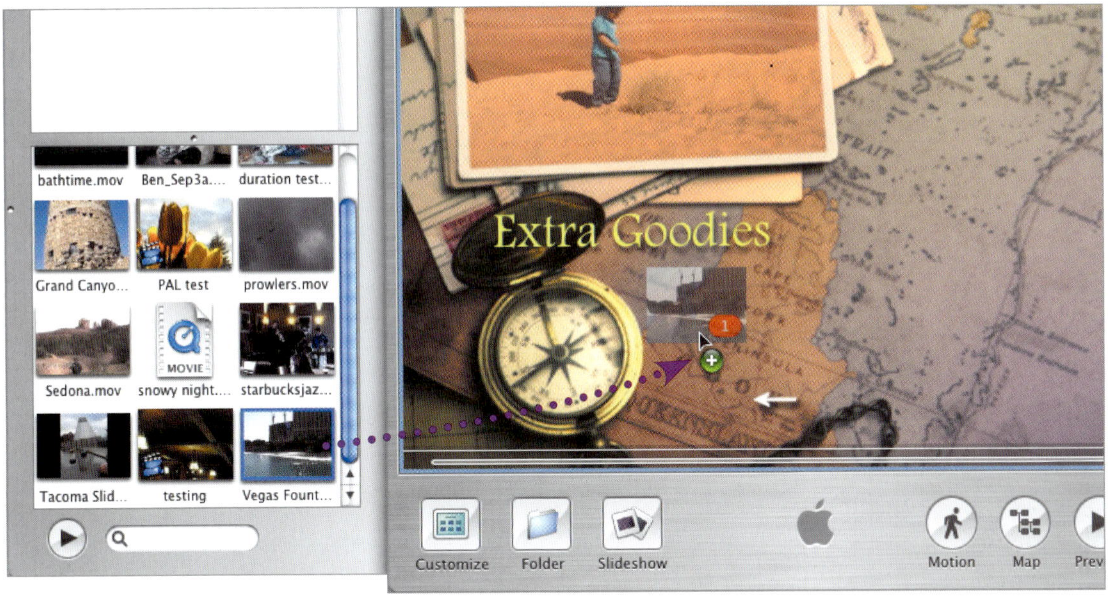

The movie appears as a new button, which you can edit as described in the last chapter.

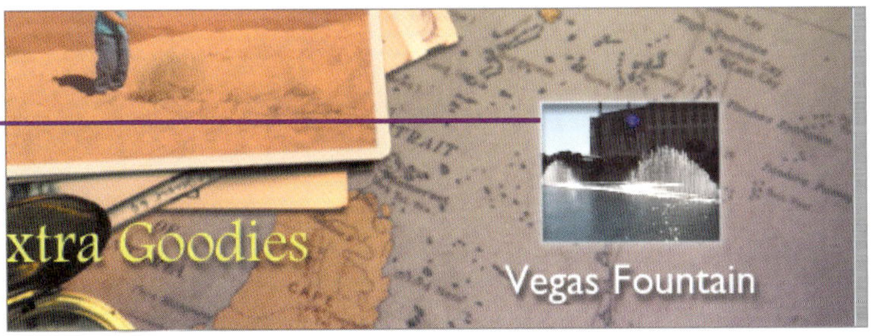

create a slideshow

In Chapter 5, you added photos to your iMovie project. Once incorporated into your movie, however, the photos get converted to video clips. In iDVD, you can build a slideshow that presents your photos sequentially, with transitions between each one and a soundtrack in the background. Although you could accomplish something similar in iMovie, it's much easier to do it here.

1 Click the Media pane, and choose Photos from the popup menu.

2 Drag an album to the menu.

In iPhoto, I made an album of my favorite photos. It's easier to drag an album into iDVD, but you can also select the photos you want and drag them in as a group to create a new slideshow.

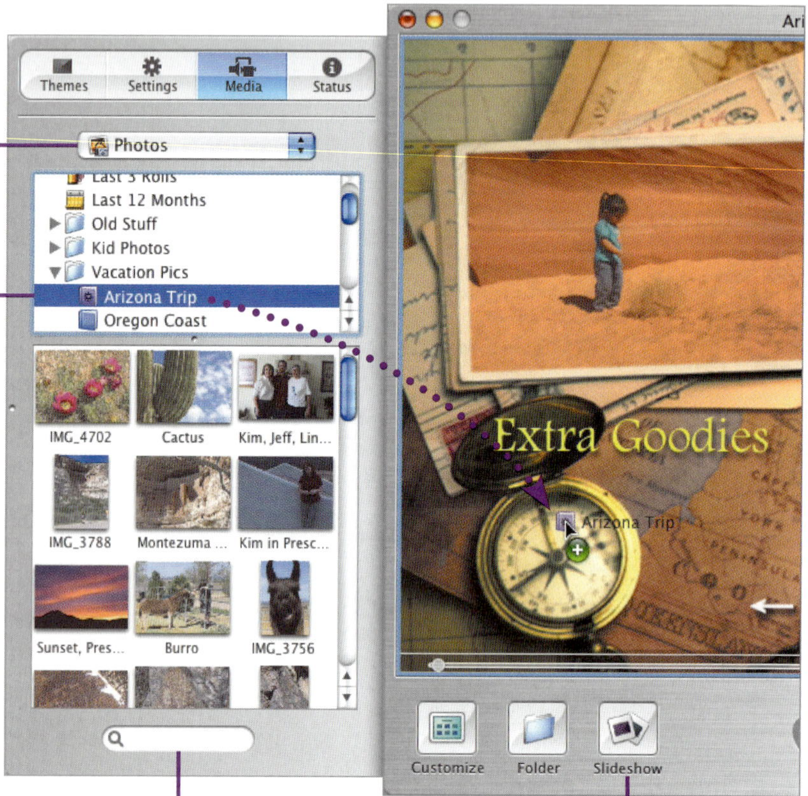

If you make a habit of naming your pictures in iPhoto, type a photo's title in the Search field to find it quickly.

You can also click the Slideshow button to create an empty slideshow, but dragging an album or photos is much easier.

3 Click the slide-show's button and use the slider to select a photo to use as an icon.

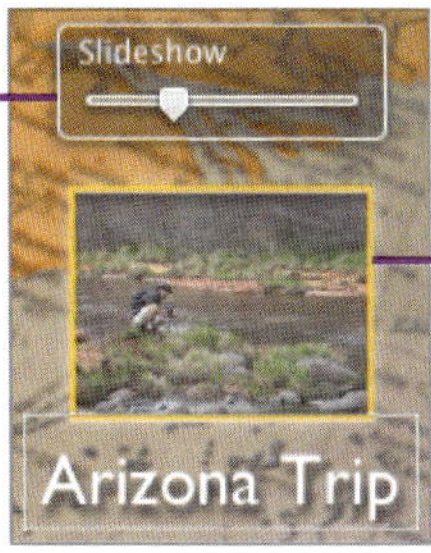

4 Double-click the new slideshow to access the Slideshow editor.

5 Set options for the slideshow.

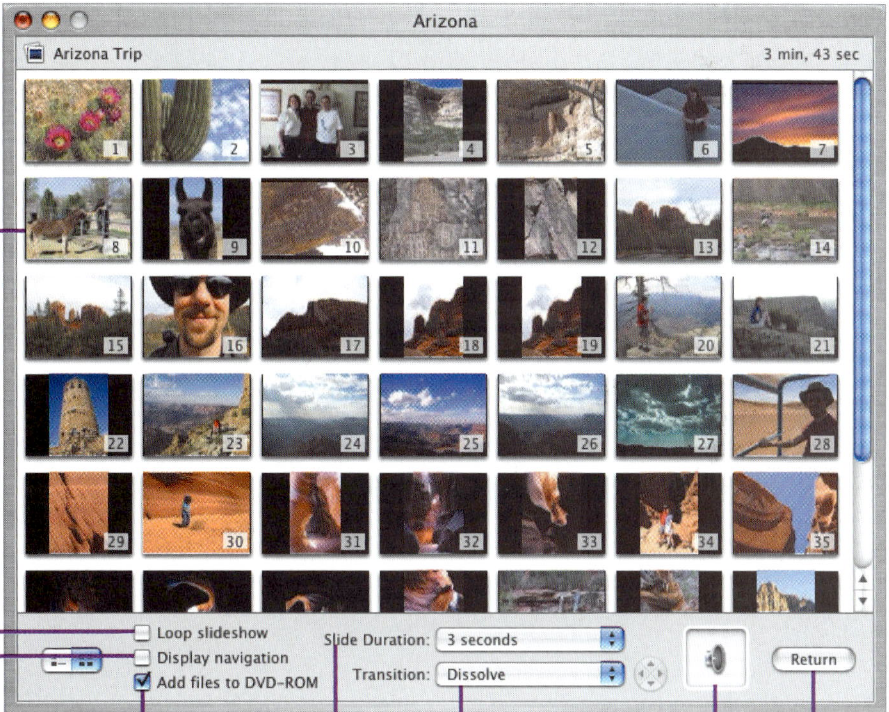

Drag photos to rearrange them, or select them and press Delete to clear them.

Click to replay the slideshow from the beginning.

Click to show navigation arrows on photos.

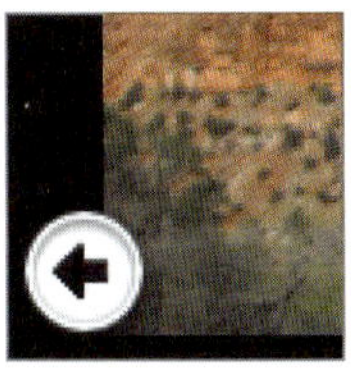

Click to include high-resolution images that someone with a computer can access.

Choose the amount of time that each slide appears.

Pick a transition type.

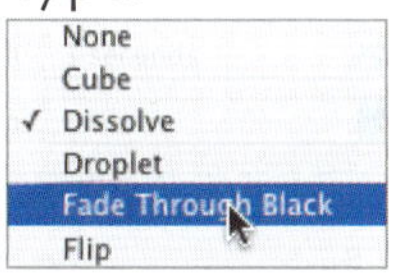

6 Go back to the menu.

Drag a song file here to set back-ground music.

add DVD-ROM content

The acronym DVD stands for "digital versatile disc" because you can store more than just movies on the shiny silver platters. iDVD can create a DVD-ROM (read-only media) area of a disc containing files that are accessible when the disc is inserted into a Mac or PC with a DVD drive.

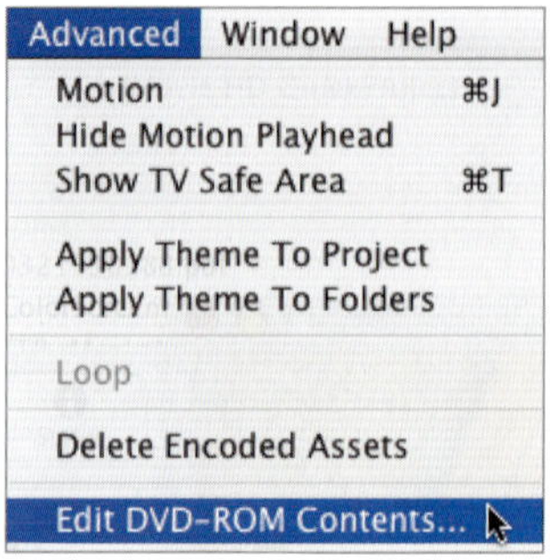

1 iDVD manages DVD-ROM content separate from its theme-driven interface. Choose Edit DVD-ROM Contents to begin.

2 Drag files from the Finder to the DVD-ROM Contents window to add them.

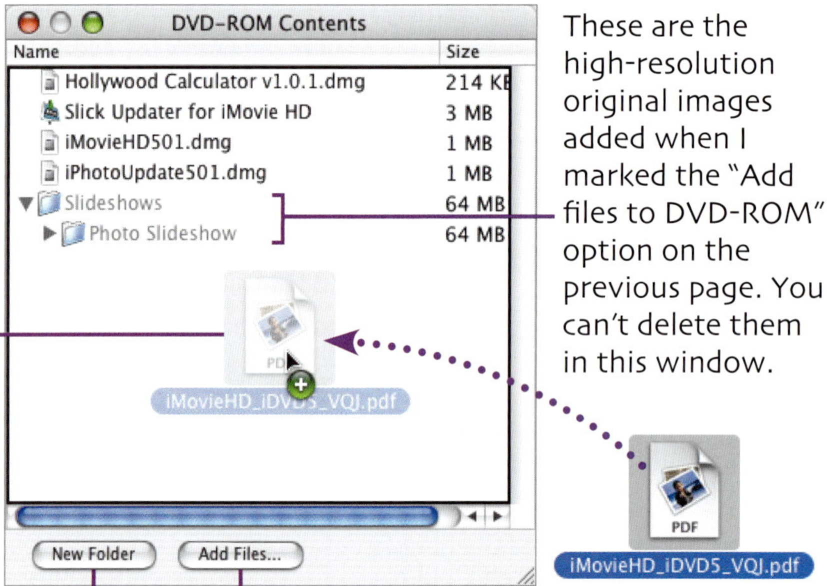

These are the high-resolution original images added when I marked the "Add files to DVD-ROM" option on the previous page. You can't delete them in this window.

Click here to make a new folder and organize the contents a bit more.

Instead of dragging files, you can click here to add files using a dialog. This is helpful if the files you want would be cumbersome to locate in the Finder.

extra bits

create a submenu p. 90

- Submenus are often created when you've run out of room for all the buttons on one menu. If you're facing button overload, move some of those items to a new submenu: select them, and choose New Menu from Selection from the Project menu. However, you can't go back and move them to the previous menu, except through the Undo command.

add movies p. 91

- When you drag a movie file from the Finder to your menu, make sure you don't release it over a drop zone.
- For the best quality, try to use QuickTime files that were saved as Full Quality DV (if they came from iMovie).
- Many DVDs these days include a short bit of video that plays before the menu loads. To do this, click the Map button and drag a movie file or group of photos to the AutoPlay well in the upper-left corner of the map.

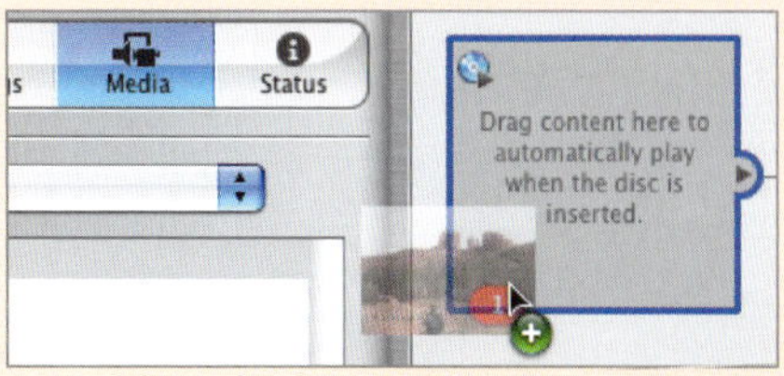

create a slideshow p. 92

- Click the Preview button while in the Slideshow editor to watch your slides without previewing the full DVD menu.
- To make photos appear better in iDVD, crop them first in iPhoto using the 4 x 3 (DVD) option under the Constrain popup menu.
- You can create slideshows by dragging photos from the Finder or even directly from iPhoto's main window.
- Consider dragging a bunch of photos to the AutoPlay well in the Map view to start your DVD with a slideshow before the menu loads.
- When picking an image to use as the slideshow button's icon, use the ← or → keys to view the photo thumbnails instead of dragging the slider.
- iDVD automatically scales slide-show photos to fit within the TV Safe Area. To use the full screen, open iDVD's preferences, click the Slideshow icon, and disable the option labeled "Always scale slides to TV Safe area."

extra bits

add DVD-ROM content p. 94

- DVD-ROM content can be nearly any file on your Mac. For example, you could include Web links (such as those created when you drag a URL out of Safari to the Desktop), PDFs containing more information about your vacation destination, maps, etc.
- Feel free to rearrange the items in the DVD-ROM Contents window by dragging them into whatever order you like.
- When you set up DVD-ROM content, iDVD only creates a link to the files you've specified; the original files aren't copied until you burn the disc. If you delete or move a file to a new location in the Finder, you'll get a "File not found" message. Either move the file to its previous location, or delete the reference in the DVD-ROM Contents window and add the file again.

14. burn the DVD

In Hollywood, shooting and editing a film is only the first half of the process. No matter how good the movie may be, without distribution it's going to sit anonymous on a shelf.

You're probably not aiming for a screening at the Sundance Film Festival, but currently your movie exists only on your hard disk. Now is the time to put that iDVD editing to work and burn your project to disc.

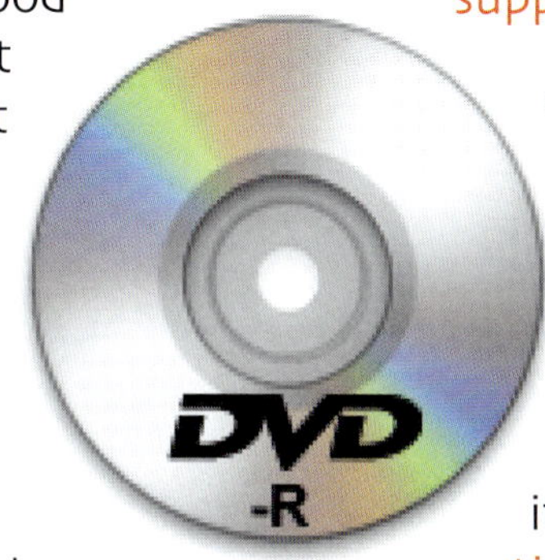

Before jumping in, I need to cover a few DVD basics.

Several flavors of blank DVDs are on the market, and iDVD 5 now supports them all: DVD-R, DVD+R, DVD+RW, and DVD-RW). The RW (rewriteable) variants are especially attractive because you can reuse them to burn copies of your project for testing.

DVD discs come in 1x, 2x, 4x, and 8x speeds. This is a measurement of how fast the SuperDrive's laser can carve data into a disc's surface. Check the specifications of your Mac at Apple's support site to determine your SuperDrive's speed: www.info.apple.com/support/applespec.html.

Also, before you burn any DVD disc, make sure your SuperDrive's firmware has been updated—on some models, using 4x-speed DVD-R media can damage the drive! Read more about it at docs.info.apple.com/article.html?artnum=86130.

(You can find the URLs above, along with other related information, at this book's companion Web site: www.necoffee.com/imovievqs/.)

If your Mac doesn't have a SuperDrive, iDVD 5 can also "burn" the project to a disc image for burning to a disc later using an external DVD burner.

Lastly, remember that a DVD disc can store roughly 4.7 GB of data (compare that to CD-Rs, which hold about 700 MB). That means you'll need to have plenty of free hard disk space available when it comes time to encode (prepare) the data and burn it.

preview the DVD

Use iDVD's Preview mode to see how the DVD will operate when played back on a DVD player.

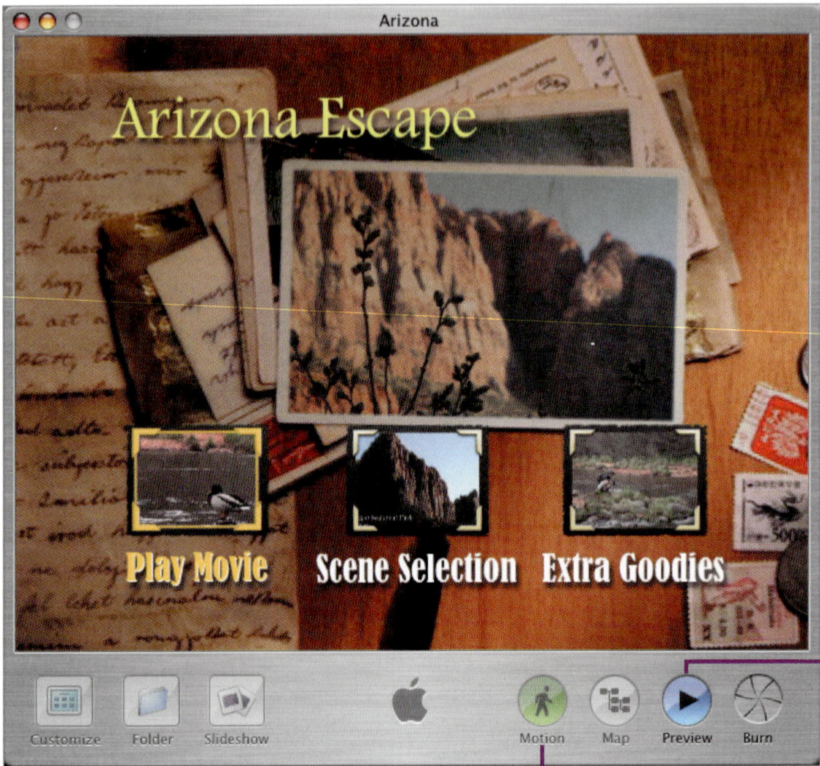

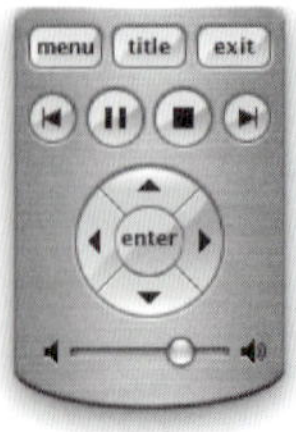

A virtual remote control device appears so you can test how the menu items will work.

Click the Preview button to enter Preview mode.

Enable Motion to see animated elements in the preview.

A slideshow or video footage plays back in iDVD's window.

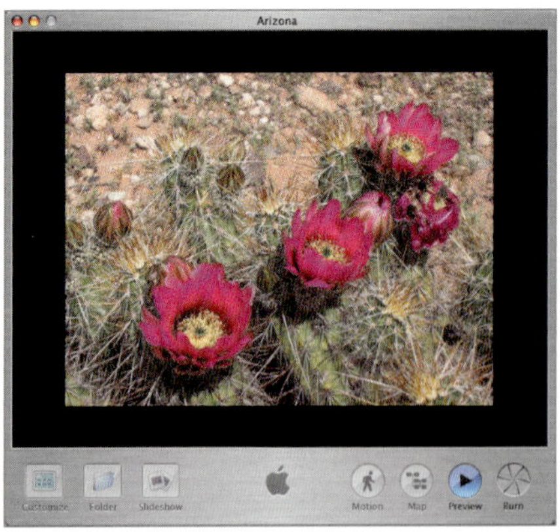

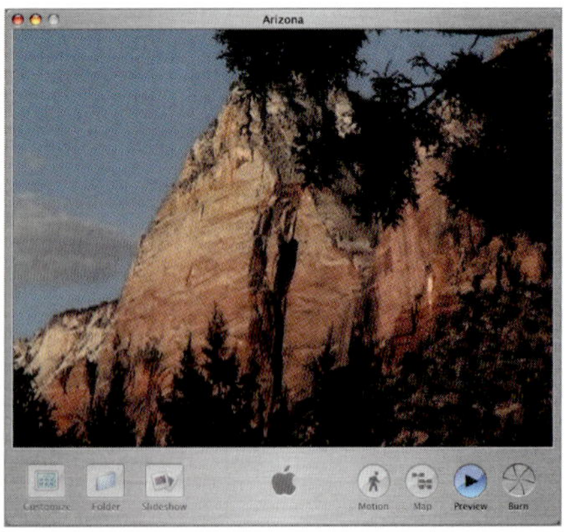

set encoding options

Before a project is burned to disc, iDVD encodes the data into a format that DVD players will recognize. This process also compresses your movie's gigabytes of video footage into a size that will fit on the disc. iDVD offers two types of encoding options, which you access from iDVD's preferences.

The default setting is Best Performance, which offers the fastest encoding time. However, your movie must be less than 60 minutes, including other assets such as motion elements.

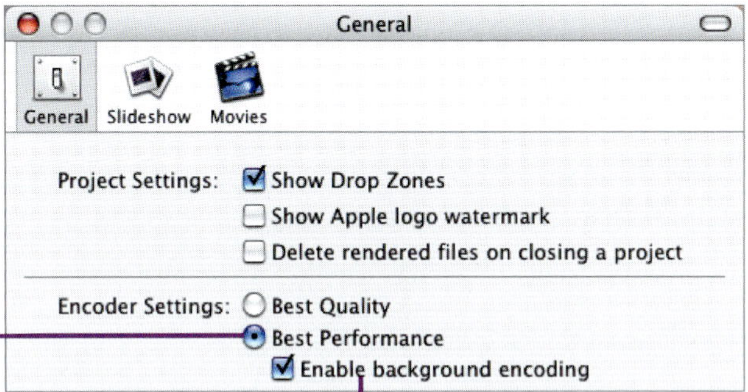

For projects of up to 2 hours in length, choose Best Quality. At burn time, iDVD analyzes the movie to determine the best level of compression while retaining image and sound quality.

An advantage of Best Performance is that iDVD can encode the data in the background while you work, shortening the overall burn time.

This means Best Quality offers no background encoding, but you gain an extra 60 minutes' worth of footage on disc.

Best Performance

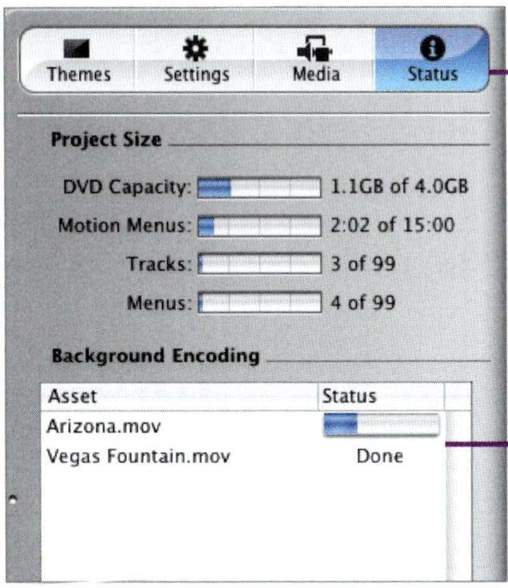

Click the Status pane to view project size and encoding progress.

Assets encoded in background

No background encoding

Best Quality

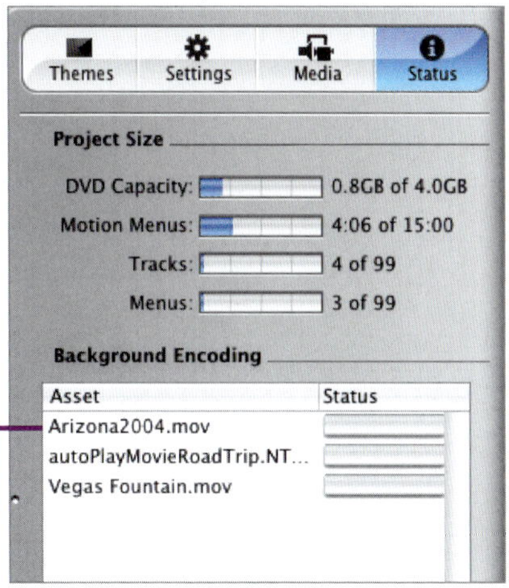

burn the DVD

1 Finally, time to burn! Click the Burn button to start the disc burning process.

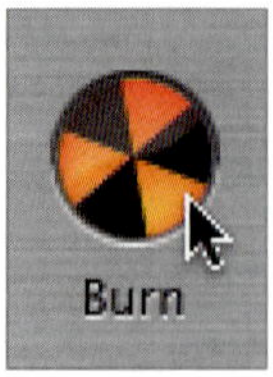

2 When prompted, insert a blank DVD disc in your Mac's SuperDrive.

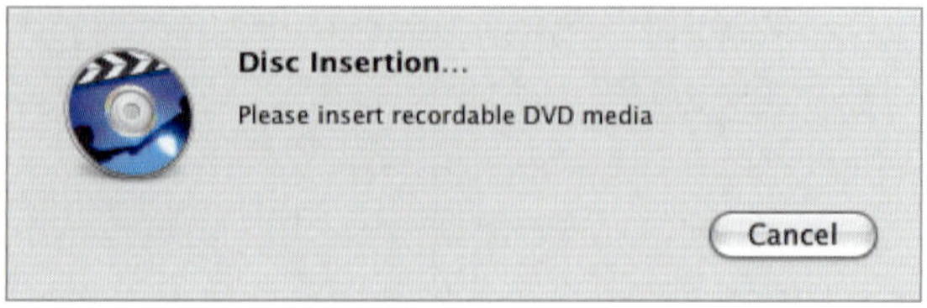

3 Wait. Get some coffee. Go to bed. Depending on your project's size, iDVD can take hours to encode and burn the disc. If you're curious, you can watch the burn process in the Creating Your DVD dialog that appears.

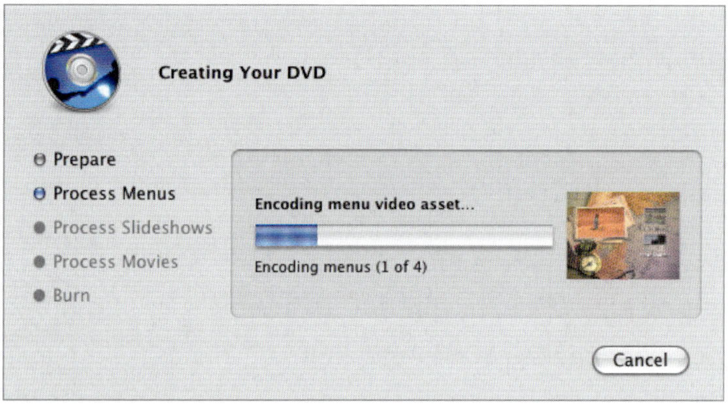

Prepare. iDVD checks that it has the pieces it needs to continue the burning process.

Process Menus. Buttons, motion menus, and other interface elements are rendered and encoded.

Process Slideshows. Slideshow photos and transitions are processed here.

Process Movies. The heavy lifting—if you're using Best Quality, the entire movie is scanned to determine the best compression quality, then the footage is rendered.

Burn. The audio and video data are combined, or "multiplexed," into a single stream that DVD players can read. The data is then etched into the disc's surface by the SuperDrive's laser.

After the Burn stage, the disc ejects and you're done!

save project to disk

What's that you say? You don't currently own a Mac with a SuperDrive? Not a problem! You can save an iDVD project as an archive, and then take that file to someone else who owns a SuperDrive. An archive is also good if you want to build a project on one computer, but do the encoding and burning on a faster Mac.

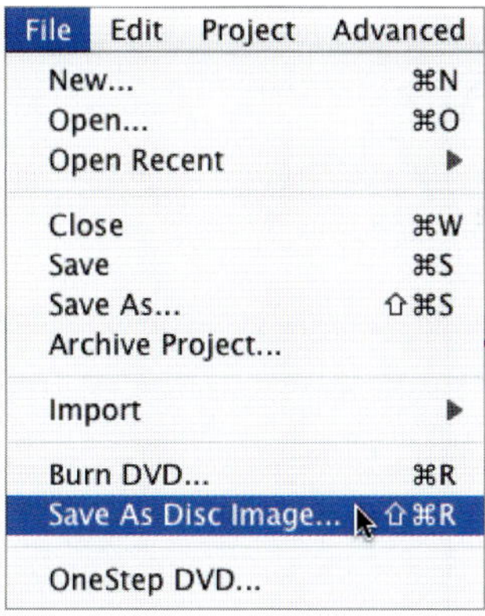

1 Choose Archive Project or Save As Disc Image from the File menu.

Or, if you own an external DVD burner, create a Disc Image that you can burn to a DVD using the Finder or an application such as Roxio Toast. (This option doesn't include the checkboxes below.)

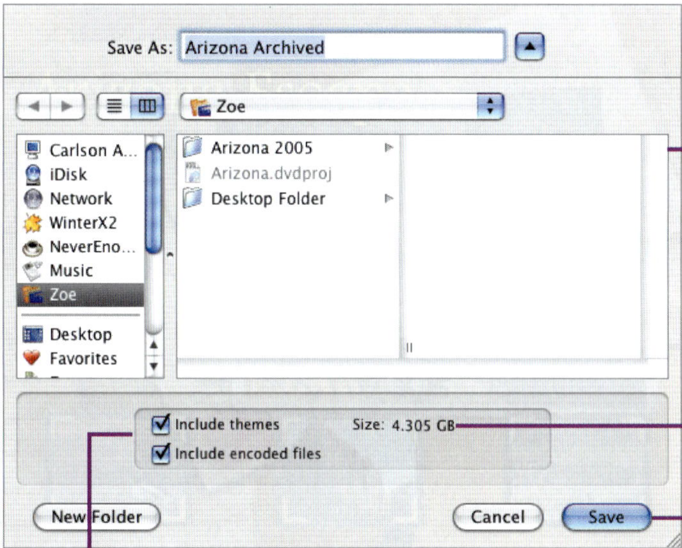

2 Select a location on your hard disk.

iDVD tells you how large the archive will be.

4 Click Save to create the archive.

3 If you've customized the theme, mark the Include themes checkbox to ensure that all of the data will be present on the destination Mac.

Select Include encoded files if you want to save the encoding that's been done already, even though it will make the archive file size larger.

extra bits

preview the DVD p. 98

- When you exit the preview during a slideshow, you're taken directly to the Slideshow editor instead of the menu.
- Clicking the Exit button on the remote control takes you out of Preview mode.

set encoding options p. 99

- Remember that Best Quality does not encode in the background. Many people mistakenly wait for the progress bars in the Status pane to appear, to no avail. Encoding begins when you burn the disc.
- If you're using Best Performance with background encoding enabled, wait until the assets have finished encoding before you burn the disc.
- Projects longer than 60 minutes are more likely to have reduced image quality due to the higher degree of compression required to fit on a disc.
- Use the DVD Capacity figure to gauge how much space your project will occupy on the disc. Also, the numbers change depending on whether or not Motion is enabled.

burn the DVD p. 100

- Make sure you have plenty of hard disk space before you burn: at least twice the size of your project.
- Enable the Motion button before burning to make sure motion elements are included.
- Blank CDs can be bought for pennies apiece, but DVDs are still on the higher edge of the price range (but dropping). However, buying in bulk from online stores such as www.shop4tech.com, or www.dealnews.com can get you prices well below $1 per disc.
- Remember that the total space occupied on the disc includes motion menus, slideshows, and the like. So, if your movie is 52 minutes long, you may still get an error message that the project is too big.
- Including transitions between menus or within slideshows increases the burning time.
- After your DVD is burned, label it with a permanent marker; adhesive labels can unbalance the disc during play and potentially damage your DVD player.
- Test the DVD on several DVD players and computers.

appendix a: troubleshooting

No one wants to run into trouble, but unfortunately it does happen. The suggestions in this appendix can help if iMovie or iDVD is crashing, or if the program's performance is choppy.

For more specific queries, turn to the Web and the large community of iMovie and iDVD users who share their experiences. The first place I look is Dan Slagel's "Unofficial" iMovie FAQ (frequently asked questions). Apple's discussion forums are also filled with information. See Appendix B for those URLs, or go to my own iMovie/iDVD Web site at www.necoffee.com/imovievqs/.

Also, make sure you're running the latest versions of iMovie, iDVD, and QuickTime (especially the latter). Apple's iLife Web page (www.apple.com/ilife/) includes links to the latest updates. To check your versions, go to the iMovie or iDVD menu in each program, and choose About iMovie or About iDVD.

For QuickTime, go to Software Preferences, click the QuickTime icon, and click the About QuickTime button.

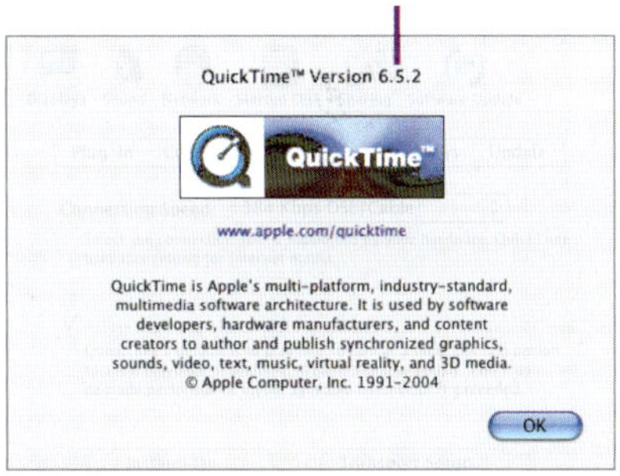

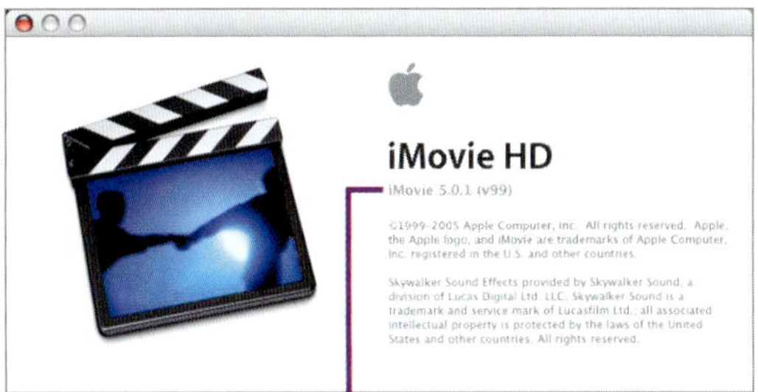

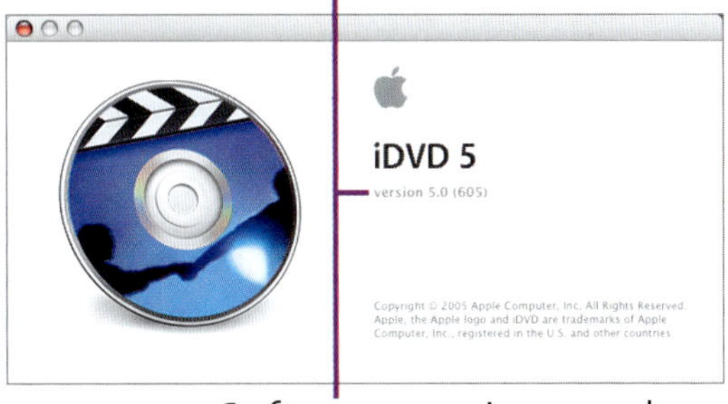

Software version numbers

improve performance

Make the iMovie window smaller. Drag the resize handle in the lower-right corner of the screen to make the window smaller.

Quit other running applications. iMovie and iDVD will gladly use as much memory and processor power as you can throw at them. If playback is sluggish, try running only iMovie or iDVD.

Delete the program's preferences. If iMovie or iDVD crashes, its preferences can become corrupted, causing more problems later. Here's how to delete preferences:

1. Quit the application.
2. In the Finder, choose Home from the Go menu.
3. Open the Library folder.
4. Open the Preferences folder.
5. Delete the following files (you may not have them all):

   iMovie Preferences
   com.apple.imovie.plist
   com.apple.iMovie3.plist
   com.apple.iDVD.plist

Turn off FileVault (Mac OS X 10.3 and later). FileVault is a technology introduced in Mac OS X 10.3 Panther that creates an encrypted version of your Home directory to secure its contents from snooping eyes. The problem is that iMovie and iDVD store their project files in the Home directory by default. So, when FileVault is active, the computer is constantly encrypting and decrypting massive quantities of data on the fly. Turn FileVault off in Mac OS X's Security preference pane.

Make sure you have plenty of available hard disk space. I can't say it enough. Digital video requires huge amounts of disk space. Consider buying an external hard drive and storing your projects there; if your Mac includes a FireWire 800 port (a faster version of FireWire), get a drive with FireWire 800 support.

troubleshoot burning

Check your DVD media. Sometimes a failed burn operation is the fault of the disc. This can happen with generic discs bought in bulk, but also occurs with more reputable vendors' discs. Try a new brand of disc, starting with the ones Apple sells (since presumably they've been vetted by the company).

Clean your SuperDrive. Accumulated dust can disrupt the laser used to burn data to a disc. Spray a little compressed air into the SuperDrive's slot to blow the dust away.

Set Energy Saver settings. Since it can take hours to burn a disc, your computer may think you've left it and go into a power-saving mode. In Mac OS X's System Preferences, set the processor performance to Highest and the hard drive to never spin down. Also turn off the option to put the computer to sleep automatically after a period of inactivity.

Burn during the day. Many people do their disc burning at night while they sleep (computers are meant to do work while we rest, aren't they?). If you're waking up to burn failures, try burning during the day—Mac OS X performs some nightly maintenance operations around 3 a.m., which could be interfering with the burning operation.

Change audio quality. iMovie and iDVD use audio set to 48.000 kHz (16-bit). However, some audio sources may record at 44.100 kHz, which has been known to cause burning problems. Take these steps to change a movie's audio quality:

1. Export your movie from iMovie to a QuickTime file using Expert Settings.
2. In the Movie Settings dialog, under Sound options, click the Settings button.
3. Click the Rate popup menu and choose 48.000.
4. Export the clip, then import it into iDVD.

troubleshoot system

Repair Mac OS X permissions. When things start going haywire under Mac OS X, I take this step first. Each file on your computer has permissions assigned to it, which dictate, for example, how the file can be changed or moved. For whatever reason, sometimes the wrong permissions get applied.

1 Open Disk Utility, which is located in the Utilities folder within your Applications folder.

2 Choose your startup disk.

3 Click to repair permissions.

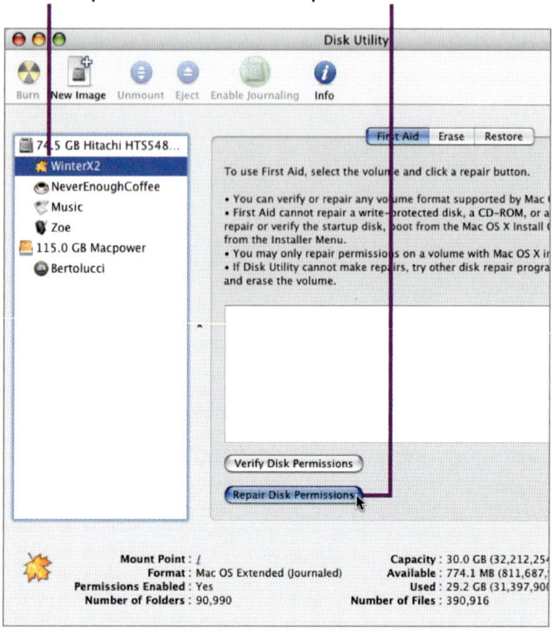

appendix b: resources

Making a Movie in iMovie HD & iDVD 5: Visual QuickProject Guide, companion Web site

http://www.necoffee.com/imovievqs/

Apple iLife

http://www.apple.com/ilife/

Apple's iMovie Support

http://www.apple.com/support/imovie/

Apple's iMovie Discussion Forums

http://discussions.info.apple.com/iMovie/

Apple's iDVD Support

http://www.apple.com/support/idvd/

Apple's iDVD Discussion Forums

http://discussions.info.apple.com/idvd/

reference and tutorials

Dan Slagle's "Unofficial" iMovie FAQ

http://danslagle.dvmix.com/mac/iMovie/

Ken Tidwell's "Unofficial" iDVD FAQ

http://www.kentidwell.com/idvd5/

MacDV Mailing List

http://www.themacintoshguy.com/lists/MacDV.html

MyMovieFest

http://www.mymoviefest.com/

HD for Indies

http://www.hdforindies.com/

Cyber Film School

http://www.cyberfilmschool.com/

DVcreators.net

http://www.dvcreators.net/

2-pop.com

http://www.2-pop.com/

Post Forum

http://www.postforum.com/

iMovie software

GeeThree

http://www.geethree.com/

Granted Software

http://www.grantedsw.com/still-life/

LQ Graphics

http://lqgraphics.com/software/

eZedia

http://www.ezedia.com/

Virtix

http://www.virtix.com/

Stupendous Software

http://www.stupendous-software.com/

cf/x

http://www.imovieplugins.com/

BKMS

http://plugins.bkms.com/

Freeplay Music

http://www.freeplaymusic.com/

Killer Sound, Inc.

http://www.killersound.com/

Sound Dogs

http://www.sounddogs.com/

iDVD software

iDVD ThemePak

http://www.idvdthemepak.com/

Blue Fusion iDVD Themetastic

http://www.idvd-themetastic.com/

glossary

Blank clips. Whether black, cobalt, or any other available hue, blank clips are placeholders added between video clips. Insert these clips to help you adjust and perfect the timing of your movie.

Burn. The (rather lengthy) process of etching data into a DVD disc's surface to create a disc that a consumer DVD player or computer with a DVD drive can read.

Clip. A segment of video or audio.

Clip fragment. Remnant of an audio or video segment, sometimes caused by overzealous cropping or trimming.

Clip Speed slider. This control, found in earlier versions of iMovie, let you adjust the speed of your footage, clip by clip. In iMovie HD, the Clip Speed slider has been replaced by the Fast/Slow/Reverse effect.

Clip Viewer. One of two modes of the Timeline, the Clip Viewer displays clips in play order, using large thumbnail previews to help you identify them.

Clip Viewer button. Filmstrip icon that appears above the Timeline. Click this icon to display the Clip Viewer.

Clips pane. This virtual display case, also known as the Shelf, sits to the right of the Monitor. Your video clips are stored here, arranged on a grid. Use the scroll bar to view more clips.

Crop. Delete frames that are outside a selected portion of a clip. Choose Crop from the Edit menu.

Crop markers. These triangular shapes appear when you position the mouse pointer just below the Scrubber Bar. Click and drag these markers to select a portion of your clip.

Cross Dissolve. Commonly used transition where the end of one clip fades into the beginning of the next clip.

Customize panel. The area where most of iDVD's options and controls are stored. It houses the Themes, Settings, Media, and Status panes.

Direct Trimming. A click-and-drag editing technique, performed in the Timeline Viewer. Shortening clips by Direct Trimming works faster than cropping, and allows unwanted frames to be hidden instead of deleted. Clips with a straight edge (or two) have been trimmed.

Drop zone. A special area in several iDVD themes where photos or movies can play within the menu to add more visual interest.

glossary

DVD. Short for Digital Versatile Disc, this plastic platter packs nearly seven times the data into the same space as a compact disc: a CD stores roughly 700 MB, while a DVD holds approximately 4.7 GB.

DVD-R. Stands for Digital Versatile Disc-Recordable. These discs can be burned once, and then played back in nearly any consumer DVD player and DVD capable computer. Use DVD-R (General) for your iDVD projects; DVD-R (Authoring) discs are not supported by iDVD. A similar format is DVD+R.

DVD-ROM. Stands for Digital Versatile Disc-Read Only Memory. The format of a digital video disc that holds data which doesn't need to be played back automatically in a DVD player. Data can be stored but not altered in this format.

DVD-RW. Stands for Digital Versatile Disc-Rewritable. These discs can be burned more than once, and are good for burning test versions of your iDVD projects. A similar format is DVD+RW.

Effect. A special visual touch to enhance your movie. Choose from a variety of styles including Black & White, Earthquake, and Fairy Dust—or layer them upon the same clip for snazzier results.

Encoding. In iDVD, the method by which your movie is compressed and formatted to fit onto a DVD disc. iDVD offers two types of encoding: Best Quality and Best Performance.

FireWire. A high-speed serial data bus that can move large amounts of data between computers and peripheral devices. Use a high-speed FireWire connection to import your footage from your camcorder into iMovie on your computer.

Footage. Movie clips, raw or edited; the stuff you download from your camcorder into iMovie and eventually turn into a finished project.

Frame. A single picture on a strip of film or video, or a single photo exposure.

Gigabyte (GB). A unit of computer data or storage space equivalent to 1,024 megabytes (MB).

HDV. A high-definition video format supported by iMovie HD. It can be shot in two varieties, depending on the camera: 1080i is an interlaced video frame at a size of 1,920 by 1,080 pixels; 720p is progressive-scan video at 1,280 by 720 pixels. The high-definition video is compressed in-camera using MPEG-2 compression, which is why HDV is considered a lower-end high-def format.

iDVD Chapter Markers. Created in iMovie, these titled thumbnails indicate a new section that will appear as a separate section in iDVD. Clicking a chapter marker in iMovie also lets you jump to specific scenes in the film.

Import. Copying video and audio from your camera to your computer's hard disk, using a FireWire cable, iMovie, and a huge amount of hard disk space.

Jump cut. Hard, quick transition between clips.

Ken Burns Effect. A method of panning, zooming in, or zooming out on a still photo; named after the acclaimed documentary filmmaker who popularized the technique.

Map. In iDVD, the Map view illustrates the DVD project's content structure.

Media pane. Part of iDVD's Customize panel, the Media pane allows you to access other iLife-related content, such as photos, movies, and music.

Mode switch. Toggle between import mode (camera icon) and edit mode (scissors icon) using this small control above the Timeline.

Monitor. Preview and edit all your video clips—or play back your entire movie—on this large screen in iMovie.

Motion. Movement or animation, added to increase your DVD's coolness quotient.

Motion Playhead. The signature feature of iDVD's Scrubber Bar, which lets you scroll through drop zone animations.

Multiplexing. The process by which audio and video data are fused into one stream that DVD players can read.

Pane. An area containing goodies that can be added to create your movie, such as clips, photos, audio, titles, transitions, and effects.

Pane buttons. Displayed below iMovie's Shelf, these icons for Clips, Photos, Audio, Titles, Transitions, Effects, and iDVD can be clicked to access all of the program's editing tools.

Playhead. Inverted triangle marker that appears on the Timeline and on the Monitor's Scrubber Bar. Drag the Playhead to any frame within your movie or clip to display it in the Monitor; the numbers beside the Playhead indicate the time location within the movie.

Preview. Just as it sounds, a preview is a chance to see how an edit or application affects your movie before you commit to accepting the change. In iDVD, click the Preview button to enter Preview mode and see what your project will look like when viewed on a DVD player.

QuickTime movie. QuickTime is a highly versatile format for sharing movies as files on your hard drive.

Rendering. The process of recreating clips in iMovie to incorporate new visual data such as transitions, titles, and effects.

Resolution. The amount of detail in an image, represented by pixels. For example, video resolution is typically more coarse than the resolution of a photo taken with a digital still camera.

Scrubber Bar. Scroll bar that allows you to move anywhere in a movie. Use the Monitor's Scrubber Bar to select a range of frames for copying, cutting, or cropping.

Settings pane. Part of iDVD's Customize panel, this pane lets you edit specific options such as text font and size, button styles, background images, and more.

Shelf. Also called the Clips pane, this display of video clips and photos appears next to the Monitor.

glossary, cont.

Slideshow. Just like Grandma and Grandpa's giant tray of vacation slides; but this one is created in iDVD by displaying pictures imported from iPhoto.

Split. To slice a clip where the Playhead is located. Place the Playhead on the desired point in a clip and choose Split Video Clip from the Edit menu.

Submenu. In iDVD, a submenu is a separate branch of the main menu, offering access to other media within your iDVD project (more movies or slideshows, for example). After creating an iDVD project from within iMovie, a button labeled Scene Selection is created; that button is actually a submenu (also known as a folder) that leads you to the chapters that comprise your movie.

Submenu theme. Visual flavor of the backdrop for your submenu. In this book's example, iDVD's Travel 2 theme is selected for the submenu.

Theme. The overall look of a menu screen, including the visual presentation (fonts, colors, etc.) as well as the way it interacts (with motion menus, etc.).

Timecode. A method all camcorders use to label and keep track of footage, where time is shown as Hours: Minutes: Seconds: Frames. In NTSC video, 30 frames equal 1 second; in PAL video, 25 frames equal 1 second.

Timeline. The row beneath the Monitor where clips, photos, and transitions are arranged and edited. Made up of the Clip Viewer and Timeline Viewer.

Timeline Viewer. Arranges the clips in order and also depicts their lengths. This viewer also includes audio tracks and controls for changing aspects of a clip.

Title (iDVD). The name you choose for your movie, which is formatted differently than other buttons and elements in an iDVD theme. Edit the title's text and position in iDVD's Settings pane.

Title (iMovie). Any clip containing text that is superimposed over footage. Accessed by the Titles pane.

Transition. Stylish method for moving from one clip to the next. Access transitions including Fade In, Fade Out, Push, or Twirl by clicking the Trans button just below the Shelf.

Trim. To shorten, as with a film clip. Also see Direct Trimming.

Waveforms (or, audio waveforms). Visual depiction of a clip's sound levels, that allows you to edit audio clips with more precision.

Zooming in. In iMovie, zooming in refers to punching up the size of your various movie components for a better view. Zooming in is helpful when you're editing small clips or transitions.

Zoom slider. Bottom left-hand gauge that determines how much of the Timeline is shown in the viewer: with the slider at the left, the entire movie appears in the Timeline. In the Photos pane, the Zoom slider dictates how much of a photo is visible.

index

2-pop.com, 108

A

Add Chapter button, 68
Advanced menu
  Edit DVD-ROM Contents, 94
  Extract Audio, 42
  Lock Audio Clip at Playhead, 43
  Paste Over at Playhead, 38
  Revert Clip to Original, 40
  Show TV Safe Area, 87
  Unlock Audio Clip, 43
albums, iPhoto, 26–27, 92
aligning title text, 77, 78, 79
"Always scale slides to TV safe area" option, 95
analog camcorders, importing footage from, 16
analog-to-digital conversion, 16
animated drop zones, 84
animation
  AutoPlay movies, 73, 95
  Motion button, iDVD, 72, 80
  motion buttons, DVD menus, 80, 87
  transitions. See transitions
Apple
  iDVD Web sites, 107
  iLife Web site, 103, 107
  iMovie Web sites, 107
  .Mac service, 65, 69
  online support discussion groups, 107
  SuperDrive support, 97
  updating firmware, 97
  updating software, 103
Apple logo watermark, 88
Apply button, 31, 61
Archive Project command, 101
archives, iDVD projects, 101
asbestos suits, 73
attachments, emailing movies, 64, 69
audio, synchronized, 43
audio backgrounds, iDVD, 81, 87, 93
audio CDs, importing songs, 32
audio clips. See also audio tracks
  editing, 42
  fading in or out, 41
  importing footage to iMovie, 4, 16
  importing from audio CDs, 32
  importing from GarageBand, 32
  importing from iTunes, 32
  importing music from iTunes, 30
  locking and unlocking, 43
  moving, 43
  restoring extracted audio, 45
  sound effects, 32
  splitting, 44
  temporary storage, 32
  volume, changing, 41, 45
  waveforms, viewing, 42, 45
Audio pane, 30, 32
audio quality settings, 105
audio tracks, 32
  extracting from video clips, 42, 45
  importing music clips, 32
  pasting clips over clips, 38
  restoring extracted audio, 45
  in Timeline Viewer, 9
audio waveforms, 42, 45
Audio well, 81, 87
AutoPlay movies, 73, 95
AutoPlay well, 73, 95

B

background encoding, 99, 102
Background well, 85, 88
backgrounds, DVDs
  audio backgrounds, 81, 87, 93
  movie backgrounds, 85, 88
  photo backgrounds, 85
  slideshows, background audio, 93
backgrounds for titles, black or colored, 56
Best Performance encoding, 99, 102
Best Quality encoding, 99, 101, 102
Billow transition, 49
BKMS, 109
black backgrounds for titles, 56
black footage, 39, 45
blank clips, 39, 45
Blue Fusion iDVD Themetastic, 110
Bluetooth, exporting videos, 70
book, companion Web site, 107
bug fix, burning 4x-speed DVD discs, 97
bugs. See troubleshooting
Burn button, 73, 100
burning DVDs, 5.
  See also DVDs; iDVD
  audio quality settings, 105

index

editing clips (continued)
- audio clips. See editing audio clips
- audio waveforms, viewing, 42, 45
- blank clips, 39, 45
- colored clips, 39, 45
- copying frames or clips, 37, 44
- cropping clips, 36, 44
- Direct Trimming, 34, 44
- duplicate projects, 45
- duration of movie, 22
- effects. See effects
- extracting audio from video clips, 42, 45
- pasting clips over clips, 38
- pasting frames or clips, 37, 44
- placeholder clips, 39
- previewing movies and clips, 33
- recovering footage, 40, 45
- renaming clips, 18
- restoring clips, 40, 45
- restoring extracted audio, 45
- selecting portions of clips, 36
- splitting clips, 35, 44
- timecode notation, 15
- Trash, emptying, 21, 23, 45
- trimming clips, 34, 36, 44
- undoing edits, 45

editing video clips. See editing clips

Effect In, Effect Out sliders, 60

effects
- applying, 61, 62
- existing effects, modifying, 62
- Fast/Slow/Reverse effect, 59
- Ken Burns Effect, 28–29, 31
- preview window, 60, 62
- removing, 61, 62
- settings, adjusting, 60, 62
- sound effects, 32

Effects pane, 60–61

Email button, 64

Email format, QuickTime exports, 67

emailing movies, 64, 69

emptying trash, 21, 23, 45

encoding
- background encoding, 99, 102
- burning DVDs, 100, 101
- encoded files in project archives, 101
- encoding options, 99, 100, 102

encryption, FileVault, 10, 104. See also compression; encoding

End switch, Ken Burns Effect, 29

Energy Saver preferences, 105

Expert Settings, QuickTime, 70

exporting movies
- to camera, 70
- to cell phones, 70
- to DV tape, 70
- to email, 64, 69
- to iDVD. See exporting to iDVD
- publishing to .Mac HomePage, 65, 69
- to QuickTime, 66–67, 70, 105
- via Bluetooth, 70

exporting to iDVD. See also iDVD
- audio quality settings, 105
- chapter markers, 5, 68, 70
- iDVD projects, creating, 68

external hard drives, 10

Extract Audio command, 42

Extract Audio when using Paste Over at Playhead option, 38

extracting audio from video clips, 45
- editing audio clips, 42
- repositioning audio clips, 43

eZedia, 109

F

fading volume in or out, 41

fast-forwarding while importing, 13

Fast/Slow/Reverse effect, 59

File menu
- Archive Project, 101
- Save As Disc Image, 101
- Save Project As, 45
- Share, 63

file size. See also compression
- emailing movies, 64, 69
- iDVD archive files, 101
- QuickTime compression settings, 66, 67, 70

files
- archive files, iDVD, 101
- audio files, importing, 30, 32
- media files. See media files
- project files, iDVD, 71, 74

FileVault, 10, 104

finding
- photos, 26

FireWire connections, 3, 10, 12

firmware update, SuperDrives, 97

Folder button, 72

Folder slider, 80

folders
- DVD-ROM folders, 94, 96
- DVD submenus, 90, 95
- Home folder, 10

fonts
- button titles, iDVD, 78
- iMovie titles, 56, 58
- menu titles, iDVD, 77

footage
- exporting. See exporting movies
- importing. See importing footage

formats
- iMovie project types and, 7

formatting text, 77, 78

formatting title text, 56

fragmented hard disks, 10

frames
- copying and pasting, 37, 44
- cropping clips, 36
- deleting, 36

frame size, Full Quality DV format, 70
Ken Burns Effect, 28–29
pasting clips over clips, 38
positioning audio clips, 30
selecting and deselecting, 44
splitting clips, 35, 44
timecode notation, 15
trimming clips, 34, 36
Free Position button, 79
free space indicator, 16
Freeplay Music, 109
Full Quality DV format, QuickTime exports, 67, 70

G

gaps, 39
GarageBand, 32, 87
GeeThree, 109
Granted Software, 109

H

hard disk space
burning DVDs, 97, 102
DVD Capacity indicator, 102
external hard drives, 10, 104
free space indicator, 16
iDVD projects, 97, 102
.Mac service, 69
partitioning disks, 10
QuickTime compression settings, 66, 67, 70
required for digital video, 3, 11, 104
HD footage
disk space requirements, 11
HD for Indies, 108
HDV 1080i, HDV 720p formats and project types, 7
help
iDVD Web sites, 107, 108
iLife Web site, 103, 107
iMovie Web sites, 103, 107, 108
online support forums, 107, 108
QuickTime support, 103
SuperDrive support, 97
troubleshooting. See troubleshooting
tutorials, 108
The "Unofficial" iDVD FAQ, 108
The "Unofficial" iMovie FAQ, 103, 108
Home folder, 10, 104
HomePage, .Mac, 65, 69

I

icons
audio lock icons, 43
effects applied to clips, 61
slideshow icon photos, 93, 95
iDisk, adding movies to, 65, 69
iDVD
burning discs. See burning DVDs
buttons. See buttons, DVD
chapters and chapter markers, 68, 70, 86
FileVault and, 104
interface, 72–73, 74
labeling burned DVDs, 102
Map view, 73, 74
menus. See menus, DVD
motion, activating, 72
OneStep DVD, 74
preferences, trashing, 104
project archives, 101
projects. See projects, iDVD
remote control, virtual, 98, 102
slideshows. See slideshows, iDVD
themes. See themes, iDVD
troubleshooting, 104, 105
The "Unofficial" iDVD FAQ, 108
iDVD button, 68
iDVD pane, 68, 70
iDVD ThemePak, 110
iDVD Themetastic, 110
image resolution, still clips, 25, 31
images. See also still clips
importing still images, 26–27
Ken Burns Effect, 28–29, 31
searching for, 26
slideshows. See slideshows, iDVD
iMovie
downloading, 103
FileVault and, 10, 104
interface, 8, 9
opening, 7
operating system requirements, 3
preferences, trashing, 104
projects. See projects, iMovie
tutorials, 108
The "Unofficial" iMovie FAQ, 103, 108
updating iMovie software, 103
iMovie Trash, emptying, 21, 23, 45
iMovie window size, 104
Import button, 14
importing
footage. See importing footage
music, 30, 32
pictures from iPhoto, 26–27, 92
importing footage, 4
adding transitions automatically, 16
disk space requirements, 3, 11
duplicated audio, troubleshooting, 16
to DVD disc, 74
FireWire connections, 12
free space indicator, 16
importing sections of tape, 16
live footage, 16
QuickTime movies, 16
reviewing before importing, 13, 16
scenes, clips created for, 14
to Shelf, 14

index

importing footage (continued)
  using analog camcorder, 16
  using digital camcorder, 12–14, 16
  from VHS tapes, 16
in-camera still photo capability, 25
interface, iDVD, 72–74, 98, 102
interface, iMovie, 8, 9
Internet
  emailing movies, 64, 69
  publishing movies to .Mac HomePage, 65, 69
  streaming movies, 67
iPhoto, 26–27, 92–93
iSight cameras, 16
iSight format and project type, 7
iTunes, adding music to movies, 30, 32

K

Ken Burns Effect
  applying, 28–29
  panning vertical photos, 31
  reversing, 31
  settings, 28, 31
keyboard shortcuts
  Clip Viewer, displaying, 9
  saving iMovie projects, 10
  Timeline Viewer, displaying, 9
Killer Sound, Inc., 109

L

labeling burned DVDs, 102
launching iMovie, 7
length of clips
  duration of movie, 22
  timecode notation, 15, 44
linked DVD-ROM files, 96
Liquid Timeline. See Timeline
Lock Audio Clip at Playhead command, 43
locked audio clips, 43
LQ Graphics, 109

M

Mac OS X
  FileVault, 10, 104
  permissions, repairing, 106
.Mac service, publishing movies, 65, 69
MacDV Mailing List, 108
Magic iMovie feature, 16
Map button, 73
Map view, iDVD, 73, 74
media files
  clips and media file storage, 8
  renaming clips, 18
Media pane, 81, 82–84, 91, 92
menus, DVD, 72
  applying themes, 76, 86–88
  drop zones, 72, 82–84, 88
  motion buttons, 80, 87. See also buttons, DVD
  motion menus, 88
  positioning menu titles, 77, 87
  previewing DVDs, 98, 102
  slide shows, 92–93, 95
  submenus, 73, 86, 88, 90, 95
  titles, formatting, 77
  transitions between menus, 88, 100, 102
MiniDV tape, 11, 70
minutes, timecode notation, 15
Mode switch, 12
Monitor, 8
monitoring movies, 8
motion
  animated drop zones and, 84
  iDVD buttons. See motion buttons
  Ken Burns Effect, 28–29, 31
  transitions. See transitions
Motion button, 72, 80
motion buttons. See also buttons, DVD
  activating and disabling motion, 80, 87
  motion duration, 87
  previewing, 80
  starting frame, 80
motion menus, 88. See also menus, DVD
Movie slider, 80
movies
  adding clips to, 18–19
  adding to DVDs, 91, 95
  AutoPlay movies, 73, 95
  in drop zones, 82, 83, 84, 88
  duration, viewing in Timeline, 22
  DVD. See DVDs; iDVD
  editing. See editing clips
  emailing, 64, 69
  exporting. See exporting movies
  as iDVD theme backgrounds, 85, 88
  previewing, 33
  publishing to .Mac HomePage, 65, 69
  QuickTime, 16, 66–67, 70, 105
  repositioning clips, 20–21, 23
  sharing. See sharing movies
moving
  chapter markers, 70
  clips, 21, 22, 23
MPEG-4 format and project type, 7
multiple text fields, 55
multiple titles, 55, 58
multiplexing DVD data, 100
music. See also audio clips
  audio CDs, 32
  background audio, DVD themes, 81, 87
  GarageBand songs, 32
  iTunes, 30, 32
MyMovieFest, 108

N

navigation arrows, slideshows, 93
New Menu from Selection command, 95
nighttime vs. daytime processing, 105

O

OneStep DVD, 74
online help. See also troubleshooting
  iDVD Web sites, 107, 108
  iLife Web site, 103, 107
  iMovie Web sites, 103, 107, 108
  online support forums, 107, 108
  QuickTime, 103
  SuperDrive support, 97
  tutorials, 108
online support forums, 107, 108
opening
  iDVD projects, 71
  iMovie, 7
  iMovie projects, 7
operating system requirements, 3
OS X
  FileVault, 10, 104
  permissions, repairing, 106
overlapping titles, 58

P

pan and zoom effects. See Ken Burns Effect
pane access buttons, 8
partitioning hard disks, 10
Paste command, 37
Paste Over at Playhead command, 38
pasting clips and portions of clips, 37, 38
pasting clips over other clips, 38
Pause button, 13
Pause slider, 55
performance issues, troubleshooting. See also troubleshooting
  audio quality settings, 105
  burning DVDs, 105
  daytime vs. nighttime processing, 105
  Energy Saver preferences, 105
  FileVault, 10, 104
  iMovie window size, 104
  Mac OS X permissions, repairing, 106
  Motion features, iDVD, 74
  preferences file, trashing, 104
  quitting other applications, 104
permissions, Mac OS X, repairing, 106
photos. See also still clips
  cropping, 31
  cropping for slideshows, 95
  in drop zones, 82–83, 84, 88
  as iDVD theme backgrounds, 85
  importing, 26–27, 31
  Ken Burns Effect, 28–29, 31
  multiple photos, adding, 31
  PICT-formatted files, 31
  previewing, 26
  searching for, 26
  slideshows. See slideshows, iDVD
  vertical photos, 31
Photos pane, 26–29
Photos slider, 82
PICT-formatted files, 31
pictures. See photos
"pillarboxed" photos, 31
pixels, square vs. rectangular, 70
placeholder clips, 39
Play button, 13, 30
  previewing movies and clips, 33
playback controls, 8, 13, 14
playback while importing footage, 13, 14, 16
Playhead
  chapters, adding to iDVD projects, 68, 70
  copying and pasting clips, 37
  pasting clips over clips, 38
  splitting clips, 35, 44
  title previews and, 54
  transition previews and, 51
positioning
  button text, 78, 79
  clips, 20–21, 23
  menu titles, 77, 87
  photos in drop zones, 83, 84
  television screen boundaries, 87
  title text, 56
Post Forum, 108
preferences, trashing, 104
Preview button, 49, 73, 98
Preview mode, iDVD, 98, 102
preview window, Effects pane, 60, 62
previewing
  clips, 33
  DVDs, 73, 98, 102
  effects, 60, 62
  imported photos, 26
  iTunes songs, 30
  Ken Burns Effect, 29
  movies, 33
  slideshows, 93, 95
  titles, 54, 56, 58
  transitions, 48, 49
Project menu, New Menu from Selection command, 95
Project Trash. See Trash
project types, iMovie, 7
projects, iDVD, 5
  archives, 101
  AutoPlay movies, 73, 95
  Best Performance encoding, 99, 102
  Best Quality encoding, 99, 100, 102
  burning discs. See burning DVDs
  chapters and chapter markers, 5, 68, 70, 86
  creating, 5, 68, 70
  drop zones, 72, 82–84, 88
  DVD-ROM content, adding, 5, 94, 96
  encoding options, 99, 100, 102
  labeling burned DVDs, 102

index

projects, iDVD (continued)
  linked DVD-ROM files, missing, 96
  motion, activating, 72
  motion buttons, 80, 87. See also buttons, DVD
  motion menus. See menus, DVD
  movies, adding to projects, 91, 95
  project files, 71, 74
  themes. See themes, iDVD
  titles. See titles, iDVD
projects, iMovie. See also movies
  creating, 7, 10
  opening, 7
  saving, 7, 10
  storage locations, 10
  types of projects, 7
publishing movies to .Mac HomePage, 65, 69
purchasing DVD discs, 102
Push transition, 49

Q

QT margins option, 56
QuickTime and QuickTime movies
  audio quality settings, 105
  compression settings, 66, 67, 70
  importing into iMovie, 16
  publishing to .Mac HomePage, 69
  QuickTime margins, 56
  sharing movies via QuickTime, 66–67, 70
QuickTime button, 66
QuickTime margins, 56

R

recovering footage, 40, 45
rectangular pixels, 70
red bar, 50
remote controls, 98, 102
removing. See deleting
renaming clips, 18, 44
rendering
  burning DVDs, 100
  canceling effect rendering, 62
  Ken Burns Effect, 29
  transition clips, 50
reordering
  clips, 20–21, 23
  photos in drop zones, 83
repositioning. See positioning
resolution, still clips, 25, 31
restoring clips, 40, 45
Reverse button, Ken Burns Effect, 31
Revert Clip to Original command, 40
reviewing footage, 13, 16
Rewind/Review button, 13
rewinding while importing, 13
rounded corners on clips, 34

S

Safe Area, TV, 87, 95
Save As Disc Image command, 101
Save Project As command, 45
saving
  iMovie projects, 7, 10
  QuickTime movies, 66
scenes, clips created for, 14
scrolling through clips, 22
Scrubber Bar, 36, 44
searching
  photos, 26
seconds, timecode notation, 15
Select None command, 44
selecting portions of clips, 36
Settings pane, 77–79, 87, 88
Share command, 63
Share dialog
  Bluetooth button, 70
  Email button, 64
  HomePage button, 65
  QuickTime button, 66
  Videocamera button, 70
"Share selected clips only" option, 63, 64, 66, 69
sharing movies, 4, 63
  on cell phones, 70
  emailing, 64, 69
  exporting. See exporting movies
  posting to Web, 65, 69
  QuickTime movies, 66–67, 70
  recording to MiniDV tape, 70
  sharing clips from Shelf, 69
  sharing selected clips, 63, 64, 66, 69
  via Bluetooth, 70
Shelf, 8
  importing footage, 14
  importing QuickTime movies, 16
  repositioning clips, 21
  sharing clips from Shelf, 69
Show Audio Waveforms command, 42
Show Clip Volume Levels command, 41, 45
Show Drop Zones option, 88
Show TV Safe Area command, 87
single titles, 55
Size slider, 79
  title text, 56
Slagle, Dan, 103, 108
Slideshow button, 92
Slideshow editor, 93
slideshows, iDVD
  adding photos, 82, 83, 88, 92
  AutoPlay movies, 95
  background audio, 93
  creating, 82–83, 88, 92
  cropping photos, 95
  deleting, 83
  as DVD-ROM content, 94
  first photo, selecting, 82
  high-resolution images, 93
  icon photo, selecting, 93, 95
  navigation arrows, 93
  previewing, 93, 95
  rearranging photos, 83, 93

removing photos, 83, 93
slide duration setting, 88, 93
Slideshow editor, 93
transitions, 93, 100, 102
TV Safe Area, 95
sluggish performance. See performance issues, troubleshooting
songs
adding to movies, 30, 32
background audio, DVDs, 81, 87, 93
Sound Dogs, 109
sound effects, 32. See also effects
soundtracks. See audio clips
spacebar, 16
special effects. See effects
speed. See also duration
DVD disc-writing speeds, 97
Speed slider, 48
title speed, 55
Split Video Clip at Playhead command, 35, 44
splitting clips, 35, 44
square corners on clips, 34
square pixels, 70
Start switch, Ken Burns Effect, 28
starting iMovie, 7
Status pane, 99
still clips. See also photos; slideshows, iDVD
adding multiple photos, 31
applying effects to stills, 62
clip duration, 27
cropping, 31
dragging to Timeline, 27
image resolution, 31
importing pictures, 26–27, 31
in-camera still photo capability, 25
Ken Burns Effect, 28–29, 31
PICT-formatted files, 31
previewing, 26
searching for, 26
vertical photos, 31
still pictures. See photos; still clips
Stop button, 13
streaming movies, 67
Stupendous Software, 109
stuttery playback, 16, 104
submenus, DVDs
applying themes, 86, 88
creating, 90, 95
motion buttons, 80, 87
starting frame, selecting, 80
transitions between menus, 88
SuperDrives, 3, 97, 105
support. See also help
iDVD Web sites, 107, 108
iLife Web site, 103, 107
iMovie Web sites, 103, 107, 108
online support forums, 107, 108
QuickTime, 103
SuperDrive support, 97
troubleshooting iMovie and iDVD, 103–106
tutorials, 108
The "Unofficial" iDVD FAQ, 108
The "Unofficial" iMovie FAQ, 103, 108
synchronized audio, 43
system requirements, 3

T

tapes
importing from VHS tapes, 16
MiniDV tape, disk space requirements, 11
recording back to DV tape, 70
technical support. See also help
iDVD Web sites, 107, 108
iLife Web site, 103, 107
iMovie Web sites, 103, 107, 108
online discussion forums, 103, 107, 108
QuickTime, 103
SuperDrive support, 97
troubleshooting iMovie and iDVD, 103–106
tutorials, 108
The "Unofficial" iDVD FAQ, 108
The "Unofficial" iMovie FAQ, 103, 108
telephones, sharing videos, 70
television screens, viewing area, 56, 87
text. See titles, iDVD; titles, iMovie
text blocks
titles, iMovie, 55
text styles, 56, 58
theme groups, 76
themes, iDVD, 5. See also titles, iDVD
animated drop zones, 84
applying, 76, 87
applying to submenus, 86, 88
background audio, 81, 87
background images, 85, 88
button styles and positions, 78–79
drop zones, 72, 82–84, 88
including in project archives, 101
motion buttons, 80, 87. See also buttons, DVD
theme groups, 76
Themes pane, 76
thumbnails, motion buttons, 80
Tidwell, Ken, 108
timecode, 15
Timeline
adding clips to movie, 18–19
Clip Viewer. See Clip Viewer
duration of movie, 22
in iMovie interface, 8, 9
importing music from iTunes, 30
previewing movies and clips, 33
scrolling through clips, 22
Timeline Viewer. See Timeline Viewer

index

Timeline Viewer, 9
  Direct Trimming, 34, 44
  importing photos, 26–27
  rendering transitions, 50
  repositioning clips, 23
  rounded corners on clips, 34
  square corners on clips, 34
  switching to Clip Viewer, 9
titles, iDVD, 72.
  See also themes, iDVD
  button titles, 78, 79, 87
  editing and formatting text, 77, 78
  menu titles, 77, 87
  positioning, 77, 79, 87
titles, iMovie
  adding to movies, 57, 58
  black or colored backgrounds, 56
  deleting, 57, 58
  duration, setting, 55
  entering title text, 54, 58
  fonts, 56, 58
  jagged text, troubleshooting, 58
  modifying, 58
  multiple text fields, 55, 58
  multiple titles, 58
  overlapping titles, 58
  pause duration, setting, 55
  positioning, 56, 58
  previewing, 54
  QuickTime margins, 56
  single titles, 55
  speed of appearance, setting, 55
  text blocks, 55
  text color, 56
  text size, 56, 58
Titles pane, 54–58
Trans button, 48
transitions
  adding automatically during import, 16
  adding to movies, 50, 51
  canceling rendering, 51
  on clips with effects, 62
  direction, setting, 49
  duration, changing, 48
  between DVD menus, 88, 100, 102
  modifying, 50, 51
  multiple transitions, adding, 51
  previewing, 48, 49
  removing, 51
  rendering transition clips, 50
  in slideshows, 93, 100, 102
Transitions pane, 48–50
Trash
  deleting clips, 21, 23, 45
  emptying trash, 21, 23, 45
  restoring clips, 23, 45
trimming clips, 9, 36, 44
troubleshooting. See also performance issues, troubleshooting; technical support
  audio quality settings, 105
  burning DVDs, 105
  daytime vs. nighttime processing, 105
  disk space requirements, 3, 104
  dropped frames during import, 16
  duplicated audio during import, 16
  Energy Saver preferences, 105
  FileVault, 10, 104
  iMovie window size, 104
  jagged title text, 58
  Mac OS X permissions, repairing, 106
  online support forums, 107, 108
  preferences, trashing, 104
  quitting other applications, 104
  stuttery playback during import, 16
  The "Unofficial" iDVD FAQ, 108
  The "Unofficial" iMovie FAQ, 103, 108
tutorials, 108
TV Safe Area, 87, 95

U

undoing edits, 45
Unlock Audio Clip command, 43
unlocked audio clips, 43
The "Unofficial" iDVD FAQ, 108
The "Unofficial" iMovie FAQ, 103, 108
Update button, 50
updating iMovie software, 103

V

VCRs, importing movies from videotape, 16
vertical photos, 31
VHS. See videotapes
video clips
  adding to movies, 18–19
  blank clips, 39, 45
  copying frames or clips, 37, 44
  cropping, 36, 44
  Direct Trimming, 34, 44
  in drop zones, iDVD, 82–84, 88
  duration of movie, 22
  effects. See effects
  extracting audio, 42, 45
  importing. See importing footage
  pasting clips over clips, 38
  pasting frames or clips, 37, 44
  pasting portions of clips, 37
  placeholder clips, 39
  repositioning clips, 20–21, 23
  restoring extracted audio, 45
  restoring to original state, 40, 45
  selecting portions of clips, 36
  splitting, 35, 44
  timecode notation, 15
  trimming, 34, 36, 44
video compression settings, QuickTime, 66, 67, 70

video formats
iMovie project types and, 7
videotapes, importing footage from, 16
View menu
Show Audio Waveforms, 42
Show Clip Volume Levels, 41, 45
Virtix, 109
virtual remote control, 98, 102
volume level bar, 41
volume markers, 41
volume of clips, 41, 45
Volume Slider (Monitor), 8, 41

W

waveforms, viewing, 42, 45
Web format, QuickTime exports, 67
Web pages, adding movies to, 65, 69
Web sites
2-pop.com, 108
Apple's .Mac service, 65, 69
BKMS, 109
Blue Fusion iDVD Themetastic, 110
cf/x, 109
companion Web site for this book, 107
Cyber Film School, 108
DVcreators.net, 108
DVD discs, purchasing, 102
eZedia, 109
Freeplay Music, 109
GeeThree, 109
Granted Software, 109
HD for Indies, 108
iDVD forums and support, 107, 108
iDVD software, 110
iDVD ThemePak, 110
iDVD Themetastic, 110
iLife, 107
iMovie forums and support, 107, 108
iMovie software, 109
Killer Sound, Inc., 109
LQ Graphics, 109
MacDV Mailing List, 108
MyMovieFest, 108
online support forums, 107, 108
Post Forum, 108
Sound Dogs, 109
Stupendous Software, 109
SuperDrive support, 97
Tidwell, Ken, 108
The "Unofficial" iDVD FAQ, 108
The "Unofficial" iMovie FAQ, 103, 108
Virtix, 109
4x-speed DVD burning bug fix, 97
Web Streaming format, QuickTime exports, 67
window size, iMovie, 104

X

4x-speed DVD burning, bug fix, 97

Z

Zoom settings, Ken Burns Effect, 28
Zoom slider, 31, 34
zooming
Direct Trimming, 34
Ken Burns Effect, 28–29, 31
Zoom slider, 31, 34